STORIES OF
PEOPLE & CIVILIZATION

ROMAN

ANCIENT ORIGINS

FLAME TREE PUBLISHING
6 Melbray Mews, Fulham,
London SW6 3NS, United Kingdom
www.flametreepublishing.com

First published and copyright © 2023
Flame Tree Publishing Ltd

23 25 27 26 24
1 3 5 7 9 10 8 6 4 2

ISBN: 978–1–80417–616–0

For Aloni
Insights from past ages can illuminate the way to the future – and the power of possibilities.
Lindsay
Your friend the historian.

Cover and pattern art was created by Flame Tree Studio, with elements courtesy of Shutterstock.
com/svekloid/Vibrands Studio/Alex Matt. Additional interior decoration courtesy of
Shutterstock.com/Babich Alexander.

Judith John (lists of Ancient Kings & Leaders) is a writer and editor specializing in literature
and history. A former secondary school English Language and Literature teacher, she has
subsequently worked as an editor on major educational projects, including *English A: Literature*
for the Pearson International Baccalaureate series. Judith's major research interests include
Romantic and Gothic literature, and Renaissance drama.

The text in this book is compiled and edited, with a new introduction. The text in Part One is
an edited version of *Rome* by William Warde Fowler (Henry Holt and Company, 1912). The
texts in Part Two are extracts from: Livy's *History of Rome*, trans. Rev. Canon Roberts (E. P.
Dutton and Company, New York, 1912); Appian's *The Foreign Wars*, trans. Horace White
(Loeb Classical Library, William Heinemann Ltd., 1899); Polybius's *Histories*, trans. W. R.
Paton (Loeb Classical Library, Harvard University Press, 1922); Plutarch's *Parallel Lives* trans.
Bernadotte Perrin (Loeb Classical Library, William Heinemann Ltd., 1919); Cicero's *Against
Verres*, trans. C.D. Yonge (George Bell and Sons, 1903); Suetonius's *Lives of the Caesars*,
trans. John c. Rolfe (Loeb Classical Library, William Heinemann Ltd., 1913); Cassius Dio's
Roman History, trans. Earnest Cary (Loeb Classical Library, William Heinemann Ltd., 1917);
Vegetius' *On Military Matters*, trans. Lieutenant John Clarke (W. Griffin, 1767); Augustus's *Res
Gestae* trans. Frederick W. Shipley (Loeb Classical Library, Harvard University Press, 1924);
Tacitus's *Annals*, trans. Alfred John Church and William Jackson Brodribb (MacMillan and
Company, 1884); Pliny the Elder's *Natural History*, trans. John Bostock and H.T. Riley (Taylor
and Francis, 1855); Frontinus's *Aqueducts of the City of Rome*, trans. Charles E. Bennett (Loeb
Classical Library, Harvard University Press, 1925); Pliny the Younger's *Letters*, trans. John B.
Firth (Walter Scott, 1900); The *Historia Augusta*, trans. David Magie (Loeb Classical Library,
Harvard University Press, 1921); Ammianus Marcellinus's *Roman History*, trans. John c. Rolfe
(Loeb Classical Library, Harvard University Press, 1940); and Orosius's *History Against the
Pagans*, trans. I.W. Raymond (Columbia University Press, 1936).

A copy of the CIP data for this book is available
from the British Library.

Designed and created in the UK | Printed and bound in China

COLLECTOR'S EDITIONS

STORIES OF
PEOPLE & CIVILIZATION
ROMAN
ANCIENT ORIGINS

Edited and Introduced by
LINDSAY POWELL
Further Reading and
Lists of Ancient Kings & Leaders

FLAME TREE PUBLISHING

CONTENTS

CONTENTS

STORIES OF
PEOPLE & CIVILIZATION
ROMAN
ANCIENT ORIGINS

SERIES FOREWORD

Stretching back to the oral traditions of thousands of years ago, tales of heroes and disaster, creation and conquest have been told by many different civilizations, in ways unique to their landscape and language. Their impact sits deep within our own culture even though the detail in the stories themselves are a loose mix of historical record, the latest archaeological evidence, transformed narrative and the unwitting distortions of generations of storytellers.

Today the language of mythology lives around us: our mood is jovial, our countenance is saturnine, we are narcissistic and our modern life is hermetically sealed from others. The nuances of the ancient world form part of our daily routines and help us navigate the information overload of our interconnected lives.

The nature of a myth is that its stories are already known by most of those who hear or read them. Every era brings a new emphasiz, but the fundamentals remain the same: a desire to understand and describe the events and relationships of the world. Many of the great stories are archetypes that help us find our own place, equipping us with tools for self-understanding, both individually and as part of a broader culture.

For Western societies it is Greek mythology that speaks to us most clearly. It greatly influenced the mythological heritage of the ancient Roman civilization and is the lens through which we still see the Celts, the Norse and many of the other great peoples and religions. The Greeks themselves inherited much from their neighbours, the Egyptians, an older culture that became weary with the mantle of civilization.

Of course, what we perceive now as mythology had its own origins in perceptions of the divine and the rituals of the sacred. The earliest civilizations, in the crucible of the Middle East, in the Sumer of the third millennium BCE, are the source to which many of the mythic archetypes can be traced. Over five thousand years ago, as humankind collected together in cities for the first time, developed writing and industrial scale agriculture, started to irrigate the rivers and attempted to control rather than be at the mercy of its environment, humanity began to write down its tentative explanations of natural events, of floods and plagues, of disease.

Early stories tell of gods or god-like animals who are crafty and use their wits to survive, and it is not unreasonable to suggest that these were the first rulers of the gathering peoples of the earth, later elevated to god-like status with the distance of time. Such tales became more political as cities vied with each other for supremacy, creating new gods, new hierarchies for their pantheons. The older gods took on primordial roles and became the preserve of creation and destruction, leaving the new gods to deal with more current, everyday affairs. Empires rose and fell, with Babylon assuming the mantle from Sumeria in the 1800s BCE, in turn to be swept away by the Assyrians of the 1200s BCE; then the Assyrians and the Egyptians were subjugated by the Greeks, the Greeks by the Romans and so on, leading to the spread and assimilation of common themes, ideas and stories throughout the world.

The survival of history is dependent on the telling of good tales, but each one must have the 'feeling' of truth, otherwise it will be ignored. Around the firesides, or embedded in a book or a computer, the myths and legends of the past are still the living materials of retold myth, not restricted to an exploration of historical origins. Now we have devices and global communications that give us unparalleled access to a diversity of traditions. We can find out about Indigenous American, Indian, Chinese and tribal African mythology in a way that was denied to our ancestors, we can find connections, plot the archaeology, religion and the mythologies of the world to build a comprehensive image of the human experience that is both humbling and fascinating.

The books in this series introduce the many cultures of ancient humankind to the modern reader. From the earliest migrations across the globe to settlements along rivers, from the landscapes of mountains to the vast Steppes, from woodlands to deserts, humanity has adapted to its environments, nurturing languages and observations and expressing itself through records, mythmaking stories and living traditions. There is still so much to explore, but this is a great place to start.

Jake Jackson
General Editor

STORIES OF
PEOPLE & CIVILIZATION
ROMAN
ANCIENT ORIGINS

INTRODUCTION
& FURTHER READING

INTRODUCTION TO
ROMAN ANCIENT ORIGINS

THE ENDURING APPEAL OF ANCIENT ROME

Agenda, **agriculture, authority**, colony, constitution, empire, genius, legislation, military, religion, republic, superstition, testament, veteran, virtue – these are among an estimated 60 per cent of words in the English language that derive from Latin. Not only words, but whole phrases used in everyday speech are Latin: from how we tell the time ('a.m.', the abbreviation of *ante meridiem* and 'p.m.', meaning *post meridiem*) to how we apply law (*habeas corpus, quid pro quo*), or from how we conduct business (*bona fide, caveat emptor,* 'i.e.', short for *id est*) to how we relate to each other (*ad hoc, inter alios, per se, status quo*) – all these and others hail from a much earlier age. That was the time of the Romans. For over 1,000 years, from Rome's legendary foundation in 753 BCE to the day the emperor was deposed in 476 CE, one city-state shaped the destiny of the Western world. How did Rome come to be so influential? What explains its extraordinary rise? How did the ancient Romans understand their own origins?

Like us, the Romans pondered deeply about who they were, where they came from and how they built an empire. Part One of this volume is William Warde Fowler's *Rome*, published in 1912. In it he tells the astonishing story of Rome and its people from the earliest times, when it was a small town defending its interests from its powerful Etruscan neighbour in the eighth century BCE, to the reign of Marcus Aurelius, who struggled to hold the Roman Empire's borders against barbarian enemies without and an invisible viral foe spreading within in the second century CE. Augmenting Fowler's study, Part Two includes extracts from translations of texts written by the Romans themselves, specially selected to bring the authentic voices of these ancient people to this sweeping survey. Arranged chronologically, they too tell Rome's story. Their peculiar history and culture shaped their responses to life and its challenges, revealing deeper universal truths that still resonate with us – indeed, we even use their words and phrases.

FROM LEGEND AND TRADITION TO ARCHAEOLOGY AND HISTORY

The Romans traced the founding of their city back to two brothers. According to legend and recorded by Livy (extract in Part Two), Romulus and Remus each built a village on one of the Seven Hills. A squabble broke out in which Romulus killed his brother. Thus the story of Rome starts with fratricide. The Hut of Romulus (*Casa Romuli*) was preserved throughout Roman history as a place of reverence, dutifully rebuilt even after its destruction numerous times (such as the fire of 64 CE, described in the extract from

Tacitus in Part Two). King Romulus needed people for his village, now called *Roma*: he welcomed men seeking a new beginning to settle in his stronghold on the Palatine Hill. They required female companions, so they abducted women from their Sabine neighbours. Thus the story of Rome also starts with rapine.

Archaeology provides some evidence of human habitation in the region going back many thousands of years. Fowler notes (in Part One, Chapter I) that Rome's 'position on the Tiber was, in fact, strategically the best in Italy'. No physical trace of the Hut of Romulus *per se* has ever been found, although postholes of a building dated *c.* 900–700 BCE were discovered on the Palatine in 1946. Pliny the Elder tells (in Part Two) how, around 600 BCE, King Tarquinius Priscus ordered construction of the *Cloaca Maxima* ('Great Sewer') to drain the swamp (*Velabrum*) between the Palatine and Capitoline Hills to the Tiber river; repaired and expanded in Roman times, it still operates to this day. The *Forum Boarium* and *Forum Romanum* were built over the resulting dry land and became the central meeting places for socializing and trading, enacting and practising law, placating and worshipping Rome's gods. As wealth from the spoils of war poured in, the great and the good of Rome erected temples, theatres, bathhouses and *fora*. In the first century CE the attention of Pliny the Elder was caught by some 18 'marvels in building displayed by our own City' (discussed in Part Two). The ruins of many of them still stand today to remind us of:

The grandeur that was Rome.
Edgar Allan Poe, 'To Helen', 1831

Historians divide the timeline of ancient Rome into five ages:

1. **Kingdom, c. 1000–509** BCE: early Iron Age people settle beside the Tiber river in Latium; according to legend, on 21 April 753 BCE, Romulus founds a city on the Palatine Hill; seven kings rule Rome in succession; Rome withstands attempts at annexation by the Etruscans.

2. **Early Republic, 509–133** BCE: the last king, Tarquinius Superbus, ousted in a coup, is assassinated by Lucius Junius Brutus; the *Res Publica* ('Commonwealth') is established with a Senate and People's Assemblies, which together enact law and annually elect consuls and magistrates; the Latins rebel, resulting in a treaty that enables Romans and Latins to conquer and colonize Italy and form military alliances; the Roman citizen army defeats Pyrrhus of Epirus (275 BCE), Hamilcar Barca and Hannibal (264–146 BCE), Philip V (197 BCE) and Antiochus III (190 BCE), acquiring parts of North Africa, Sicily, Spain, Macedon, Greece and parts of Asia Minor.

3. **Late Republic, 133–31** BCE: violent struggles break out in Rome between the Patrician and Plebeian orders over the division of power, farmland and proceeds of empire; land reform advocates, the Gracchi brothers, are assassinated (133 and 123 BCE); slaves revolt in Sicily (132 and 103–101 BCE); Romans and allies stop Cimbric and German invasions of Italy (113–101 BCE); as the outcome of the Social War (91–89 BCE), Roman citizenship is granted to Italian allies; Caius Marius and Lucius Cornelius Sulla fight to rule Rome (83–81

BCE); Marcus Licinius Crassus defeats the army of Spartacus in the Third Servile War (73–71 BCE); Cnaeus Pompeius Magnus annexes more territory in Asia Minor (66–63 BCE), while Caius Julius Caesar conquers Gaul (58–50 BCE); civil war ensues, leading to Caesar being appointed *Dictator Perpetuo* – and to his assassination (Ides of March 44 BCE); after defeating the assassins (42 BCE) Caesar's heir, Octavian, establishes his power in a three-way alliance with Marcus Antonius and Marcus Aemilius Lepidus (43–32 BCE).

4. **Early Empire, 31 BCE–192 CE:** Antonius allies with Cleopatra VII, leading to civil war, their defeat at Actium (31 BCE), their deaths (30 BCE) and the annexation of Egypt; Octavian agrees a pact with the Senate dividing up the Roman Empire and is named Augustus (27 BCE); Augustus professionalizes the Roman army, which acquires territory in Spain, northern Italy, the Balkans and up to the Rhine and Danube rivers; Augustus and his Julio-Claudian successors consolidate imperial power in their position as *princeps*; Jesus of Nazareth is crucified (30/33 CE); Claudius invades Britain (43 CE); fire destroys the centre of Rome (64 CE); after Nero's suicide, civil war ensues (68–69 CE); the First Jewish War (66–73 CE) results in Jerusalem being razed; Trajan annexes land north of the Danube and east of the Euphrates rivers (98–117 CE); Hadrian abandons Trajan's conquests (117 CE), builds a wall in Britain (119/22–126/130 CE) and defeats Jewish rebels in the Second Jewish War (132–136 CE); Marcus Aurelius fights the Marcommani (166–180 CE).

5. **Late Empire, 192–476 CE:** after a civil war, the unstable rule of the Severan Dynasty (193–235 CE) leads to political

turmoil (235–284 CE); Diocletian divides the empire into East and West sectors (286 CE); Constantine I declares tolerance for Christianity (313 CE) and moves the capital of the Empire from Rome to Byzantium (Constantinople, 330 CE); the Empire is split again upon the death of Theodosius I (395 CE); Romulus Augustus, the last emperor of the West, is ousted from Rome (4 September 476 CE) by Odoacer.

SPQR: THE COMMONWEALTH AND ROMAN CITIZENSHIP

Arguably the most recognizable symbol of ancient Rome is the group of four initials 'SPQR'. Visitors to modern Rome still see SPQR on buildings and public service infrastructure owned and operated by the city council. The letters stand for the Latin phrase *Senatus Populusque Romanus*. It means 'Roman Senate and People' and represents the two parts of Roman government. The division of political power (*imperium*) between the Patricians and Plebeians – the two classes that made up Roman society – was fought over for centuries. Fowler calls the Senate 'perhaps their greatest political institution' (in Part One, Chapter II). Writing in the second century BCE, Polybius describes (in Part Two) Rome's constitution as a unique hybrid of a democracy and a monarchy.

What the Romans most feared was the oppression (*dominatio*) of a king (*rex*) and the threat to their freedom (*libertas*). When Julius Caesar was perceived as becoming too ambitious, he was assassinated on the Ides of March 44 BCE, as recorded by Suetonius (in Part Two). After the ensuing civil wars (43–42 BCE), the victor Augustus claimed to have 'restored liberty to the *Res Publica*, which had been oppressed by the tyranny of a faction [i.e. the conspirators]' (in Part Two); but from that time on *imperium* came to be concentrated in the person of the emperor (*princeps*), as observed by Cassius Dio (in Part Two). The Senate still met and advised the *princeps*, issuing decrees (*Senatus Consulta*) from time to time, but the People's Assemblies (*comitia*) were eventually suspended.

The Roman Empire was an evolving amalgam of cultures. Latins, Etruscans, Greeks, Gauls, Iberians, Syrians, Egyptians, Judaeans, Germans, Africans and Britons all contributed their uniqueness to the project that was Rome. It placed Roman citizenship (*civitas*) front and centre. Even a slave had a chance of being freed and his children could then become enfranchised citizens, able to participate fully in society. (Only men could be full citizens, participating in politics and military life in Roman society; the status of a woman was defined by her father and/or husband.) Finally, in 212 or 213 CE, Emperor Caracalla issued an edict (*Constitutio Antoniniana*) granting Roman citizenship to all free-born men of the Empire. A citizen could participate in passing laws, vote in elections for city magistracies and enrol in the legions, but, as Fowler notes (in Part I, Chapter III), 'the first duty of a citizen was obedience to constituted authority'. 'The Roman citizen was the one most highly privileged person in the civilized world of that day,' he writes (in Part One, Chapter V), on account 'of the legal protection of his person and his property, wherever he might be in the Empire'. The three most powerful words in the ancient world were *civis Romanus sum!* ('I am a Roman citizen!'), as the case against Caius Verres, prosecuted by Cicero in 70 BCE, illustrates (in Part Two).

PAX AUGUSTA: WARFIGHTING AND PEACEKEEPING

From the earliest times, Roman armies were recruited from Roman citizens. The legion was a citizen militia. Adult males were picked by lot to serve for a campaign season in the ranks of two legions (from the Latin *legio*, 'levy'), each consisting of between 4,200 and 4,500 infantry and 300 cavalry. Led to war by consuls or praetors, the legion was subdivided into *manipuli* ('maniples' or 'companies') comprising two *centuriae* ('centuries'), commanded by the senior of two centurions. There were maniples of three different kinds of soldiers: *hastati*, lightly armed, relatively inexperienced troops, forming the front battle line; *principes*, better equipped and more experienced soldiers forming the second line, to whom the *hastati* would fall back if overwhelmed; and *triarii*, heavily armed soldiers, battle-hardened from several campaigns, held in reserve at the rear. The army was supplemented with infantry and cavalry from Italian allies (*socii*), obliged by treaty with Rome to provide manpower in wartime when called upon. This was the combined army led by Scipio, which defeated Hannibal at Zama (202 BCE).

By the time of Marius and Julius Caesar, in the first century BCE, in response to fighting many enemies in different theatres of war the format of the Roman legion had transmuted to one based on *cohortes*. A legion, now commanded by a legate, had 10 cohorts, each comprising six centuries. The *centuria* of 80 soldiers (*milites*) was the backbone of the legion, with the *centurio* in charge being key to its operational success. A legion employed up to 6,000 *legionarii* with officers, as well as 120 cavalry. Auxiliaries (*auxilia*) came to match the number of legionaries. By the time of Augustus the Roman army had increased to 300,000 men-at-arms and included a navy.

Augustus created the standing army of professional troops. Men served fixed terms and were paid a stipend, as explained by Dio Cassius (in Part Two). A professional army required policies for recruitment and training, described by Vegetius (in Part Two). There were operational failures: mutinies were uncommon, but they did occur, and the loyalty of the legions or the Praetorian Cohorts could be bought for a price in times of civil war – of which there were increasing numbers of incidents during the Early and Late Empire.

By agreement with the Senate, under Augustus the legions were deployed to areas of greatest risk of unrest. These locations changed over time, as observed by Cassius Dio and Tacitus (extracts in Part Two). In the provinces the army acted as a police force, with centurions frequently adjudicating in civil disputes.

The Roman Empire had grown initially by accident. Obliged to assist its allies by treaty, Roman armies were involved in wars in Italy, then overseas. War fighting became imperial policy. After the Punic Wars, and especially under the emperors, Roman commanders engaged in foreign wars of choice, for the glory (*gloria*) of victory (*victoria*) – and with it the booty (*praeda*) – and as a means of retaining power through the loyalty of the army (*fides exercituum*). Achieving peace (*pax*) required the successful prosecution of war: 'peace was born from victories,' states Augustus in his *Res Gestae*.

The Romans now had to protect their far-flung territories. The *Historia Augusta* (in Part Two) notes that from Emperor Hadrian's time in the second century CE, the Empire's military strategy became more defensive in posture. Frontier walls and defences were built in Britain, Germany and North Africa. From the third century CE border forces (*limitanei*) and mobile field armies (*comitatenses* and later *palatini*), led by counts, replaced the old military structure. Barbarian warriors were also recruited to serve Rome in the fight against other barbarians.

PAX DEORUM: RELIGION AND TRADITION

The Romans considered themselves to be a religious people. Their religion (*religio*) was about ritual, prayer and the offering of sacrifices or votive objects, rather than matters of belief or doctrine. Public ceremonies were led by the *Pontifex Maximus* (later a role of the emperor) as Chief Priest and colleges of priests; they conducted traditional rites to maintain peace with the gods (*Pax Deorum*) or to influence them in ways favourable to the community. 'If this peace, or covenant, were not kept up, it was believed that the State could not prosper – the very life of the State depended on it,' writes Fowler (in Part I, Chapter III). Across the Empire, Roman colonies (*coloniae*) had temples to the Capitoline Triad – Jupiter, Juno and Minerva – replicating the ones on the Capital Hill in Rome. *Religio* was transactional: in return for a good outcome, such as victory in battle, an individual supplicant might offer to set up an altar or a temple to a god in willing fulfilment of a vow (*votum solvit libens merito*).

A profound respect for tradition and custom (*mos maiorum*) informed Roman society and its norms. Suetonius writes in

Rhetoricians that 'These innovations in the customs and principles of our forefathers do not please us nor seem proper.' The all-female Vestal priesthood actually predated Rome itself; the women tended to Vesta's hearth to ensure the sacred flame always burned.

The Romans were animists. They believed in spirits of place (*genii loci*), which had to be respected and placated. Every home had a shrine to the household gods (*lares* and *penates*) for daily worship, and a cupboard for the ancestors' death masks (*imagines*), which were worn at funerals. Combats between gladiators were originally held in honour of the shades (*manes*) of deceased relatives. In the Late Republic and Early Empire wealthy individuals sponsored funeral games (*munera*), attended by the public in remembrance of notable family members.

Romans studied omens and portents: priests called *augures* watched the flight of birds, while *haruspices* inspected the entrails of sacrificed animals to interpret the will of the gods. Certain days were deemed *dies fasti* on which business could be conducted; others were *dies nefasti* on which business was suspended.

As the Romans annexed territory (*territorium*), they encountered new, yet familiar, gods and spirits. Rather than seeing them as different, the Romans understood them to be local manifestations of their own deities and combined their attributes into composite identities. In Britain the goddess of the spring at Bath (Aquae Sulis) was perceived as Minerva, becoming Sulis Minerva, while the tribal protector god of Britons and Gauls was regarded as Mars, becoming Mars Toutatis. Finding *similarity* between religious and political systems was one reason for Rome's success in pacifying conquered peoples.

With growing exposure to foreigners, new religions and cults appeared in Rome. The oldest synagogue of the Jews – generally respected for the antiquity of their religion – was built at Ostia around the time of Emperor Claudius. Mystery cults from the East, such as those of the Egyptian goddess Isis or the Persian god Mithras, gained in popularity, offering their worshippers a deeper spiritual life. Christians initially met in secret. In the second century CE Pliny the Younger sought advice from Trajan (in Part Two) about how to deal with them. A century later, Constantine I tolerated Christians, permitting them to worship in the open – a fact celebrated by Orosius (in Part Two).

QED: PRACTICAL TECHNOLOGY AND REALISTIC ART

The spread of Roman civilization was enabled by several key technologies. Perhaps foremost of them was the road (*via*). The first was the *Via Appia* ('Appian Way', 312–264 BCE), built by Appius Claudius Caecus to link Rome to the seaport at Brundisium (Brindisi). By 117 CE there were an estimated 80,000 km (50,000 miles) of roads crisscrossing the Empire. The Romans did not invent the road, but they perfected its construction, using layers of compacted gravel and stone for durability and a camber and gullies for drainage. Usually laid down by the army as highways to expedite the supply of men and matériel between camps, the roads were famously straight – the result of using the *groma*, a surveying tool. Roads also enabled the public mail service (*cursus publicus*), established by Augustus, with rest stops at change and repair stations (*mutationes*), to relay expeditiously official government and military correspondence between Rome and its outposts.

Rivers were traversed with well-engineered bridges. For military campaigns Julius Caesar built a temporary pontoon bridge across the Rhine twice – in 55 and 53 BCE (noted by Suetonius in Part Two). Trajan subsequently erected a permanent segmental arch bridge across the Danube (103–105 CE). Key to a permanent bridge's stability and load-bearing capacity was the arch. Again, the Romans did not invent the arch, but they perfected its round or semicircular form. Arches supported and graced the interior and exterior walls of halls (like the *Basilica* of Maxentius), theatres (such as the Theatre of Marcellus) and amphitheatres (like the Colosseum).

Roman aqueducts carried conduits of fresh water atop arcades, often tiered, across valleys and plains. The Aqueducts at Segovia and Pont du Gard near Nîmes still stand to a height of 28.5 m (93.5 ft) and 48.8 m (160 ft) respectively. Julius Frontinus wrote a treatise on the aqueducts of Rome (extract in Part Two), boasting:

> *With such an array of indispensable structures carrying so many waters, compare, if you will, the idle Pyramids or the useless, though famous, works of the Greeks!*

Water brought by aqueducts flowed continuously over settling tanks, then on to distribution towers and through lead pipes to supply public drinking fountains, baths and private residences. Waste water and untreated sewage flowed through channels buried beneath the streets, such as the *Cloaca Maxima*, and out into nearby rivers.

While Romans used stone and marble extensively in construction, mass-produced, kiln-fired bricks and tiles were *the* essential building materials. Layers of brick, or brick and stone in various combinations, with infills of rocky material, were bonded together using lime mortar. Arches of brick were often embedded into the walls to distribute the weight above. Outer surfaces could be left undecorated or plastered and painted or covered with marble; Pliny the Elder describes (in Part Two) how machines sliced slabs of marble to decorate buildings. Cement (*opus caementicium*) – a mixture of 85 per cent volcanic ash (*pozzolana*), lime and water – could be poured into wooden forms to construct vaults (such as at Trajan's Market, Rome) and domes (such as the Pantheon, still the largest unsupported dome in the world). Remarkably, Roman concrete hardened in sea water. A study by Massachusetts Institute of Technology and Harvard University, published in 2023, suggests that it was self-healing because its 'lime-casts' chemically sealed cracks when made wet by rain or sea.

'The Romans were, in fact, the most practical people in history,' writes Fowler (in Part One, Chapter I). In both the sciences and the arts they drew upon the discoveries of the Etruscans, Greeks and Egyptians. From the Etruscans they learned about hydraulic engineering and road construction, and from the Greeks about architectural and artistic styling. Julius Caesar brought the solar-based calender of 365 days plus a leap year from Egypt to Rome, officially replacing the domestic lunar calender on 1 January 45 BCE. The Romans were experts at scaling up mechanical innovations. Their achievements included the hillside mill at Barbegal, with its cascading, 16 water-powered grindstones to make flour for the community at Arles, and the massive, man-powered cranes, operated with arrays of multiple pulleys to erect tall buildings in Rome.

In the first century CE the Roman engineer Vitruvius wrote in his treatise on architecture that buildings should display three attributes: *firmitas* (strength), *utilitas* (utility) and *venustas* (beauty). Stonemasons graced them with carved inscriptions of great clarity and elegance using the Latin alphabet – the same letters in which this book is printed. Roman artists celebrated realism. Decorating their buildings, portrait busts and statuary represented accurate, lifelike reproductions of people in painted marble or polished bronze. The walls of private homes were often adorned with naturalistic landscapes or fantasy architectural illusions. In Romanized Egypt, artists painted portraits of deceased persons in encaustic on wood to enhance mummies, producing facial images of a quality not seen again until the Renaissance.

THE LEGACY OF ANCIENT ROME

After the fall of Rome in 476 CE, and with it the Empire in the West, Roman civilization continued in the East. Its Greek-speaking citizens there still called themselves Ῥωμαῖος (*Romaios*, Romans). This Byzantine Empire had a Roman administration, a predominantly Greek culture and a Christian state religion. It lasted until the fall of Constantinople on 29 May 1453.

Many of the Empire's *coloniae* survived to become urban centres in the emerging countries of Europe – Rome's direct successor, Christendom. The Roman Church's influence extended into all aspects of life. While Greek books circulated in the East, Latin books in the West were preserved and copied by hand by monks in Christian monasteries. After the 1440s many texts were reproduced as printed copies, which circulated among scholars and the intelligentsia. Pliny the Elder's *Natural History* became a go-to reference book in the Middle Ages and the Renaissance. Niccolò Machiavelli studied Livy's Roman history and deduced principles for modern men in positions of power to follow. In England William Shakespeare found inspiration for his tragedies in Thomas North's 1519 translation of *Parallel Lives of the Noble Greeks and Romans* by Plutarch. Some countries adopted or adapted Roman law. The men of the Age of Enlightenment read the works of Caesar, Cicero, Polybius and Tacitus. The 'Founding Fathers' studied them at school and used their insights to draft, in 1787, the constitution for a new republic: the United States of America.

Learning Latin was a crucial part of an Englishman's education. After school, taking the Grand Tour – which included Italy – became highly fashionable for young men of means. Edward Gibbon benefited from such travels, his visit to Rome inspiring him to write his monumental *The Decline and Fall of the Roman Empire* (1776–1789). These travellers brought back the romance of the ancient civilization's now faded glory. Inspired by the rediscovery of Vitruvius's books on architecture, Andrea Palladio, Inigo Jones, Christopher Wren and Ottone Caledari designed palaces and stately homes across Europe in the grand style, complete with arches, columns, domes and pediments. To decorate them, antiquities such as busts and statues found their way into the halls and libraries. Images of the ruins of Rome, reproduced in souvenir paintings by Giovanni Paolo Panini or in prints by Giovanni Battista Piranesi, often adorned their walls.

Ancient Rome, which rose from a village in Latium to rule an empire on three continents, came to be shorthand for the ambition of imperial power. In this vein, from *Lays of Ancient Rome*, a popular collection of narrative poems, comes this stirring verse:

> *Where Atlas flings his shadow*
> *Far o'er the western foam,*
> *Shall be great fear on all who hear*
> *The mighty name of Rome.*

**Thomas Babington Macaulay, *Prophecy*
of Capys XXXI, 1842**

The aura of Caesar continued to dominate political circles. In eighteenth-century Russia the emperor was called Tsar, while in nineteenth-century Germany he was named Kaiser. Twentieth-century authoritarian regimes appropriated Rome's potent symbols to bolster their dubious credentials: Benito Mussolini took the *fasces*, the symbol of a Roman magistrate's legal authority, to be the logo of his National Fascist Party; Adolf Hitler adapted the Roman god Jupiter's *aquila* holding thunderbolts to be the swastika-clutching *Adler*, which hung over the stage at Nazi Party rallies.

In the rush towards the future, we risk forgetting the past. As Fowler rightly observes:

We may be apt at the present day, when science has opened out for us so many new paths of knowledge, and inspired us with such enthusiasm in pursuing them, to forget the value of the inheritance which Rome preserved for us.
William Warde Fowler, *Rome*, Chapter X

Two millennia after the height of the Empire, the Romans continue to inspire new generations about the opportunities that come from applying determination, discipline, fortitude, order and resilience. The Romans also inform us about the responsibilities that come with citizenship, liberty, patriotism, power and privilege. Tellingly, all of these words derive from ones the Romans themselves used.

FURTHER READING

ANCIENT TEXTS

Anon, various (trans. Robin Birley), *Lives of the Later Caesars: The First Part of the Augustan History, with Newly Compiled Lives of Nerva & Trajan* (Penguin Books, 1976)

Appian (trans. Brian McGing), *Roman History*, Volumes I–VI (Loeb Classical Library, Harvard University Press, 2020)

Augustus (trans. P.A. Brunt *et al.*), *Res Gestae Divi Augusti: The Achievements of the Divine Augustus by Augustus; Emperor of Rome* (Oxford University Press, 1969)

Caesar (trans. Kurt A. Raaflaub), *The Landmark Julius Caesar: The Complete Works: Gallic War, Civil War, Alexandrian War, African War, and Spanish War* (Broadway Books, 2019)

Cassius Dio (trans. Ernest Cary), *Roman History*, Volumes I–IX (Loeb Classical Library, Harvard University Press, 2020)

Catullus (trans. Daisy Dunn), *The Poems of Catullus* (HarperCollins Publishers, 2016)

Cicero (trans. Michael Grant), *Selected Works* (Penguin Books, 2004)

Horace (trans. David West), *The Complete Odes and Epodes* (Oxford University Press, 2008)

Livy (trans. J.C. Yardley), *History of Rome*, Volumes I–XIV (Loeb Classical Library, Harvard University Press, 2017)

Lucan (trans. Susan H. Braund), *Civil War* (Oxford University Press, 2008)

Lucretius (trans. Frank O. Copley), *On the Nature of Things* (W. W. Norton & Company, 2011)

Marcus Aurelius (trans. Martin Hammond), *Meditations* (Penguin Books, 2006)

Ovid (trans. Anne and Peter Wiseman), *Fasti* (Oxford University Press, 2013)

Sallust (trans. John T. Ramsey and J.C. Rolfe), *The War with Catiline. The War with Jugurtha* (Loeb Classical Library, Harvard University Press, 2013)

Suetonius (trans. Catherine Edwards), *Lives of the Caesars* (Oxford University Press, 2009)

Tacitus (trans. Alfred John Church and William Jackson Brodribb), *The Annals and The Histories* (The Modern Library, 2003)

Vegetius (trans. N.P. Milner), *Epitome of Military Science* (Liverpool University Press, 1997)

Vitruvius (trans. Ingrid D. Rowland and Thomas Noble Howe), *Ten Books on Architecture* (Cambridge University Press, 2001)

MODERN TEXTS

Balsdon, J.P.V.D., *Life and Leisure in Ancient Rome* (Phoenix, 2002)

Barrett, Anthony A., *Rome Is Burning: Nero and the Fire That Ended a Dynasty* (Princeton University Press, 2020)

Beard, Mary, *SPQR: A History of Ancient Rome* (W.W. Norton and Company, 2015)

Butterworth, Alex and Laurence, Ray, *Pompeii: The Living City* (St. Martin's Press, 2013)

Carandini, Andrea, *Atlas of Ancient Rome* (Princeton University Press, revised edition, 2017)

Clarke, John. R., *Roman Sex 100 BC–AD 250* (Harry Abrams, 2003)

Connolly, Peter, *Greece and Rome at War* (Frontline Books, illustrated edition, 2016)

DeLaine, Janet, *Roman Architecture* (Oxford University Press, 2023)

Drogula, Fred K., *Commanders and Command in the Roman Republic and Early Empire* (The University of North Carolina Press, 2015)

Fischer, Thomas (trans. Bishop, M.C.), *Army of the Roman Emperors* (Casemate, illustrated edition, 2019)

Flower, Harriet I., *Roman Republics* (Princeton University Press, 2011)

Gabriel, Richard A., *Scipio Africanus: Rome's Greatest General* (Potomac Books, illustrated edition, 2008)

Galinsky, Karl, *Augustus: Introduction to the Life of an Emperor* (Cambridge University Press, 2012)

Goldsworthy, Adrian, *The Punic Wars* (Cassell, 2001)

Heather, Peter, *The Fall of the Roman Empire: A New History* (Pan Books, 2006)

Holland, Tom, *Rubicon: The Triumph and Tragedy of the Roman Republic* (Abacus, 2004)

Kershaw, Stephen P., *The Enemies of Rome: The Barbarian Rebellion Against the Roman Empire* (Pegasus Books, 2021)

Knapp, Robert, *Invisible Romans: Prostitutes, outlaws, slaves, gladiators, ordinary men and women ... the Romans that history forgot* (Profile Books, 2013)

Luttwak, Edward, *The Grand Strategy of the Roman Empire: From the First Century* CE *to the Third* (Johns Hopkins University Press, revised and updated edition, 2016)

Matyszak, Philip, *Gladiator: The Roman Fighter's (Unofficial) Manual* (Thames and Hudson Ltd., illustrated edition, 2011)

Powell, Lindsay, *Augustus at War: The Struggle for the* Pax Augusta (Pen and Sword Books, 2018)

Rook, Tony, *Roman Building Techniques* (Amberley Publishing, 2013)

Rüpke, Jörg, *Pantheon: A New History of Roman Religion* (Princeton University Press, 2020)

Scheidel, Walter (ed.), *The Science of Roman History: Biology, Climate and the Future of the Past* (Princeton University Press, 2019)

Scullard, H.H., *From the Gracchi to Nero: A History of Rome 133 BC to AD 68* (Routledge, 2010)

Sherwood, Andrew N. *et al.*, *Greek and Roman Technology: A Sourcebook of Translated Greek and Roman Texts* (Routledge, second edition, 2019)

Strauss, Barry, *The Death of Caesar: The Story of History's Most Famous Assassination* (Simon & Schuster; illustrated edition, 2016)

Sumner, Graham and D'Amato, Raffaele, *Arms and Armour of the Imperial Roman Soldier: From Marius to Commodus, 112 BC–AD 192* (Frontline Books, illustrated edition, 2009)

Syme, Ronald, *The Roman Revolution* (Oxford University Press, 2002)

Ward-Perkins, Bryan, *The Fall of Rome and the End of Civilization* (Oxford University Press, illustrated edition, 2006)

Wolff, Greg, *Rome: An Empire's Story* (Oxford University Press, 2012)

Lindsay Powell (Introduction, editor) is a historian and author who writes about the conflicts, commanders and campaigns of the ancient world. He edited, and wrote the introductions for, the volumes *Hannibal*, *Julius Caesar* and *Greek Ancient Origins* for Flame Tree Publishing. His critically acclaimed books include the biographies *Marcus Agrippa*, *Eager for Glory*, *Germanicus* and *Bar Kokhba*, as well as the military histories *Augustus at War*, *Roman Soldier versus Germanic Warrior, 1st Century AD* and *The Bar Kokhba War, AD 132–136*. He is news editor of *Ancient History* and *Ancient Warfare* magazines. His articles have also appeared in *Military History*, *Strategy and Tactics* and *Desperta Ferro* magazines. Lindsay is a regular guest on the *Ancient Warfare* and *History Hit* podcasts. He is a 10-year veteran of the Ermine Street Guard, the world's leading Roman army re-enactment society. He has a BSc (Hons) in managerial and administrative studies from Aston University, England. Born in Cardiff, Wales, he divides his time between Austin, Texas and Wokingham, England.

PART ONE

PART ONE

ORIGINS & HISTORY OF THE ROMANS

The Romans have been closely studied by scholars for centuries. Among the best was William Warde Fowler MA (1847–1921). A British historian and classicist, he contributed significantly to the study of the religions and social history of ancient Rome.

Born in Langford Budville, Somerset in England, Fowler was educated at Marlborough College (1860–1866). He entered New College, Oxford (1866) and, after a term, won a scholarship to Lincoln College (1866–1870). Elected to a Fellowship of Lincoln (1872), he tutored ancient history at the college, later becoming Sub-Rector (1881–1904). Fowler became vice president of the Society for the Promotion of Roman Studies (now the Roman Society) for 1913–14, and served as president of the Classical Association in 1920.

He published several influential works on ancient Rome, including *Julius Caesar and the Foundation of the Roman Imperial System* (1892), *The Roman Festivals of the Period of the Republic* (1899) and *Social Life at Rome in the Age of Cicero* (1908). His series of 20 Gifford Lectures, given at The University of Edinburgh, appeared in print as *The Religious Experience of the Roman People, from the Earliest Times to the Age of Augustus* (1911).

Fowler's critically acclaimed *Rome* (1912), a lightly edited version of which is presented here, is a history of the city from its foundation in the time of the Etruscans to its zenith in the age of the Antonine emperors.

ROME

I
THE FIRST ROMANS

Let us suppose an ordinary person, with no special knowledge of Classical History, to be looking at a collection of Roman antiquities in the cases of a museum. They will probably not linger long over these cases but will pass on to something more likely to attract their interest. The objects they are looking at are, for the most part, neither striking nor beautiful, and the same are presented for his inspection over and over again as collections from various Roman sites. These are chiefly useful things, implements and utensils of all kinds, and fragments of military weapons and armour. In the coins they can take no delight, because, apart from the fact that, uninterpreted, these have no tale to tell them, these do not excite their admiration by beauty of design and workmanship. If, indeed, they were visiting a museum at Rome, they would find plenty of beautiful things in it; but these are works of Greek artists, imported by wealthy or tasteful Romans in the later ages of Rome's history. A typical collection of genuine Roman antiquities would probably have the effect I describe. Utility, not beauty, would seem to have been the motive of the people who left these things behind them.

The Highest Good: The Powerful, Not the Beautiful

The same motive will also be suggested to us if we visit any of the larger Roman works either in Britain or on the European Continent. Most of us know the look of a Roman road running straight over hill and valley, and meant mainly for military purposes, to enable troops to move rapidly and to survey the country as they marched. In the towns which have been excavated, we usually find that the most spacious and striking buildings must have been the meeting-halls (*basilicae*), in which business of all kinds was transacted, and especially business connected with law and government. Very often, though not in the comparatively poor province of Britain, this characteristic of utility is combined with another – solidity and imposing size. In this well-watered island the Romans did not need aqueducts to bring a constant supply of water to their towns, but in Italy and the south of France these great works are sometimes unnecessarily huge and imposing. Even when they left the path of strict utility, as in their triumphal arches and gateways, for which we must go to Trier in Germany, or to Orange in the south of France, or to Italy itself, they held strongly to the principles of solidity and imposing size. A writer who knew their art well has said that their notion of the highest of all things, their *summum bonum*, was not the beautiful, but the powerful, and that they thought they had as a people received this notion from heaven.

It would, indeed, be wrong to say that there is no beauty in Roman art; but it is quite in accordance with what has just been said, that even in the best of it there is a strong tendency to realism, to matter of fact. In their sculpture they were especially strong in portraiture, and in depicting scenes of human life they never or rarely idealise. A battle scene, or a picture on stone of life in a city, is crowded with figures, just because it really was so, and the work is without that restfulness for the eye which the perfect grouping of a Greek artist so often supplies. So, too, in literature; all their greatest poetry has a strictly practical object, and bears directly on human life. The great philosophical poem of Lucretius was meant to rescue the Romans from religious superstition; the object of the *Aeneid* of Virgil, of which I shall have more to say in another chapter, was to recall the degenerate Roman of that day to the sense of duty in the home and in the State. Their one original invention in literary form was satire, by which they meant comment, friendly or hostile, on the human life around them. Their myths and legends, of which there was no such abundant crop as in Greece, dealt chiefly with the founding of cities, or with the heroic deeds of human beings. On the whole they excelled most in oratory and history; and their prose came to perfection earlier than their poetry.

People of Action

One other feature of their character shall be mentioned here, which is entirely in keeping with the rest, and often escapes notice. If in the works of their hands and their brains they were not an imaginative people, we can well understand that they had not this gift in practical life. Imagination in action takes the form of adventurousness, as we may see in our own history; the literary imaginativeness of Elizabethan England has its counterpart in the adventurous voyages of Elizabethan seamen. The Romans were not an adventurous people; they were not imaginative enough to be so. They penetrated, indeed, into unknown countries; Caesar reached Britain and bridged the Rhine, but that great man, a true Roman born, had a temperament rather scientific than romantic. He did as almost all conquering Romans had done before him, and were to do after him – he advanced solidly, making his way safe behind him and feeling carefully in front of him. His book about his wars in Gaul was written without a touch of imagination, and for strictly practical purposes. There is, indeed, in the generation before Caesar, an exception so striking that it may be said to prove the rule; he who reads Plutarch's charming life of Sertorius, an Italian from the mountains of central Italy, will find both romance and adventure in his story.

It is plain, then, that we have to do in this volume with a people not of imagination, but of action: a people intensely alive to the necessities and difficulties of human life. The Romans were, in fact, the most practical people in history; and this enabled them to supply what was wanting to the civilization of the Mediterranean basin in the work of the Greeks. They themselves were well aware of this quality, and proud of it. We find it expressed by the elder Cato quite at the beginning of the best age of Roman literature; his ideal Roman is *vir fortis et strenuus* – 'a man of strong courage and active energy'. Tacitus, in the later days of that literature, says that all designs and deeds should be directed 'to the practical ends of life' (*ad utilitatem vitae*). Midway between these two, we have the great Latin poets constantly singing of the hardihood and the practical virtues which had made Rome great, and Italy great under Rome's leadership:

Our babes are hardened in the frost and flood,
Strong is the stock and sturdy whence we came.
Our boys from morn till evening scour the wood,
Their joy is hunting, and the steed to tame,
To bend the bow, the flying shaft to aim.
Patient of toil, and used to scanty cheer,
Our youths with rakes the stubborn glebe reclaim,
Or storm the town. Through life we grasp the spear.
In war it strikes the foe, in peace it goads the steer.

Virgil, *Aeneid* 9.607–613
(E. Fairfax Taylor's translation)

These lines, though applied to an Italian stock, were meant to remind the Roman of a life that had once been his. The words in which the Romans delighted as expressing their national characteristics, all tell the same tale: *gravitas*, the seriousness of demeanour which is the outward token of a steadfast purpose; *continentia*, self-restraint; *industria* and *diligentia*, words which we have inherited from them, needing no explanation; *constantia*, perseverance in conduct; and last, not least, *virtus*, manliness, which originally meant activity and courage, and with ripening civilization took on a broader and more ethical meaning. Quotations might be multiplied a thousandfold to prove the honest admiration of this people for their own nobler qualities. As exemplified in an individual, Plutarch's *Life of the Elder Cato* will give a good idea of these.

But it is essential to note that this hard and practical turn of the Roman mind was in some ways curiously limited. It cannot be said that they excelled either in industrial or commercial pursuits. Agriculture was their original occupation, and trade-guilds existed at Rome very early in her history; but the story of their agriculture is rather a sad one, and Rome has never become a great industrial city. Their first book about husbandry was translated from the Carthaginian, and their methods of commerce they learnt chiefly from the Greeks. It was in another direction that their genius for practical work drew them: to the arts and methods of discipline, law, government.

The Power of Ruling: Discipline, Law, and Government

We can see this peculiar gift showing itself at all stages of their development: in the agricultural family which was the germ of all their later growth, in the city-state which grew from that germ, and in the Empire, founded by the leaders of the city-state, and organized by Augustus and his successors. It is seen, too, in their military system, which won them their empire; they did not fight merely for spoil or glory, but for clearly realized practical purposes. As Tacitus says of a single German tribe which possessed something of this gift, the Romans did not so much go out to battle as to war. True, they constantly made blunders and suffered defeat; they often 'muddled through' difficulties as we do ourselves; but they refused to recognize defeat, and profited by adverse fortune. Listen once more to a few words of old Cato; in his *Origins of Rome*, written for his son, he wrote, 'Adversity tames us, and teaches us our true line of conduct, while good fortune is apt to warp us from the way of prudence.' Thus, they went on from defeat to victory, conquest, and government. It is worthwhile not only to lay to heart, but to learn by heart, the famous lines in which Virgil sums up the Roman's conception of his own work in the world:

> Others will mould their bronzes to
> breathe with a tenderer grace,
> Draw, I doubt not, from marble a vivid life to the face,
> Plead at the bar more deftly, with sapient wands of the wise,
> Trace heaven's courses and changes, predict us stars to arise.
> Thine, O Roman, remember, to reign over every race!
> These be thine arts, thy glories, the
> ways of peace to proclaim,
> Mercy to show to the fallen, the proud with battle to tame!
> **Virgil, Aeneid 6.847–853**
> **(Charles Bowen's translation)**

It was this power of ruling, which itself implies a habit of discipline, that marked out Rome as the natural successor of Greece in European civilization; and it grew naturally out of the purely practical bent of the early Romans, who were unhampered in their constant activity by fancy, reflection, or culture. Without it, we may doubt if the work of the Greeks would have been saved for us when the storms from the north, invasions of barbarian peoples, fell at last upon the sunny lands filled with the spirit of Greek thought and the divine works of Greek artists. To Roman discipline, law, and government, we owe not only much that even now is every day of practical benefit to us, but the preservation of what we still possess of the treasures of Hellenic genius.

Greek Influence

For this reason I assume that this book will be taken up by most readers after they have made some acquaintance with the history and thought of the Greeks. It is true that the history of the two peoples is best looked at as one great whole; there is a general likeness in their institutions; the form of the State, and the ideas of government, with which each grew to maturity, were in the main the same. But Roman mental development was much slower than Greek; and Greece was already beginning to lose her vitality when Rome was still illiterate and unable to record her own history adequately. Thus Greek influence was the first to tell upon the world; the basin of the Mediterranean was already permeated by the Greek spirit when Roman influence began to work upon it; and there can be no doubt that he who begins with Roman history and then goes on to Greek is reversing the natural order of things.

I will also assume that those who have begun to read this book are provided with some knowledge of that Mediterranean basin which is the scene of Graeco-Roman history; such as can be gained by frequent contemplation of a good map. They will be familiar with Sicily and south Italy, which were teeming with Greek settlements when Roman history really begins. They will probably have realized how short a step it is from Italy to Africa, whether or no Sicily be taken as a stepping-stone; Cato could show fresh figs in the Roman senate which had been grown in Carthaginian territory. They will have realized that you can pass from the 'heel' of Italy to the Hellenic peninsula in a single night, as Caesar did when he embarked

his army at Brindisi to attack his rival; such geographical facts
are of immense importance in explaining not only the foreign
policy of Rome, but also the development of her culture. And
thus furnished, they will begin to be curious about the destiny
of the Italian peninsula, of which Greek history has had little
to tell them. Leaving that question for the present, they will
wish to know why the Greeks did not colonize the centre and
north of Italy as they did the south and south-west, but left
room enough for a new type of civilization to grow up there.
And above all, they will wish to know how and why a single
city on the western coast should have succeeded in building
up a great power in Italy quite independent of Greece, and
destined eventually to supersede her, which may be reckoned
as a factor almost as important in the making of our modern
civilization as Hellas herself.

This last question is the one which I must try to answer in
the earlier part of this book; in the later chapters I shall have
to deal with another one – how this single city-state contrived
to weld together the whole Mediterranean civilization,
strongly enough to give it several centuries of security against
uncivilized enemies in the north, and half-civilized enemies
in the east. But for the moment let us see why the Greeks
did not permeate Italy with their own civilization as they did
Sicily: how it was that they left room for a new power, capable
eventually of shielding them and their work from destruction.
To answer this question we must consider the nature of the
Italian peninsula, and the character of the races then living
in it.

The simple fact is, that though the shrewd commercial
Greek had seized on all the best harbours in the long, narrow

peninsula, these harbours were all in the south coast, about the 'heel' of Italy, or in the south-west coast, in the volcanic region of the modern Naples, which was itself one of these Greek settlements. The east coast north of the 'heel' is almost harbourless, as will be realized by anyone who takes the route by rail to Brindisi on his way to Egypt or India. *Italy is a mountainous country* – a fact never to be forgotten in Roman history – and its mountains, the long chain of the Apennines, have their spinal ridge much nearer the east than the west coast, and descend upon the sea so sharply on that side that for long distances road or railway only just finds a passage. All along this east coast there was nothing to tempt Greeks to settle, and as they rarely or never penetrated far inland from their settlements, their influence never spread into this mountainous region from the many seacoast towns of Magna Graecia, as their part of Italy was called. On the Bay of Naples they had, indeed, a better chance; here there was a rich fertile plain stretching away to the hills, which on this side come down less steeply than on the eastern; this we shall hear of again as the Plain of Campania, in which Greek influence was very strong and active, capable of penetrating beyond its limits northward. But north of this again they left no permanent settlements; good harbours are wanting, and such as there are were occupied about the eighth century BCE by a people at that time as enterprising as themselves, the Etruscans. These, too, had been recent immigrants into the peninsula from the east, and together with the Greeks they formed the only obstacles to the growth of a native Italian power – a power, that is, belonging to the older races that had long been settled there. The Greeks were not likely to interfere with such a growth, as

we have seen; whether the Etruscans were to do so we have
yet to see.

Born of Italian Geography

It was, in fact, this Etruscan people who first gave an Italian
stock the chance of rising into a great Mediterranean power;
and in order to understand how this was, we must look at a
good map of central Italy, which gives a fair idea of the
elevations in this part of the peninsula. Looking at such a
map, it is easy to see that the long, narrow leg of Italy is cloven
in twain about the middle by a river, the Tiber, the only river
of considerable size and real historical importance, south of
the Po. It is formed of several streams which descend from the
central mass of the Apennines, now called the Abruzzi, but
soon gathers into a swift though not a wide river, and emerges
from that mountainous district some five-and-twenty miles
from the sea, into what we now call the Roman Campagna,
the Latium of ancient times; skirting the northern edge of
this comparatively level district it falls into the sea, without
forming a natural harbour, about half-way up the western
coast of the peninsula. To the north of it and of the plain
were settled a number of cities, more or less independent of
each other, forming the Etruscan people, whose origin we
do not yet know for certain, and whose language has never
been deciphered from the inscriptions they have left behind
them; a mysterious race, active in war and commerce, who had
subdued but not exterminated the native population around
them. To the east and south of the Tiber, stretching far along
the mountainous region and its western outskirts, was a race

of hardy mountaineers, broken up, as hill peoples usually are, into a number of communities without any principle of cohesion except that of the various tribes to which they belonged. The northern part of this sturdy hill-folk was known as Umbrians and Sabines; the southern part as Samnites or Oscans. They all spoke dialects of the same tongue, a tongue akin to those which most European peoples still speak. Lastly, immediately to the south of the Tiber in the last part of its course, occupying the plain which stretches here between the mountains, the river, and the sea, there was settled another branch of this same stock, speaking another dialect destined to be known for ever as Latin. These three sub-races of a great stock – Umbrians, Samnites, and Latins – are meant when we speak of a native Italian population as opposed to Greek or Etruscan immigrants. Doubtless they were not the aboriginal inhabitants of the country, but of older stocks history knows nothing that concerns us in this book. These are the peoples who were destined to be supreme in the Mediterranean basin, and eventually to govern the whole civilized world.

Rome the Organizer

It is as well to be quite clear at once that the acquisition of this supremacy was not the work of one only of these peoples, the Latins, or of one city only of the Latins, *i.e.* Rome. It was the work of all these stocks which I have called native Italian. Roman is a convenient word, and Rome was all along the leader in action and the organizing power; but the material, and in a great part as time went on the brainpower also, was contributed by all these peoples taken together. They had first to submit to the great leader and organizer, Rome, a fate against which, as we shall see, they struggled long; but no sooner had they submitted than they were added to the account of Italian development, and with few exceptions played their new part with a good courage.

So much, then, for the Italian peoples who were to supersede the Greeks in the world's history. But let us now return for a moment to the Tiber, and fix our eyes on the last five-and-twenty miles of its course, where it separates the plain of Latium from the Etruscan people to the north. The Latin-speaking stock were far more in danger from these Etruscans than the Umbrian and Samnite mountaineers; nothing but the river was between them and their enemies, for enemies they undoubtedly were, bent on pushing farther south, like the Danes in England in the ninth century of our era. The Latins had, indeed, a magnificent natural fortress in the middle of their plain, in the extinct volcano of the Alban Mountain, some 3,000 feet above sea-level; and here, according to a sure tradition, was their original chief city, Alba Longa. But this was of no avail against an invader from the north; it was the river that was the vital concern of Latium when once the Etruscans had become established to the north of it. Now at one point, some 20 miles by water from the river's mouth, was a group of small hills, rising to a height of about 160 feet, three of them almost isolated and abutting on the stream, and the others in reality a part of the plain to the south, with their northern sides falling somewhat steeply towards the Tiber. Here, too, was an island in the river, which might give an enemy an easy chance of crossing. On this position there arose at some uncertain date, but beyond doubt as a fortress against the Etruscan power, a city called *Roma*; and there a city has been ever since, known by the same name. It is likely enough that it was an outpost founded by the city of Alba Longa, which eventually itself vanished out of history; and this was the tradition of later days. If we can accept the motive of the foundation – the defence of Latium against her foe, we need not trouble about the many legends of it.

Rome started on her wonderful career as a military outpost of a people akin to her, and face to face with an enemy with whom she had no sort of relationship. If she could but hold her position there was obviously a great future for her. The position on the Tiber was, in fact, strategically the best in Italy. It is, as a great Roman historian said, just in the centre of the peninsula. There was easy access to the sea both by land and water, and a way open into central Italy up the Tiber valley – the one great natural entrance from the sea. She was far enough from the sea to be safe from raiders, yet near enough to be in communication with other peoples by means of shipping. If enemies attacked her from different directions inland, she could move against them on what in military language we may call 'inner lines' – she could strike simultaneously from a common base. From the sea no power dared attack her, until in her degenerate days Genseric landed at Ostia in 455 CE. On the whole, we may say that no other city in Italy had the same chance, as regards position, of dominating the whole of Italy, and that in those early days of her history the Etruscans unwittingly taught her how to use this great advantage. This way the Romans became a leading people in Italy by virtue of having to withstand the Etruscans.

II

THE ADVANCE OF ROME IN ITALY

Rome and Latium Overwhelm the Etruscans

I said in the last chapter that if Rome could only hold the line of the lower Tiber against the Etruscans, great possibilities of advance were open to her. How long she held it we do not know; but there is hardly a doubt that in course of time – some time probably in the sixth century BCE – she lost it, and even herself fell into the hands of the enemy. The tale is not told in her legendary annals; but we have other convincing evidence. The last three kings of Rome seem to have been Etruscans. The great temple of Jupiter on the Capitoline Hill, which was founded at this time, was in the Etruscan style, and built on foundations of Etruscan masonry, some of which can still be seen in the garden of the German embassy in modern Rome. Below this temple, as you go to the river, was a street called the street of the Etruscans, and there are other signs of the conquest which need not be given here. On the whole we may believe that this persistent enemy crossed the Tiber higher up, where she already had a footing, and so took the city in flank and rear.

Fortunately, the Etruscans were not in the habit of destroying the cities they took: they occupied and made use of them. They seem to have used Rome to spread their influence over Latium: they built a temple of Jupiter on the Alban hill, the old centre of a Latin league: and there is strong evidence that they made Rome the head of another and later league, with a religious centre in a temple of Diana, who was not originally a Roman deity, on the Aventine hill overlooking the Tiber. All events in this Etruscan period are very dim and doubtful, but it looks as if the very loss of the line of defence had only given the conquered city a new lease of life, with a widened outlook and fresh opportunities. But was she to continue as an Etruscan city?

At this time it seems that the Etruscans were being harassed from the north by Gallic tribes, who had already spread over northwest Europe, and were conquering the valley of the Po and pressing farther south. This may account for the undoubted fact that about the end of the sixth century BCE Rome did succeed in throwing off the Etruscan yoke: that the old Roman families united to expel their foreign king, and to establish an aristocratic republic. Henceforward the very name of king (*rex*) was held in abhorrence by the Romans, and the government passed into the hands of two-yearly elected magistrates, with absolute power as leaders in war, and a limited power within the city. In the next chapter I will explain this new form of government more fully: here it will be enough to say that they were called consuls, and that they had an advising body (as the kings probably had before them) of the heads of noble families, called *senatus*, or a body of elderly men (from *senex*, 'old man'). At present let us go on with the story of Rome's advance in Italy.

According to the legend, the Etruscans made a vigorous attempt to recover Rome. This is a picturesque story, and is admirably told in one of Macaulay's famous *Lays of Ancient Rome*. But we must pass it over here, for we have no means of testing the truth of it. Soon afterwards we come upon what seems to be a real historical fact, a treaty between Rome and the other Latin cities, the text of which was preserved for many centuries. This treaty shows plainly that henceforward we have to reckon Rome and Latium as one power in Italy; and this is the first real forward step in the advance of Rome. It guaranteed in, the first place, mutual support in war; Rome needed support against the Etruscans, and the Latin cities at the southern end of the plain were liable to be attacked by hill tribes from the east and south. Still more important as showing the advance of civilization was the sanction of a common system of private law. Any citizen of a Latin city (including, of course, Rome) was to be able to buy and sell, to hold and inherit property, in any other city, in full confidence that he would be protected by the law of that city in so doing; and if he married a woman of another city his marriage was legitimate and his children could inherit his property according to law. This was going a long way towards making a single state of the whole of Latium. All the communities were on equal terms, and all had certain legal relations with each other; and these are two of the chief features of a true federation. Now all federations were an improvement on the isolation of the single city-state, which was helpless in those days of turbulence and invasion. This one looks like the work of a statesman; and if that statesman was a Roman, Spurius Cassius, as tradition asserted, then Rome had achieved her first victory in the arts of statesmanship and diplomacy with which she was destined to rule the world.

The Fortunate Location of Latium

Before we go on with our story let us notice how well Latium was geographically fitted to develop a federation, as compared with the more mountainous districts of Italy. Latium was a plain, as its name seems to imply; and like Boeotia in Greece it was naturally suited for federative union, while tribes living in the highlands always found it difficult to unite. Again, the Latins were jammed into a comparatively small space between the hills and the sea, and their strength was concentrated by their position: while the Etruscans, and the various Italian stocks, were continually moving onward to look for better quarters, and losing their strength and their cohesion in doing so.

In these early federations of cities there was always a tendency for one particular city to slip into the position of leader, just as in modern federations, that of Switzerland for example, there is a continual tendency for the central authority to extend its influence. In Latium there can be no doubt that Rome very soon began to assume some kind of headship. Her position on the Tiber, and the constant strain that she had to undergo in resisting the Etruscans, gave her an advantage over the other Latin cities, who had to resist less constant annoyance from less highly civilized enemies. I mean that the Roman people had both nerve and brain so continually exercised that they developed not only brute courage, but endurance, diplomatic skill and forethought. For a whole century after they expelled their Etruscan kings they had to keep up a continual struggle with the great Etruscan city of Veii, which was only a few miles to the north of the river, on very high ground, and with the smaller town of Fideae on the Tiber above Rome, which the Veians could make use of to attack them from that side. No wonder that when at last they succeeded in taking Veii they burnt it to the ground. It is said that they thought of migrating to that lofty site themselves, and abandoning the position on the Tiber; but they wisely gave up the idea, and Veii was sacked and her goddess Juno brought to Rome. The site is a deserted spot at the present day.

It was this prolonged struggle, in which the Latins were of course called upon to help, that placed Rome in the position of leader of the league, and from the moment it was over we find her attitude towards the Latins a changed one. It is likely enough that she had long been growing overbearing and unpopular with the other cities, but of this, if it was so, we have no certain details. What we do know is that at the beginning of the fourth century BCE, when a terrible disaster overtook Rome, the Latins failed to serve her.

This disaster was the capture and sack of Rome by a wandering tribe of Gauls from the north, who descended the valley of the Tiber, took the Romans by surprise, and utterly routed them at the little river Allia, 12 miles from the city. These Gauls were formidable in battle and fairly frightened the Romans; but, like other Celtic peoples, they were incapable of settling down into a solid State, or of making good use of their victories. They vanished as quickly as they had come, and left nothing behind them but an indelible memory of the terror they had inspired, and many stories of the agony of that catastrophe. The most characteristic of these shows the veneration of the Romans for what was perhaps their greatest political institution, the Senate. The citizens had fled to the Capitol, where they contrived to hold out till relief came; but meanwhile the older Senators, men who were past the age of fighting, determined to meet their death, and devoted themselves, according to an old religious practice resorted to

in extreme peril, to the infernal deities. Each then took his
seat in state robes at the door of his house. There the Gauls
found them and marvelled, taking them for more than human.
At last a Gaul ventured to stroke the beard of one of them
named Papirius, who immediately struck him with his ivory
wand: he was instantly slain, and of the rest not one survived.
We need not ask whether this story is true or not, for it is
impossible to test it: but it is truly Roman in feeling, and from
a religious point of view it falls in line with others that were
told of the sacrifice of the individual for the State.

This experience was a terrible discipline for the Romans,
but no sooner had the Gauls departed than they began to
turn it to practical account. They saw that they must secure
the country to the north of them more effectually, and they
did so by making large portions of it Roman territory, and
by establishing two colonies there, *i.e.* garrisoned fortresses
on military roads. Then they turned to deal with their own
confederates, who perhaps had felt a secret satisfaction in the
humiliation of a leader of whom they were jealous, and were
now, especially the two great neighbouring cities of Tibur and
Praeneste (Tivoli and Palestrina), beginning to rise in open
revolt. Knowing what happened afterwards, we can say that
these Latin cities were standing in the way of Italian progress:
but to the ancient city-state independence was the very salt
of life.

All public records and materials for history, except those
engraved on stone, were destroyed in the capture and burning
of Rome by the Gauls, so that up to this time Roman "history"
is not really worthy of the name. But from this time onward
certain official records were preserved, and we gradually pass

into an age which may truly be called historical. In detail it will still be questionable, chiefly owing to the tendency of Roman leading families to glorify the deeds of their own ancestors at the expense of truth, and so to hand on false accounts to the age when history first came to be written down. But in the fourth and third centuries BCE it becomes fairly clear in outline. I said in the last chapter that the Romans were curiously destitute of the imaginative faculty. But no people is entirely without imagination, and it is most interesting to find the Romans using their moderate allowance in inventing the details of noble deeds and honourable services to the State. Provoking as it is to us, and provoking even to the Roman historian Livy himself, who was well aware of it, this habit has its own value as a feature of old Roman life and character.

Italian Neighbours and Allies

But I must return to the story of the advance of Rome in Italy. It seems clear that after the Gallic invasion the Latins became more and more discontented with Roman policy, which probably aimed at utilising all the resources of the league and at the same time getting complete control of its relations to other powers. We have the text in Greek, preserved by the historian Polybius, of a treaty with Carthage, then the greatest naval power in the Mediterranean, which well illustrates this: the date is 348 BCE Rome acts for Latium in negotiating this treaty; and Carthage undertook not to molest the Latin cities, *provided that they remained faithful to Rome*; nay, even to restore to the power of the leading city any revolting Latin community that might fall into their hands. This plainly shows that revolt was expected, and a few years later it became general. But in spite of the support of the Campanians in the rich volcanic plain farther south, and indeed of danger so great that it gave rise to another story of the *devotio* of a Roman consul to the infernal deities on behalf of the State, the Latins were completely beaten at the Battle of Mount Vesuvius, and the Romans were able so to alter the league as to deprive it of all real claim to be called a federation.

We saw that any citizen of a Latin city could buy and hold property, marry and have legitimate children, in any other Latin city, knowing that he was protected by the law in the enjoyment of these rights. But after the rebellion this was all changed. A citizen could enjoy these rights in his own city, or at Rome, but nowhere else, while a Roman could enjoy them everywhere. A citizen of Praeneste, for example, could enjoy them at Praeneste or Rome, but not in the neighbouring cities of Tibur or Tusculum: while a Roman could do business in all these cities, and be supported in all his dealings by the Roman law, which now began gradually to permeate the whole of Latium. Rome thus had a monopoly of business with the other cities, which were effectually isolated from each other. To us this seems a cruel and selfish policy, and so in itself it was. But we must remember that Rome had been all but destroyed off the face of the earth, and that the Latins had done nothing, so far as we know, to help her. To resist another such attack as that of the Gauls, it was absolutely necessary for Rome to control the whole military resources of Latium, and this she could not do in a loose and equal federation. She was liable not only to assaults from the Gauls, but from Etruscans, and, as we shall see directly, from Samnites, and, if we find that in the struggle for existence she was at times unjust, we may remember that there has hardly been a successful nation of which the same might not be said. She saw that Latium must become Roman if either Rome or the Latins were to survive, and she devised the principle of isolation with this object.

From this time all Latins served in Roman armies nominally as allies, but in reality as subjects; and all Latins who became Roman citizens served in the Roman legions. When a military colony was founded, it might be either Roman or Latin; but a Latin colony meant not necessarily a collection of Latins; it might admit anyone – Roman, Latin or other, who threw in his lot with the new city and accepted the two rights of trade and marriage described above. Thus the term Latin came to mean not so much a man of a certain stock as a man with a certain legal position, and so it continued for many centuries, while the new power rising to prominence in the world came to be known not as Latin, but as Roman.

The last and decisive battle with the Latins took its name, as we saw, from Mount Vesuvius, and the reader who knows the map of Italy will ask how it came to be fought so far south of Latium, in the large and fertile plain of Campania, near the modern city of Naples. The answer is that a powerful State, such as Rome was now becoming, is liable to be appealed to by weaker communities when in trouble; and the Campanians, attacked by the hill-men from the central mountainous region of the Samnites, had appealed for help to Rome. This was given, but the Romans found it necessary to make peace with these Samnites, and left the Campanians in the lurch, and then the latter threw in their lot with the Latins, and the Latin war drifted south to Campania. At the end of that war they were treated in much the same way as the Latins; and thus Rome now found herself presiding with irresistible force over a territory that included both the plains of western Italy and all its most valuable land, and over a confederacy in which all the advantages were on her side, and all the resources of the members under her control.

Struggles with the Samnites

But to be mistress of these two plains was not as yet to be mistress of Italy. Those plains, and especially the southern and more valuable one, had to be defended from the mountaineers of the central highlands of the peninsula: a region which the reader should at this point of our story study carefully in his map. Towards the end of the Latin war these highlanders, Samnites, as the Romans called them, had ceased raiding the Campanian plain, for they in their turn had to defend southern Italy against an unexpected enemy. The strong and wealthy Greek merchant-city of Tarentum, just inside the 'heel' of Italy, destined to play an important part in Italian history for the next century, had lately had its lands raided by the Samnites and their kin the Lucanians to the south of them, and had called in Greeks from oversea to help them. Here we come into touch with Greek history, just at the time when Alexander the Great was the leading figure in the Greek world. A Spartan king came over to aid Tarentum, and lost his life in so doing; then Alexander of Epirus was induced to come, an uncle of the great conqueror: and after a period of success against the Samnites, he was assassinated. It is said that Rome came to an understanding with him, and it is likely enough; there must have been men in the great Council at Rome who were already accustomed to look far ahead, and keep themselves informed of what was going on far away in Italy and even beyond the Italian seas. Her long struggle for existence had taught her venerable statesmen the arts of diplomacy, and we are not surprised to learn that after the death of Alexander she began to form alliances in that far country between the Samnites and Tarentum, much of which was rich and fertile, in order that when the inevitable struggle with the hill-men should come, she might have them enclosed between two foes – herself and Latium on the north and west, and the Apulians and Greeks in the south and east. It seemed as if her power and prestige must continually go forward, or collapse altogether; the same alternative that faced the English in India in the eighteenth century and later. In neither case did the advancing power fully realize what the future was to be.

The inevitable struggle with the Samnites came, and lasted many years. We need not pursue it in detail, and indeed the details are quite untrustworthy as they have come down to us; but one episode in it is told so explicitly and has become so famous, that it deserves a place in our sketch as showing that hard feeling of national self-interest, without a touch of chivalry, that is gradually emerging as the guide of Roman action in her progress towards universal dominion.

A strong Roman army, under the command of both consuls, was pushing to the south through the mountains, and fell into a trap in a defile called the Caudine Forks, a name never forgotten by the Romans. All attempts to escape were vain, and they were forced to capitulate. The terms dictated by Pontius the Samnite general were these: the consuls were to bind themselves on behalf of the Senate to agree to evacuate Samnium and Campania and the fortresses (*coloniae*) which had been planted there, and to make peace with the Samnites as with an equal power. The consuls bound themselves by a solemn rite, and the army was allowed to go home, after being sent under the yoke, *i.e.* under a kind of archway consisting of one spear resting on two upright ones: this was an old Italian custom of dealing with a conquered army, which may have originally had a religious signification. When the disgraced legions reached Rome, and the consuls summoned the Senate to ratify their bond with Pontius, the Fathers, as they were called, positively refused to do so. The consuls and all who had made themselves responsible for the terms were sent back to Pontius as his prisoners, *but not the army*. His indignation was great, for he knew that Samnium had lost her chance, and would never have it again. The consuls, of course, had no power to bind the Senate, and the Samnite terms were such as the Senate could not accept as the result of a single disaster caused by a general's blunder: that was not the way in which the Romans carried on war. But the disgraced army should have been sent back too, and the Senate and People knew it. The speech which the later Roman historian puts into the mouth of Pontius to express his indignation, shows that some feeling of shame at this dishonourable action had come down in the minds of many generations.

Roman Genius for Organization

The last effort of this long struggle against Rome was a desperate attempt to combine the forces of Samnites, Etruscans and Gauls: the idea was to separate her armies and thus crush her in detail. Even this was a failure, and without going into the doubtful stories of the fighting, we may ask why it was so. Beyond all doubt the Roman power was for a time in very great peril; but in the end it prevailed, and this is a good moment for pausing to think about the advantages that Rome's genius for organization had secured for herself; advantages which no other Italian stock seemed able to acquire.

First, she had learnt how to use with profit her geographical position; to north, south and east she could send armies to strike in different directions at the same time; and she must have devised some means (though we do not know the method) of keeping up communication between these armies. The stories seem to suggest that the commanders of this period belonged to a very few noble families whose members had spent their whole lives in fighting – not indeed merely in fighting battles, but in carrying on war: the Fabii and Papirii are particularly prominent. These veterans must have come to know the art of war thoroughly, as it could then be applied in Italy, and also the details of the country in which they had to fight.

Secondly, the efforts of these tough old heroes were admirably seconded by the home government, i.e. the Senate, because this assembly consisted of men of the like military experience, and the leaders among them were themselves generals, men who had been consuls and had led armies. Though at this very time, as we shall see, there was a strong tendency towards popular government, yet in the direction of war we find no sign that the monopoly of the old families was questioned; and as their interests and their experience were all of the same type, they could act together with an unanimity which was probably unknown to their enemies. The fact that Rome always at this time, and indeed at all times, negotiated and kept in touch with the *aristocracies* in the Italian cities, shows how completely the noble families had gained control over the management of diplomacy as well as war.

Thirdly, Rome was now beginning to learn the art of securing the conquered country by means of military roads and *coloniae*: an art to which she held firmly throughout her history, and to which the geography even of Roman Britain bears ample testimony. My readers will do well to fix their attention for a moment on three of these colonies which were founded during this long war; they are by no means the only ones, but they serve well to show the extent of the Roman power in Italy at this time, as well as the means taken to secure it. The first is Narnia, far up the Tiber valley (founded 299 BCE) on a military road afterwards known as the Flaminian Way: this was an outpost, with quick communication with Rome, against both Etruscans and Gauls. The second, Fregellae, a city with a sad future, was some 70 miles to the south-east of Rome, on a road called the Latin Way, but beyond the limits of Latium proper, commanding, in fact, the passes between Latium and Campania; it was in a beautiful situation near the junction of two rivers, and became in time a most prosperous city. For the third colony we must look much further south on the map, at the south-eastern end of the mass of the Samnite highlands: this was Venusia, with 20,000 colonizts, destined to separate the Samnites from the Greeks and other inhabitants of the heel and toe of Italy. It stood on the most famous of all the great roads, the Via Appia, which after leaving Rome ran nearer the coast than the Latin Way, but joined it in

Campania, and then ran across the hilly country to Venusia, and eventually to Brundisium (Brindisi), which also became a colony 50 years later.

These three advantages, duly considered, will help the reader to understand to some extent how the prize of Italian presidency fell to Rome and not to another city: and they will also explain why Rome emerged safe and stronger than ever from another peril that was now to threaten her existence.

The Struggle for Tarentum

The great colony of Venusia, as we saw, was meant to separate the Greeks of southern Italy from the highlanders of Samnium. Of the Greek cities by far the most powerful was Tarentum, then ruled by a selfish and ill-conditioned democracy, apt to be continually worrying its neighbours. That Rome should sooner or later come into collision with Tarentum was inevitable; but the Senate tried to avoid this, knowing that the Tarentines would appeal to some Greek power beyond sea to help them. Now just across the Adriatic, in Epirus, there was a king of Greek descent who was looking out for a chance of glory by imitating Alexander the Great; for Alexander's marvellous career had stirred up a restless spirit of adventure in the freelances of the generation that succeeded him. Pyrrhus seems to have fancied that he could act the part of a knight-errant in freeing the Greeks of the west from the barbarians – from the Romans that is, and the Carthaginians, who were at the moment in alliance. When the inevitable quarrel with Rome came, and Tarentum invited him, he crossed the sea with a small but capable force, determined to put an end to this new power that was threatening to swallow up the Greek cities. But he had to learn, and through him the Greek world had to learn as a whole, that the new power was made of sterner stuff than any that had yet arisen in the Mediterranean basin.

Pyrrhus began with a victory, not far from Tarentum; it was won chiefly by some elephants which he had brought with him to frighten the Roman cavalry. This shook the loyalty of many Italian communities, but the Senate was unmoved. The ablest diplomatist in Pyrrhus's service made no impression on that body of resolute men, trained by long experience to look on a single defeat as only a 'regrettable incident' in a long war. 'Rome never negotiates while foreign troops are on Italian soil;' so, according to the story, the aged Appius Claudius told the Greek envoy in the Senate-house. Then Pyrrhus tried a march on Rome; but he had to learn, like another invader after him, that the nearer he drew to the city the more difficult his task became. A second victory was far less decisive and almost fruitless, and Pyrrhus most unwisely evacuated Italy. Tarentum had turned against him, unwilling to submit to his discipline, and now that wayward city fell a victim to the Roman power. The king crossed to Sicily to deliver the Sicilian Greeks from Carthage, and this he did brilliantly, but there, too, the fickle Greeks grew tired of him. Returning to Italy, he fought one more battle with the Romans, at Beneventum in Samnium, and lost it. Foiled everywhere, he left Italy, with Rome more firmly established than ever in the supremacy of the whole peninsula: for Tarentum, with its fine harbour, its almost impregnable citadel, and its fleet, fell soon afterwards into the hands of the Romans.

Almost the whole Italian peninsula was now Roman; or perhaps it is truer to say that Rome had become an Italian state. It was a wonderful work: perhaps the most wonderful that Rome ever achieved. The military part of it was the result mainly of *constantia*, steady perseverance and refusal to accept defeat; the political organization was the result of good sense and good temper combined with an inflexible will, and a shrewd perception of the real and permanent interests of Rome. In the third century BCE, at which we have now arrived, Italy may be described as a kind of federation, in which each city has its own alliance with the leading one, and no alliance with any other. Each has its own government and administers its own law, but places all its military resources at the disposal of the Roman government. The fighting power of the future was to be Italy under Roman leadership, and all questions of foreign policy were decided by Rome alone. There was no general council of the whole confederacy. The Roman Senate controlled an ever-increasing mass of detailed and varied business, having to deal with Latins, Italians of the old stocks, Etruscans, Greeks and Gauls. How the business was done we cannot tell: not a single contemporary record of it is left. One glimpse of that wonderful Senate at work would be worth all descriptions of the battles of that century.

Before the close of the third century BCE that Senate, instead of directing a further steady advance, had been forced to defend the State against an invader, in the most terrible life and death struggle ever experienced by any people. But in the next chapter I must pause to try and explain wherein consisted the nerve-power, the mental and material fibre, of the people destined to rule the world.

III
THE TRAINING OF THE ROMAN CHARACTER

Discipline and Duty

have mentioned some outward circumstances which gave Rome an early training in war and diplomacy, and in particular her geographical position, exposing her to constant attack, and yet giving her good chance of striking back and advancing. But to accomplish all that was told of her in the last chapter, more than this was surely needed. There must have been a quality in this people, individually and as a whole, fitting them to withstand so much storm and stress, and to emerge from disaster with renewed strength to take in hand the work of conquest and government. We need not, indeed, assume that the people of this one city were naturally of stronger character than others, than their kinsfolk of the Latin cities or other Italians of the same great race. All these immigrating stocks, which spread themselves, long before history begins, over a primitive population of which we know little or nothing, were probably much the same in physical and mental build; a fact which will help us to understand how they all came eventually to be able to unite together as the centre of a great empire. But the quality or character, which I am to try and explain in this chapter, was more strongly stamped upon the citizens of Rome than on those of other cities, owing to the more continual call for them in her case; for all our qualities and habits can be made more sure and lasting by constant exercise.

Discipline and duty are the two words which best explain, if they do not exactly express, the quality here meant; the habit of obedience to authority, which is the necessary condition of the power of governing, and that sense of duty which lies at the root of the habit and the power. This aptitude for discipline and this sense of duty can be traced both in the private and the public life of early Rome, in the life of the family and in the life of the State. Let us be clear at once that the individual as such was not as yet an important item of society; society was based on a system of groups, and the individual played no part in it in these early times except as the member of a group, either a group of kin (*gens*), or a local and administrative group (*pagus, curia*). But the only group with which we are concerned in this little book, the smallest of all, was the *familia*, another of those immortal words which we have inherited from the Latin language. This shall be explained first, in order to find the discipline and duty of that family life: then we will take the State, and follow out the same habits reproducing themselves in a more complicated social and political union.

Familia: The Roman Household

This word *familia* did not mean exactly what we mean by family; household would perhaps come nearer to it, if we understand by household a group of individuals supporting itself on the land. It meant not only father, mother, and children, but also their dependents, whether bond or free. These, if bond, were slaves (*servi*), prisoners of war and the children of such prisoners, or persons who had forfeited their liberty by debt: if free, they were clients, who for some reason had become attached to the *familia* in an inferior position, and looked to it for subsistence and protection. And our picture is not complete unless we take into account also the divine members of the group, dwelling in the house or on the land, to whom the human members looked for protection and prosperity in all the walks of life. Chief among these were the spirit of the hearth-fire, Vesta; Penates, the spirits of the store-closet and its contents: the Lar, the guardian spirit of the cultivated land, or, as some think, of a departed ancestor; and the Genius of the head of the family, which enabled him to beget children and so continue the collective life of the group. Though these spirits – they are hardly yet deities – naturally seem to us mere fancies of the primitive Roman mind, they were to that mind itself as real and active as any human member of the group, and we must try to think of them as such, for they played a very important part in the development of the quality we wish to realize.

Now this group, or rather the human part of it, lived under a very simple and effective form of government. It was under the absolute control of a head, the father and husband; or, if more than one family lived together, the oldest living father and husband. Over wife and children he had a father's power (*patria potestas*), and they were said to be in his *hand*; over the slaves he had a master's power (*dominium*): to his clients he was *patronus*, or quasi-father. His power over wife and children was absolute, but it was kept from being arbitrary by a wholesome custom, of immense importance in all its results throughout Roman history, of seeking the advice of a council of relations before taking any extreme step in the way of punishment for serious offences. This was an obligation, a duty, on his part, enforced by no law, but by what may be well called an even more powerful sovereign than law – the custom of the ancestors (*mos majorum*). His power over his client, or his freed slave if he had any such, was restrained by customs of mutual obligation, which eventually found their way into law. His power over his slaves was, however, not only absolute but arbitrary, and so continued down to the latest period of Roman history; yet the slave, we must not forget, was really a member of the *familia*, and as such was probably treated as a human being, necessary to the life of the group, and even partaking to some extent in its religious worship.

Let us see how this system of government would work out in the practical life of a *familia* settled on the land, as all such groups were during at least a great part of the period we have been tracing: for the city itself was mainly used as a fortress, into which the farming families would come in time of peril, and in which they would in course of time possess a town dwelling as well as a farm, like the leading families of our English shires in the Middle Ages. The paterfamilias directed all the operations of the farm, no one disputing his authority: and he decided all quarrels among his subjects and punished all offences. The necessary work of the house, the cooking, and the spinning of wool for the garments of the members (which were then entirely woollen), he left to his wife and daughters: and thus the wife came to exercise a kind of authority of her own, which raised her far above the position of a "squaw," and gave her in course of time a great influence, though an indirect one, in social life. And not only had all the members their work to do, under this strict control, in keeping themselves alive and clothed, but they all had their duties to the divine members, on whom they believed themselves dependent for their health and wealth. There were simple acts of worship every day and at every meal, in which the children joined; we may almost think of the Head as a priest and of the children as his acolytes. And at certain days, fixed in ancient times by a Council of Heads, and later in the city by a calendar, the families of a district (*pagus*) would join together in religious festivities, after harvest, for example, or after the autumn sowing, to honour and propitiate the spirit of the harvested grain or of the sown seed. These were often accompanied by games and races, and so the life was saved from becoming too sombre and monotonous. But though discipline was not allowed to destroy freedom and enjoyment, the life was on the whole a routine of command and obedience, of discipline and duty.

Growing Up Roman

What of the education which should perpetuate these habits? Unluckily we have no contemporary record of it for these early times, and must guess at it chiefly from what we know of the bringing up of his son by the elder Cato, a strenuous believer in the old methods, in the second century BCE. As we might expect, it seems to have been an education in the active practical life of the farm, and in reverence, obedience, and modesty of demeanour. Cato taught his boy not only to work, to ride, to box, and to swim, but to shun all indecency; and was himself 'as careful not to utter an indecent word before his son, as he would have been in the presence of the Vestal virgins.' He wrote histories for his son in large letters, so that he might learn something of the illustrious deeds of the ancient Romans, and of their customs. In his time an education of the mind was beginning to come into vogue, as well as one of the will; but in the period we have been surveying this must have been of the most meagre kind. Yet it is possible that the idea of active duty to the State and its deities, as well as to the family and its presiding spirits, was all the more vividly kept up in the absence of intellectual interests. As life in the city became more usual, the boys of good families had more opportunity of learning what was meant by duty to the State; they accompanied their fathers to hear funeral orations on eminent citizens, and were even admitted to meetings of the Senate. In this way they must have developed a shrewdness and practical sagacity invaluable to them in after life.

There is a story of a Roman boy, preserved by Cato, which so well illustrates this and other features of that early Roman life, that I shall insert it here, whether or no it be strictly true. A boy who had been with his father to the Senate was asked by an inquisitive mother what the Fathers of the Senate had been discussing. The boy answered that he was strictly forbidden to tell, which only excited his mother's curiosity the more, and made her press him hard. At last he invented what Cato calls a shrewd and witty falsehood: he said that the Senate had been discussing whether it were better for the State that one man should have two wives, or one wife two husbands. Much alarmed, she went and told other matrons, and next day they crowded weeping to the Senate House, to petition that one wife might have two husbands rather than one husband two wives. The astonishment of the senators was dispelled by the boy, who stood out in the midst and told his tale; and from that time no boy was allowed to be present at debate save this one, who was thus rewarded for his honesty and shrewdness.

This good old Roman story may aptly bring us to the second part of my subject in this chapter, the training of the citizen in the service of the State. But let us pause here for a moment to consider what was the Roman idea of the State and its function.

Strength Through Struggle and Endeavour

In Italy, as in Greece, the State took the form of a city, with more or less of territory on which to subsist; in the heart of the city was the life of the State. And it is true of Italy as of Greece that the process of rising to the city from the life of farm or village was one of immense importance for humanity, enabling man to advance from the idea of a bare material subsistence to that of moral and intellectual progress. This is the advance to what Aristotle called 'good life' as distinguished from life simply. He meant that in the lower stage man has not time or stimulus to develop art, literature, law, philosophy: all his strength is spent in struggle and endeavour – struggle partly with Nature, partly with human enemies whom he is ill able to resist. The city-state supplied him not only with opportunity for a higher life, but with nutriment to maintain it.

But the Italians never drew from this new form of social life the same amount, the same quality of nutriment, as did the Greeks. Rome did indeed draw enough to fertilize the germs of much that was most valuable in her own character, and to educate herself for the practical work she was to do in the world. But the last chapter will have shown that, unlike most Greek city-states, she was forced by circumstances to continue for centuries a life of struggle and endeavour. She had constant difficulty in keeping herself alive and free, and as we shall see, she was hardly ever without internal as well as external perils. In Greece many States found leisure to rest and enjoy the exercise of their higher instincts – enjoyment which led to the production of works of art and literature: leisure, too, to reflect and inquire about Nature in man and outside him, and so to develop philosophy and science for the eternal benefit of mankind. But all the strength of Rome was used in the struggle for existence, which gradually led her on to conquest and dominion. As we left her at the end of the last chapter, the leading city of Italy, she might indeed have passed from struggle to leisure, and so to thought and inquiry, turning to account the gifts of the various peoples of Italy, Etruscans, Gauls, Greeks, as well as her own kin. But the long and terrible struggle with Carthage, to be told in the next chapter, effectually destroyed this chance. Her strength was spent when it was over, and when her chance came to sit down (so to speak), and think, she could not do it. Still, her long training in practical endeavour had its due result; and the ideas of duty and discipline, of law and order, which had carried her through so many perils, never wholly vanished from the Roman mind. Let us turn to trace the progress of those ideas in the life of the city-state of Rome.

Imperium: Power

When we first begin to see clearly into the working of the Roman State, what chiefly strikes us is the unlimited power of the magistrate in all the departments of government. Just as the head of the family had an absolute power over its members, so had the king (*rex*) an unlimited power over the citizens. In the family the word for this power was *potestas*, but in the State it was called *imperium* – one of the greatest words ever coined, surviving to the present day in many familiar forms. For the Roman it expressed more strikingly than any other the idea of discipline in the State: it stamped on his mind the inherited conviction that lawful authority must be implicitly obeyed. Not unlawful authority, ill-gotten by fraud or violence; for such power the word *imperium* could never be used: but authority entrusted to an individual by the human members of the State, and sanctioned by the consent of its divine members. For the *imperium* must be conferred upon its holder by an act of the People, and the gods must give their consent by favourable omens; both processes, the passing of the law, and the obtaining of the *auspicia*, must be gone through according to certain traditional methods, and the slightest flaw in these would make the choice of the magistrate invalid. But once legally in his hands, the *imperium* was irresistible; its outward symbol, the *fasces* (rods and axes) of the lictors, accompanied its holder wherever he went, to remind the Roman that the first duty of a citizen was obedience to constituted authority.

This word *imperium* stood for three different kinds of power. First, the king was supreme in matters of religion, for he was responsible for the good relations between the human and divine inhabitants of the city, for 'the peace of the gods' (*pax deorum*) as it was called. If this peace, or covenant, were not kept up, it was believed that the State could not prosper – the very life of the State depended on it.

But now let us note a point of the utmost importance in the development of Roman public life. The king could not perform this duty entirely by himself; no single man could have the necessary knowledge of all the details of ancient religious custom. So he was assisted by a small board of skilled experts called *pontifices*, perhaps also by another board of *augurs*, skilled in the methods of discovering the divine will by omens. Thus the *imperium* in religious matters, though still legally unlimited, was saved from becoming arbitrary and violating ancestral custom: the king is entrusted with power which he uses in accordance with the advice of sages.

Secondly, *imperium* stood for the supreme judicial power, for the maintenance of peace between individual citizens. The king had an unlimited power not only in deciding disputes but in inflicting punishments, even that of death. But here again, though his power was absolute, it was not arbitrary. Custom governed the State even more than he did, and his work was to see that custom was obeyed. In order to make sure that this duty was rightly performed, he was provided with a council of elderly men (*senatores*), fathers of families, whose advice custom compelled him to ask, though it did not compel him to take it. Here, then, the exercise of discipline was combined with a sense of duty and obligation, as in the life of the family; the Senate of the State was the same in principle as the council of relations in the family.

Thirdly, *imperium* stood for the absolute power of the commander in war: and here, as we might expect, custom seems hardly to have interfered with it. A Roman king in war was outside the custom of his own State, beyond the reach of the protection of his own deities, and under the influence of unknown ones. Both before starting on a campaign, and before entering the city on its return, the army had to undergo certain religious rites, which show how nervous even Romans were about leaving their own land and gods. Custom could not rule here, and the power of the general in the field remained throughout Roman history not only absolute but arbitrary. Doubtless he could, and often did, not only ask advice but take it, but he was never even morally obliged to do so: in this one department of State activity the wise judgment of the Romans left the *imperium* practically unhampered.

Such, then, was the *imperium* in the hands of the chief magistrate, the foundation-stone of the Roman government in all periods. But what of the people who obeyed it? Of the people we unluckily know hardly anything until nearly the end of the monarchical period. We do, indeed, know that, as in many Greek city-states, there was a privileged and an unprivileged class, and of these two classes a word shall be said directly. What needs here to be made clear is how this population was placed as regards duty and discipline, and our first real knowledge of this dates traditionally from the reign of the last king but one. Here we find the whole free population, privileged and unprivileged, serving in the army as a civic duty, and paying such taxes as were necessary mainly for military purposes. They served without pay, and the infantry – that is, by far the greater part, provided their own arms and equipment; the cavalry were provided with horses by the State, for horses were expensive. Those who had most property were considered as having the largest stake in the State, and therefore as bound to bear the heaviest burden. This may be seen in the order of the army for battle, for those who could afford the best equipment fought in front, the poorest and worst armed in the rear. This was the wholesome principle that governed the Roman army during the period of advance and conquest in Italy. It was an army of citizens (*populus*), all of whom served as a matter of duty, and paid taxes as a matter of duty according to their means, leaving all command to the holder of *imperium*, and the officers whom he appointed to carry out his orders.

Thus when the last king was expelled, and the kingship came to an end, the people were thoroughly well trained in the ideas of duty and discipline, and the practical results of such a training were obedience as a habit, respect for authority and knowledge, steadiness and coolness in danger. This people did not give way to excitement, either in civil or military crises. They not only obeyed their rulers, but trusted them. They were not much given to talking, but contented themselves with action: and as talk is a more effective stimulus to quarrelling than action, they did not as yet quarrel. Though Rome was destined to pass through many political as well as military dangers in the generations to come, it was nearly four centuries before blood was shed in civil strife in her streets.

Res Publica: The Roman Commonwealth

I must close this chapter with a very brief sketch of the political history of the period of advance in Italy, in order to show how their training in duty and discipline kept the people steady and sound at home.

After the expulsion of the last king the Roman State became a *res publica* – that is, literally translated, a 'public thing' – or as we may perhaps call it, a free State. This is another of the immortal words bequeathed to modern European language by Latin speech, and its meaning is still the same for us as it was for the Romans. When Cicero, almost at the end of the life of the Roman free State, wrote to a friend, 'We have completely lost the *res publica*,' he meant that it had passed from public management into the hands of private and irresponsible individuals. What were the essential marks of this 'public thing,' or free State? As we might expect, they are to be found in the treatment of the *imperium*, the governmental centre of gravity, by the founders of the *res publica*.

Firstly, to abolish the *imperium* was out of the question; no Roman ever dreamed of such a thing, for it would be like digging up the foundations of a building already in part constructed. But the *imperium* was no longer to be held for life, nor to be held by a single person. It was now to be entrusted to two magistrates instead of one, and for a year only; at the end of the year the holders, henceforward to be called Consuls or Praetors, were to lay down their insignia and resign their power, becoming simply private citizens again. Meanwhile new consuls had been elected; and the voice of the whole people was to be heard in the election, for it was to be effected by the army of citizens, arranged according to property as in military service. Every Roman who was to obey the *imperium* was to have a voice in the election of its holders, but those who had most stake in the State, and served in the front ranks in war, were to have a preponderating voice.

Secondly, the dread *imperium* was now not only limited in the period of its tenure, but the possibility of an arbitrary use of it was averted in two ways. First, the two consuls had a veto on each other's action, and both at home and in the field they took it in turn to exercise the *imperium*. Secondly, they could not put a citizen to death in the city unless the people in their assembly sanctioned it; in the field the Romans wisely left the *imperium* unlimited, feeling, as we still feel, that military discipline needs a more forceful sanction than civil. And besides these two restrictions, the council of elders, the Senate, was retained to act as a general advising body for the consuls, who, however, themselves had the power of filling up vacancies in it from time to time. We do not know exactly what its composition was at this time; but it is certain that all who had held the *imperium* had seats in it, as men whose service and experience best entitled them to advise and criticize their successors. This principle, that ex-magistrates should be members of the Senate, was adhered to at all times, and eventually made this great council into the most effective assembly of men of capacity and experience in practical life that the world has ever seen.

The Time-Limited Power of the *Dictator*

Before we leave the *imperium*, for the present, one interesting fact must be noted. The Romans were not afraid to withdraw for a time these restrictions on the magistrate's power, and to revert to absolute government, if they thought it necessary for the safety of the State. In moments of great peril, civil or military, the consul, on the advice of the Senate, would appoint a single individual to hold office for a fixed time with unlimited *imperium*; and in this case the assembly was not called on even to ratify the choice, so great was the trust reposed in the Fathers of the State. They did not call this single magistrate by the hated name of *rex*, but used another word well known in Latium, *dictator*. The institution was of the utmost value to a people constantly in a state of struggle and endeavour, and shows well the practical sagacity which along training in duty and discipline had already developed.

Patricians and Plebeians

But this practical sagacity was to be put to many a hard test in the period we sketched in the last chapter. No sooner was the *res publica* established, than a great question pressed for solution, that of the mutual relations of the privileged and unprivileged classes. What was really the origin of this distinction of class we do not yet know, and perhaps never shall. Here the fact must suffice, that the privileged, the patricians as they were called, the representatives of families belonging to the old clans (*gentes*) were alone deemed capable of preserving the peace between citizens and gods, or between the citizens themselves, and therefore they alone could hold the *imperium* and take the auspices. Both classes served in the army and voted at elections, but without the chance of holding the *imperium* the plebeians were helpless. Yet it is quite certain that they had grievances of their own, and real ones. We must think of them as in the main small holders of land, with little or no capital, and constantly obliged to borrow either in the form of money or stock. They became debtors to the rich, who would usually be the patricians, and the old customary law of debt was hard and even savage.

The result of this was, according to the traditional story, that once at least, if not twice, they actually *struck*; they left their work and went off in a body, threatening to found a new city some miles farther up the Tiber. They knew well that they were indispensable to the State as soldiers, and the patricians knew it too. Fortunately, the plebeians also knew that the State, with all its traditions of religion and government, of duty and discipline, was indispensable to themselves. They knew nothing of the forms and formulas which were deemed necessary for the maintenance of peace with gods and men. They could not carry away with them the gods of the city, under whose protection they and their forefathers had lived. They would simply be adrift, without oars or rudder, and such a position was absolutely unthinkable. So they returned to the city – so the story runs – and the result was a compromise, the first of a long series of compromises which finally made Rome into a compact and united commonwealth, and enabled her to tide over three centuries of continual struggle and endeavour. The story of these compromises is too long and complicated to be told in this book, but the successive stages can briefly be pointed out.

Soon after the strike, or secession, the plebeians were authorized to elect magistrates, or more strictly officers, of their own, to protect them from any arbitrary use of the *imperium*; these were called Tribunes, because the assembly that chose them was arranged according to tribes, local divisions in which both patricians and plebeians were registered for taxpaying purposes. The good-will of the patricians in making this concession is seen in the fact that the tribunes of the plebs (as they were henceforward called), were placed under the protection of the gods (*sacrosancti*), so that anyone violating them was made liable to divine anger. As the plebeians grew more numerous and indispensable, their assembly and officers became steadily more powerful, and eventually won the right to pass laws binding the whole State.

Again, it was not long before their ignorance of the customary law and its methods of procedure found a remedy. A code of law was drawn up in 12 tables, containing partly old customs now for the first time written down, partly new rules, some of them perhaps imported from Athens. Of this code we still possess many fragments, which show plainly that it was meant for all citizens, whatever their social standing. 'The idea of legislating for a class ... is strikingly absent. The code is thoroughly Roman in its caution and good sense, its respect for the past, which it disregards only when old customs violate the rules of common sense, and its judicious disregard of symmetry.' As the historian Tacitus said of it long afterwards, it was 'the consummation of equal right.' And it was the source of the whole mighty river of Roman law, ever increasing in volume, which still serves to irrigate the field of modern European civilization.

There was to be a long and bitter contest before the plebeians forced their way into the central patrician stronghold of the *imperium*, but even this was accomplished without civil war or bloodshed. We hear of a series of evasive manoeuvres by the patricians, who naturally believed that all would go wrong if the duty of keeping 'the peace of the gods' were committed to men whom the gods could not be supposed to take count of. But these patrician consuls and senators were responsible for the State's existence, and it could not exist without the plebeians; the two classes were authorized by law to intermarry, which (strange to say) had been unlawful hitherto, and then the old class-feeling and prejudice, far exceeding in force any such feeling known to us now, gradually subsided. By the middle of the fourth century BCE, not only could a plebeian be consul, but one of the two consuls *must* be a plebeian. And before that century was over the old patrician nobility was beginning to disappear, giving way to a new one based on the leading idea of *good service done for the State*. If a man had held the consulship, no matter whether he were patrician or plebeian, he became *nobilis* – *i.e.* distinguished – and so, too, did his family. The great Roman aristocracy of later times consisted of the descendants of men who had thus become distinguished.

The Role and Responsibilities of the Censor

I will conclude this chapter with a few words about one remarkable institution which well illustrates the Roman instinct for duty and discipline. It was in this period, 443 BCE, according to the traditional date, that a new magistracy was established, intended at first merely to relieve the consuls of difficult duties for which in that warlike age they had no sufficient leisure, but destined eventually to become even a higher object of ambition than the consulship itself. The Roman love of order made it necessary to be sure that every citizen was justly and legally a citizen, that he fulfilled his duties in the army, and paid his taxes according to a right estimate of his property. Every four or five years an inquiry had to be made with this object in view, and two censors, holding office for a year and a half, were now elected to undertake it. These censors, though they had no *imperium*, were irresponsible; their decisions were final, and they could not be called to account for any official act. They were almost always – in later times invariably – reverend seniors who had held the consulship, men in whose justice and wisdom the people could put implicit confidence. And such confidence was needed; for their power of examination easily became extended from details of registration to the personal conduct of the citizen in almost every relation of life. All heads of families might be questioned about their performance of family duties, and any shameful cruelty to a slave, or injustice to a client, or neglect of children, might be punished by removal from the list of tribesmen; and this meant loss of civil rights, and *infamia* (civic disgrace), a terrible word, greatly dreaded by the Roman. Neglect of land or other property, useless luxury, bad faith in contracts or legal guardianship – all came in course of time to be taken count of by the censors. A senator might have his name struck off the list of the Senate, and a cavalry soldier might be removed from the roll, if the horse provided him by the State were ill cared for, or if in any other way he were deemed unworthy of his position.

It may be hard for us to understand how such a power of inquisition can have been submitted to in a free State. But apart from the age and standing of the holders of this office, and the Roman habit of obedience to constituted authority, there are two facts that will help us to understand it. One is simple: the censors were *collegae* like the consuls; each had a veto on the action of the other, and if that veto were not used, if they were unanimous in condemning a citizen, the authority of their decision was naturally irresistible. The other fact is harder for a modern to understand. There was a religious element in the work of the censors; the final act of a censorship was the religious 'purification' (*lustratio*) of the whole citizen body, with sacrifice and prayer, in the field of Mars outside the walls of the city. What exactly a Roman of that day believed, or rather felt, to be the result of this rite, we can only guess; but we can be sure that he was convinced that the life of the State would be imperilled without it, and that this conviction was strong enough to compel him to submit to the whole process of which it was the consummation.

IV
THE STRUGGLE WITH CARTHAGE AND HANNIBAL

Clash of Civilizations

In these days sober students of history wisely leave the oft-told stories of war and battle, and busy themselves rather with questions of social life, public and private economy, and the history of religion, morals and scientific inquiry. But there are a few wars, great struggles of nation against nation, which will always have an absorbing interest: partly because of their dramatic character, partly because of their far-reaching consequences; and the long fight between Rome and Carthage is assuredly one of these. On the Carthaginian side it produced two of the most extraordinary men, father and son, of whom history has anywhere to tell; and on the Roman side it gives us a vivid picture of the most marvellous endurance during long years of extreme peril that we can find in the annals of any people. And probably no war was ever so pregnant of results for good and ill alike. It welded the whole of Italy south of the Alps into a united country under the rule of Rome, and launched the Romans on a new career of conquest beyond the sea; it laid the foundations of the Roman

Empire as we now think of that great system. Yet it left Italy in a state of economic distress from which it is hardly untrue to say that she has never fully recovered, and it changed the character of the Roman people, rich and poor alike, for the worse rather than the better.

In order to see clearly how it came about, we must once more look at the map of Italy; a map of modern Italy will do well enough. Let the reader remember that as yet Rome had control only over the central and southern parts of the whole of what is now the kingdom of Italy, and that two other parts of that kingdom, which every Italian now regards as essential to its unity, were in other hands. These were: first, the great alluvial plain of the river Po (Padus); secondly, the island of Sicily: strategically speaking, these lie on the two flanks of the Roman dominion, to north and south respectively. Any power holding central Italy, to be safe from invasion, must be in possession of these two positions, as a long series of wars has clearly shown, beginning with the two now to be sketched. The magnificent plain of the Po, stretching from the great Alpine barrier to the Apennines which look down on the Gulf of Genoa, the richest land in all Italy, was then in the hands of warlike Gallic tribes, who had settled there before the time when they struck southward and captured Rome itself; these might again become a serious danger, as indeed they proved to be in this very war. The island of Sicily was, and had long been, a bone of contention between the Greek settlers who had long ago built cities on the most favourable points of its coast, and the traders of the Phoenician city of Carthage just opposite to it on the coast of Africa. Sicily was rich in harbours, and like the plain of the Po, also rich in corn, olive, and vine; and the Greeks had held on to it so persistently that with the recent help of Pyrrhus they had for a moment been in almost complete possession of the island. But they foolishly deserted Pyrrhus at the critical moment, and now again the Carthaginians had recovered it, all but the kingdom of Hiero of Syracuse, stretching along the eastern coast under Mount Etna. Carthaginian fleets cruised round the island, and were often seen off the coasts of Italy as well. For Carthage was the mistress of the seas in all the western part of the Mediterranean basin.

Carthage was a daughter of the Canaanite city of Tyre, belonging to that seafaring people known in history as Phoenicians, whom the Israelites had pushed down to the coast of Palestine without subduing them. The genius of the Phoenicians was for trade, and the splendid position of Carthage, near the modern Tunis, with a rich corn-growing country in the rear, had helped her merchant princes to establish by degrees what may loosely be called an empire of trading settlements extending not only along the African coast, but over that of Sardinia and southern and eastern Spain, and including Sicily, as we have seen. To maintain this empire she had to keep up great fleets, and huge docks in her own port; but as her Phoenician population was largely occupied with trade, she had to rely for her crews and also for her land forces largely on the native Africans whom she had subdued, or on mercenaries hired from other races with whom she came in contact. Though this was a weak point in her armour, she was far the greatest power in the western seas, and any other people ambitious of power in that region would have to reckon with her. So far she had been on friendly terms with Rome, and we still have the text of three treaties between the two states; but the latest of these shows signs of mutual distrust, and Rome had now risen so high that a collision was all but inevitable. A people ruling in Italy cannot afford to have a rival in Sicily and also in undisputed command of the sea.

The collision came in the year 264 BCE, and it was the immediate result of an act of bad judgment and also of bad faith on the part of the Romans. There would be no need to mention this here if it did not illustrate a trait in the Roman character which is becoming more marked as Rome is drawn more and more into diplomatic relations with other states. The habit of order and discipline at home did not bring with it a sense of justice and honour in dealing with foreigners. The Roman practical view of life, which did not include education of the mind and feeling, was not favourable to the growth of generous conduct except towards a fellow citizen. The Latin word *virtus*, which expresses the practical duties of a citizen, does not suggest honourable dealing outside the civic boundary. Some mental imagination was needed for higher aims to make themselves felt in public life; slenderness is too often characteristic of Roman diplomacy; and hardness, not always stopping short of cruelty, is henceforward constantly to be found in their conduct towards a beaten foe.

A rascally band of mercenaries, Italians by birth, who had been in the Syracusan service, had seized on the old Greek city of Messana – the same Messina which quite recently met with so terrible a fate in the great earthquake. The city lay on the Sicilian side of the strait which still bears its name, and looked at from an Italian point of view, might be called the key to Sicily. Exactly opposite to it was Rhegium (Reggio), another Greek city which had been treated in the same way by another band of brigands; but these had been at once cleared out by orders from Rome. In the case of Messana the task naturally developed on Hiero, the king of Syracuse, a young man of ability who had lately made a treaty with Rome; but when he made the attempt, the brigands appealed for help both to Rome and to Carthage. The plain duty of the Senate was to support their ally Hiero, or to leave the applicants to their fate. But the Carthaginians might then establish themselves at Messana, and that must have seemed to a Roman a thing not to be permitted. The Senate hesitated for once, and finally referred the matter to the people, who voted to support the mercenaries against an ally of the Roman State. This act of bad faith and bad policy cost the Romans a valuable ally, and a war with Carthage that lasted without a break for 23 years.

First Punic War

It would be waste of space in this little book to go into the details of this long and wearisome war, which can be read in any history of Rome. It was, of course, in the main a naval war, and the Romans had as yet no fleet to speak of. But now was seen the advantage of a united Italy. The difficulty was overcome by enlisting the services of Greek and Etruscan sailors and ship-builders; a Carthaginian war-vessel, wrecked on the Italian coast, served as a model, and a large fleet was soon ready for sea, with which, strange to say, the Roman commanders succeeded in the course of a few years in clearing the Italian and Sicilian seas of the enemy, and even contrived to transport an army of invasion to Carthaginian territory. This astonishing feat was accomplished simply by the invention of a device for grappling with the enemy's ships, so that they could be boarded by Roman soldiers acting as 'marines'. And during this first half of the war they also renewed their alliance with Hiero, and conquered the whole of Sicily, with the exception of the strong city of Lilybaeum (now Marsala).

But all these good results were thrown away by the folly of the Roman Senate. Now that they had crossed the sea and entered on a new sphere of action, they seemed for the moment to have lost the prudence and wisdom that had won them the headship of Italy. They had two consular armies in Africa which seemed to have Carthage herself in their grip; but when she sued for peace they offered her impossible terms, and about the same time actually recalled one of the two consuls with his army to Italy. The old Phoenician spirit revived, and turned to desperate courage: an able Greek soldier of fortune, Xanthippus, took the Carthaginian army in hand, and before long, the remaining Roman army was utterly destroyed and its commander Regulus was a prisoner. This is the Regulus of one of the most famous of Roman stories, and one of the most beautiful of Horace's *Odes*. He is said to have gone to Rome on *parole* with an embassy, and on its failure to have returned a captive to Carthage, where he was put to a cruel death. Many critics now reject this tale as pure legend, without sufficient reason. It is probably true in outline, and it is certain that it took firm possession of the Roman mind. It thus bears witness to the strong Roman feeling of the binding power of an oath, even when given to an enemy; for Regulus had sworn to return if the mission failed.

It took Rome many years and enormous efforts to recover from this disaster, and from the destruction of her fleets by tempests which unluckily followed and gave Carthage once more the mastery of the sea. Carthage, too, had found a man of genius, Hamilcar Barca, whose intense hatred of Rome, ever growing as she gradually prevailed, inspired his people to continue the struggle by sea, and his own forces to hold on grimly to a mountain fortress in the north-west of Sicily, Mount Eryx, the scene of the games in the fifth book of Virgil's *Aeneid*. Both sides were exhausted and indeed permanently damaged; but the strength of Rome was more enduring, and in 241 BCE Hamilcar consented himself to negotiate a peace, by which Sicily and the adjacent smaller islands passed into the hands of Rome for ever. Soon afterwards, taking advantage of a deadly war which Carthage had to wage with her own mercenaries, Rome contrived, in that spirit of 'slenderness' already noticed, to get possession of both Sardinia and Corsica. This shows that the Senate understood the importance of these islands for a power in command of the western seas; but unjust dealing brought its own reward. It is possible that the great Hamilcar might have forgiven Rome her injuries to his country but for this. As it was, his hatred of her sunk into his soul more deeply than ever, and that hatred, springing up afresh in the breast of his son Hannibal, all but destroyed his enemy off the face of the earth. He retired to Spain, to organize a Carthaginian dominion there, of which he was himself practically king, and which he destined as a base of operations against Rome in another war; and before he started, as Hannibal himself told the story long afterwards, the father made his boy of nine years old take a solemn oath to cherish an eternal hatred of the enemies of his country.

Second Punic War

The plan of invading Italy from Spain was forced upon Hamilcar by the fact that Rome was in command of the sea; it was no longer possible for Carthage to strike at her from Africa without a greater effort to recover that command than her government of merchant princes was now disposed to make. And the fact that Hannibal was actually able to carry out the invasion by land was due to the genius and personal influence of his father in building up a solid dominion in southern Spain with New Carthage (now Cartagena) as its capital. Some historians have thought that of these two extraordinary men the father was the greatest; and it is at least true that his was a noble work of construction, while his son's brilliant gifts were wasted in the attempt to destroy the great fabric which Rome had reared in Italy. The attempt was unavailing; the solid Roman structure survived all the assaults of the greatest captain of the ancient world. The glamour of Hannibal's splendid victories must not blind us to the fact that he made two serious miscalculations: he believed that the Italians hated Rome as he did himself, and would join him to crush her; and he hoped, if he did not believe, that Carthage would give him substantial help. Had he judged rightly on the former point, Rome's fate was sealed. But the Italian kinsmen of Rome, who had come to recognize in her their natural leader, never even faltered in their loyalty, and Carthage did but little to help him till it was too late. Thus we have in this terrible war the strange spectacle of a single man of marvellous genius pitting himself against the whole strength of a united Italy with military resources, as we know from the accurate Greek historian, Polybius, amounting to some 770,000 men capable of bearing arms.

Fascinating as we may find Hannibal's wonderful career, much as we may admire his nobility of character, a sober judgment must lead to the conclusion that no great man ever did less for the good of his fellow creatures. During the 15 years of his stay in Italy he did irreparable damage to the fair peninsula, and he hardened the hearts of the Romans for all their future dealings with their foes. When at last he left it he was unable to save his own country, and spent his last years in exile, ever plotting against the enemy that had escaped him. A man who is actuated all his life through by a single motive of hatred and revenge, can never be reckoned among those who have done something for the benefit of humanity.

While Hannibal was gaining the loyalty of the southern Spaniards, and organizing their resources, Rome was occupied in trying to extend her power over the Gauls settled in the plain of the Po, and so to make sure of her northern flank, as she had already secured Sicily in the south. The Senate knew something of Hannibal's design, and hoped to anticipate him in getting a hold on that valuable region, the strategical key to Italy. But here there was no question of gaining the loyalty of the tribes; the Gauls were restless and hostile, and had quite lately made another determined attempt to reach Rome; they actually came within three days' march of the city before they were defeated in a great battle. In 219-218 BCE Roman armies were still busy in driving roads northward, and planting two colonies, Placentia and Cremona, on Gallic soil and on the Po, when Hannibal descended on them from the Alps. He had found a pretext for war, gathered a force of 100,000 men, passed the Pyrenees and reached the *Rhône* before the Senate knew what he was about, and eluded a consular army dispatched to stop him. Scipio, its commander, with true military instinct, sent his army on to Spain, to cut his communications with the base he had been preparing so long. This line of communication Hannibal never recovered for 10 years, and was forced to maintain and recruit his army on Italian soil.

That army, from a purely military point of view, was without doubt one of the best known to history. It consisted chiefly of thoroughly trained Spanish infantry, officered by Carthaginians, and of the best cavalry in the world, recruited from the Numidians of the western region of North Africa. It was one of those armies that can go anywhere and do anything at the bidding of its general, because entire trust in him was the one motive actuating it. It was a professional army, a perfect instrument of war, a weapon admirably fitted to destroy, but without constructive value – with no sap of civilization giving it permanent vital energy. Luckily for Rome, this army had shrunk to very moderate dimensions when it reached Italy; the length of the march, the necessity of leaving some troops in Spain, and the terrible trials of the crossing of the Alps, where the native tribes combined with rock, snow and ice to wear it out, had reduced it to less than 30,000 men.

Yet after a few days' rest Hannibal went straight for the nearest Roman force. This force was now on the north bank of the Po under Scipio, who had returned from the *Rhône* to Italy. Pushing it back to the new *colonia* of Placentia, where it was joined by that of the other consul Sempronius, Hannibal utterly defeated the combined Roman armies on the little river Trebbia which runs down to that city (now Piacenza) from the Apennines. The Roman power in the plain of the Po was instantly paralysed by this defeat, and the victor at once set himself to organize alliances with the Gallic tribes while he rested and recruited his weary troops. But from the Gauls he got no substantial help; that fickle people had no great reason to welcome an invader when once he was in their territory. And perhaps this was fortunate for him; for if he had marched into central Italy as leader of a Gallic army he would have strengthened, not weakened, the resistance of the whole Italian federation that Rome had so solidly organized. His knowledge of the motives which held this federation together must surely have been seriously imperfect.

But in the spring he crossed the Apennines, and made his way through the marshy and malarious district around the lower Arno, where it is said he lost an eye from ophthalmia, to meet the consul Flaminius, who had been sent to cover the approach to Rome with a large army. Slipping past Flaminius, Hannibal concealed his army among the hills and woods on the eastern shore of the lake of Trasimene, along the western bank of which the railway now runs on its way from Florence to Rome; and here he lay in wait for his prey. Flaminius walked into the trap laid for him; his army was totally destroyed, and he himself was killed. There was now nothing to stop the conqueror if he chose to march straight on Rome.

But Hannibal's plans did not include a siege of Rome; he had brought no siege apparatus, and at no time during the war did he succeed in getting any from Carthage, or in making it in Italy. His real object was to bring the Italians over to his side, to isolate Rome, and to put a free Italy (so he is said to have phrased it) in place of a Roman dominion. So he turned his back on Rome, and made his way at leisure down the eastern coast of central Italy to the corn-lands of Apulia, which were henceforward to serve as his chief base of operations. Hence he might easily reach the great sea-ports of Tarentum and Croton, and so get into touch once more with Carthage, and perhaps, too, with another power from whom he was already looking for help, Philip, king of Macedon. But during this southward march he learnt, apparently for the first time, that Italy was studded with Roman and Latin colonies, each a fortress, each provisioned and ready to resist him: each, too, a miniature Rome, disseminating among the Italians the honour and pride of Roman citizenship, and the animating spirit of Italian unity under Roman leadership. One or two of these fortresses he vainly tried to take, and he must at this time have begun at last to realize that the mortal hatred of an individual is no match in the long run for the organized vitality of a practical people.

His one chance was to win another great battle, and so to overawe south Italy, to make his base absolutely secure, and to force gradually northward the leaven of anti-Roman feeling on which he calculated. For the rest of that year, 217 BCE, he could not get this chance; the Senate, still cool-headed, had appointed a cool-headed dictator, who knew that his slow and steady citizen soldiers were no good match for a mobile professional army skilfully handled, and steadily refused to accept battle. Not even when Hannibal forced his way northward to the rich plain of Campania, and tried to gain over the wealthy city of Capua, would Fabius be tempted to fight; he dogged the enemy's footsteps, and once tried to catch him in a snare, from which Hannibal escaped by a clever ruse. But next year the Senate dispatched the two new consuls, with an army not far short of 100,000 men, to deal with the enemy in southern Italy; and here, reluctant though one at least of them was, Hannibal enticed them into a battle by seizing a valuable depot of stores at a town called Cannae, near the sea, in the plain of Apulia. Though far inferior in numbers, he contrived by consummate tactics to draw the solid Roman legions into a net, and then used his mobile Numidian cavalry to prevent their escape to the rear. The fight became a butchery, in which 80,000 Romans are said to have fallen. The largest army ever yet sent out from Rome was totally destroyed, and it would seem as if she could no longer escape from her deadly foe.

Roman Resilience

At this point, the high-water mark of Hannibal's successes, we may pause to see how the Senate met the news of this most terrible disaster. At no moment in Roman history is the sterling quality of the Roman character and spirit so conspicuously shown. The Senate had to meet not only the immediate military crisis in Italy, but the problems of military and naval policy in Spain, in Sicily, and in the plain of the Po. At home, too, they had to deal with what we may call a religious panic; the people, and especially the women, were beginning to lose nerve, and to fancy that their gods had forsaken them. We can believe the Roman historian when he says that any other people would have been crushed by a catastrophe like this. But the wise men of the Senate simply sat down to repair it, never dreaming of giving in. The city was made safe, fresh legions were enrolled, and thanks were voted to the surviving consul 'for not despairing of the Republic.' They would not ransom the prisoners in Hannibal's hands, nor receive the officer whom he sent for this purpose. They were not moved even by the news that southern Italy, the Bruttians, Lucanians, Apulians, and most of the Samnites, had joined the enemy, and that isolated towns farther north had deserted them. Capua, the second city of Italy, was betrayed to Hannibal, and he was thus enabled to advance his base from Apulia into the plain of Campania, without leaving an enemy in his rear: but the Senate did not despair. In due time the ranks of this Senate, sadly thinned since the war began, were filled up by a dictator with the best and most experienced citizens available. All possible means were adopted of keeping up the idea of 'the peace of the gods'; an embassy was even sent to Delphi; the religious panic speedily quieted down. At the beginning of the next year provision was made as usual for the military commands in Sicily, Sardinia, and Spain, and also for a fleet which was being got together at Ostia, the port at the mouth of the Tiber. Within a few months after the battle all was going on in Rome as usual.

So the overwhelming defeat of Cannae did but lead the Romans to victory – to a victory of all the nobler elements in their character over momentary doubt and despair. A people that could recover from that disaster, and go quietly about the work of repairing it, was not likely to be crushed out of existence even by a Hannibal; and though he was to remain as a standing menace for many years on Italian soil, it may fairly be said that henceforward he had no real chance of ultimate success. Two moments of grave anxiety were still to come, but Rome survived them both. One of these came three years later, when a desperate effort was being made to snatch Capua out of Hannibal's grasp. To induce the Roman government to raise the siege, he made a sudden march on Rome, knowing that no covering army was between him and the capital. He encamped on the Anio, three miles above the city, and rode with an escort of cavalry right up to the gates. But it was all in vain; the Senate had gathered levies amply sufficient to hold the walls, and after plundering the Roman lands Hannibal fell away again, like a sea-wave spent and broken on a rocky shore.

The last moment of extreme peril came five years later, in 207 BCE. The wise foresight of the Senate at the outset of the war had so far secured the Roman hold on Spain, and no reinforcements had reached Hannibal from that source. At last his loyal and able brother Hasdrubal eluded the Roman army there, and by taking a new route avoided all opposition from the Romans in northern Spain. Communications with Italy were now at last open, though not by sea, as they should have been had the government at Carthage thrown its whole strength into the work of building up its naval power afresh. Hasdrubal was forced to cross the Alps, and this he did with better knowledge and with less loss than his brother. He made his way through the Gallic territory and reached Ariminum (Rimini). Hannibal was in Apulia, where one consul was holding him in check and dealing with disaffected Italians; the other was waiting for the invader on the great coast road south of Ariminum. Hasdrubal sent dispatches to his brother informing him of his arrival and suggesting plans of co-operation; but there were Roman troops everywhere, and the messengers fell into the hands of the enemy. The consul in the south, Claudius Nero, discovering thus the danger, took a step, without orders from the Senate, which has made his name for ever famous. He left sufficient force to hold Hannibal, and slipped away with 7,000 picked men, without being discovered even by the most wily of commanders. He marched into the camp of Livius, the other consul, by night, after a march of some 200 miles, all the loyal people of central Italy feeding and blessing his army as he went. Two days later the most decisive battle of the war was fought on the banks of the little river Metaurus, which runs into the sea from the Apennines a few miles south of Ariminum. The Romans were this time completely victorious; the invading army was utterly destroyed, and Hasdrubal was killed fighting hard to the last. Nero went swiftly southwards to his original station, and flung the head of Hasdrubal – so it was said – into his brother's camp. For the first time during the long weary years of the war Rome was mad with joy; and almost for the first time in her history we note a genuine outburst of gratitude to the gods for this their inestimable blessing. Gratitude, whether to god or man, was not a conspicuous trait in the Roman character; but now, in a moment of real religious emotion, the first thought is one of thankfulness that 'the peace of the gods' is fully restored. It was not only that the Senate ordered a public thanksgiving of three days, but that men and women alike took advantage of it to press in crowds to the temples, the mothers, in their finest robes, bringing their children with them.

Scipio: Rome's Greatest General

The rest of the war story is soon told. The man who had let Hasdrubal escape him in Spain was a young Scipio, son of a Scipio who had done good work and lost his life there earlier in the war. He himself was a young man of real ability, whose character has always been to some extent a mystery. He was a new type of Roman, one not wholly without imagination, and the long years that he spent in Spain without rivals to check him had perhaps made him cherish and develop his own individuality more than was possible for the staid Roman noble of the old type at home. He believed profoundly in himself, and had the gift of making others believe in him. Returning home the year after the Metaurus battle, he was elected consul, though not yet of the legal age, and had Sicily given him as his province, where after many vicissitudes the Romans were now supreme. He at once proposed to invade Africa, and so to force Hannibal to leave Italy; and the Senate, though they could not or would not risk a large force, gave him leave to make the attempt.

Scipio crossed to Africa in 204 BCE, and ere long the Carthaginian government recalled Hannibal. The great general obeyed, sadly and unwillingly, and in 202 met Scipio in battle at Zama and was beaten; the undisciplined levies given him by the government were no match for Roman veterans. He himself now advised his people to make peace, and conducted the negotiations, thus doing what he could to make up for the irreparable damage done her in the war by his own implacable hatred of her rival. Carthage was no longer to be a naval power – that was definitely secured by the terms accorded her. She surrendered Spain to the victors, and agreed to pay a large war indemnity by instalments during 50 successive years. Her foreign policy was to be guided by Rome: she could no longer be called an independent State.

So ended this great trial of Roman endurance. No people has ever gone through a harder test and survived. The sense of duty and discipline never once failed them; Romans and Italians alike were ready to face death at any moment in defence of their country. But war, always mischievous, when prolonged can sow the seeds of much evil in the future; and we must confess with regret that we are to see but little more of the heroic qualities that had carried Rome through this great struggle.

V
DOMINION AND DEGENERACY

The Accidental Imperialists

It is hard for young nations, as for young men, to realize the need of rest, and all the harder in ancient Italy, where fighting had hardly ceased to be looked on as 'the natural industry of a vigorous State.' The Roman Senate was not ripe enough in knowledge of human nature to understand the mischief, moral as well as material, that a long war can cause, especially if the enemy has been in your country harrying and devouring, no one knowing when his turn will come to be ruined. And, indeed, we may doubt whether even if Rome's leading men had been able to understand the nature of the mischief, they would have had the skill to discover and apply the necessary remedies.

This mischief and its results must be the subject of this chapter, for without getting some idea of it we cannot understand the perils to which civilization was exposed in the next 200 years by Roman degeneracy, or the way in which they were eventually overcome. But I must just glance, to start with, at the policy actually pursued by the Senate in the period following the war, which placed Rome in the position of arbiter of the whole Mediterranean world, and mistress of a territory many times as large as Italy.

The two recent invasions of Italy by formidable enemies must have taught the Senate the necessity of making it impossible that there should be another. But another might yet be looked for – so at least they believed – not from Spain or Africa, but from the great military power of Macedon. Philip of Macedon had been among Rome's enemies since Cannae; but not even Hannibal could persuade him to attack her with vigour, and he missed his chance. Roman diplomacy had stirred up the Greeks against him, and he had plenty to do at home. But no sooner was Carthage crushed than the Senate coaxed the tired and unwilling People into declaring war against him, and this led in the course of the next half-century to the overthrow of the Macedonian kingdom, and finally to its absorption into what we must now begin to call the Roman Empire. At the same time, Rome acquired a protectorate over the whole of Greece, at first honestly meant to defend her against Macedon, but destined to pass rapidly into dominion. The Greeks in their leagues and cities were never again really free. If they could have kept from quarrelling among themselves, they might have endured this protectorate with profit; but ere Rome had done with them they were to feel her heavy hand.

Thus the 'peasants of the Tiber' became masters of the Balkan peninsula as well as of that of Italy. In the same period they completed the conquest of Italy up to the Alps, not without difficulties and defeats, and went on driving their roads and planting colonies in all parts. In the Spanish peninsula, from which the Carthaginians had been finally driven, they now established two permanent commands (*provinciae*), one in the basin of the Ebro in the north-east, and the other in the fertile valleys of the Guadiana and Guadalquivir, as the two great rivers of southern Spain are now called. From these they slowly but persistently, after their manner, and in spite of many defeats and even disgraces, pushed up into the high tablelands of central Spain, until they had brought the greater part of the peninsula under their sway. Here they had to deal with a people very different from the weary and exhausted Greeks and Macedonians; a people only half civilized, but lively, intelligent and capable of making excellent soldiers, as Hannibal had found. It is to the credit of the Romans that, in spite of much cruelty and misgovernment, they gave this peninsula a real civilization, of which the traces are still abundant especially in the south, and a beautiful language, which descends directly from their own.

In order to maintain their communications with Spain by land as well as by sea, they also had to look to the coast between the western Alps and the Pyrenees. Here they made a lasting alliance with the ancient and flourishing Greek colony, Massilia (Marseille); and in defending Massilia from the attacks of mountain tribes they were gradually drawn into the acquisition of a permanent hold on the lower valley of the Rhône. This, again, in due time very naturally became the starting point for fresh advance into the heart of modern France. No one who has seen the Rhône from Lyons to Marseilles can resist the conclusion that a power in possession of its lower reaches must inevitably advance along it northward.

There is yet a fourth peninsula in this land-locked sea, known for want of a better name as Asia Minor, which juts out from the Asiatic continent, and forms a meeting place for Eastern and Western civilizations. This was in the last three centuries BCE the fighting-ground of the successors of Alexander the Great, kings of Macedon, Pergamum, Syria and Egypt, who wasted the vigour of humanity in wars that to us seem needless. The Romans were soon drawn into a war with the king of Syria, an ally of Philip of Macedon, and won a great victory in this peninsula in the year 190 BCE. But they annexed no territory here until the last king of Pergamum left his kingdom to Rome by will some 60 years later. The Senate preferred to act as arbitrator, to make alliances, to reward friendly states, to use diplomacy rather than force; and on the whole they succeeded. Their policy was often tortuous, sometimes even mean, but in the long run it did more good than harm to humanity that a young and virile people should interfere among these monarchies.

Asserting Roman Influence

Thus, whether we look west or east in the Mediterranean, we find the Roman power predominant everywhere within 80 years from the end of the war with Hannibal. It is not easy to explain in a few words what drove this power onwards. It was not simply the commercial motive, as with Carthage. It was not simply the desire to conquer and annex, for the Senate was slow to undertake new duties of government abroad if their object could be attained in some other way. But what was that object? Undoubtedly it was self-defence to begin with; but self-defence, once successful, only too easily slips into self-assertion. This self-assertion, as we see it in Roman policy, was the determination to have a voice in all matters within their 'sphere of interest'. No Roman senator had a doubt that his people were the strongest and most competent to control the world. And the constant assertion of this proud conviction brought many suitors and suppliants to Rome, whose presence flattered Roman pride, and whose diplomacy sometimes involved the government in new wars, giving ambitious consuls their opportunity of increasing the fame and the wealth of themselves and their families. So in due time there arose a dominion of the following military commands or provinces: one in Sicily, one in Sardinia, two in Spain, one in southern Gaul, one in Macedonia with Greece attached to it, one in Asia Minor, and one in Africa, after the destruction of Carthage by her old enemy in 146 BCE. Of the method of governing these provinces I will say something in another chapter. Now let us try to estimate some of the results of these continuous wars in distant parts, taken together with the long struggle with Carthage. We shall find a change in every department of the people's life, and in almost all a change for the worse.

The Impact of Empire on Roman Society

First, let us look at that family life which formed the essential fibre of the old body politic, and provided the most powerful factor in the Roman character. We have but to think of the immense numbers of citizens killed or captured in war, or carried off by the pestilences that always follow war, to see what paralysis of family life there must have been. Fathers and grown-up sons innumerable never came home at all; and long service far from home would, in any case, deprive the family of the natural influence and authority of its head. Mothers might do much to fill up the gap, and the tradition of the dignified and righteous Roman lady was not as yet wholly weakened; but there are signs that the women in this period were getting steadily more excitable, more self-asserting, more luxurious. It is in this age that divorce begins to make its appearance, a sure sign of the decay of the old family life. There were rumours, too, of the poisoning of husbands by their wives, and on one occasion two noble ladies were put to death for this crime by the verdict of a council of relations. In an extraordinary attempt to introduce into Italy the exciting orgies of the Greek religion of Dionysus, women were among the most prominent offenders. The changing position of women at this time is illustrated by a famous saying of Cato, that 'all men rule over women, we Romans rule over all men, and our wives rule over us.'

With the decay of the old family life, the wholesome training of the children in manly conduct (*virtus*) and sense of duty (*pietas*) could not but suffer, too. Old-fashioned families would keep it up, but among the lower classes it was hard to do so owing to bad housing and crowding in the city; and in the noble families there was undoubtedly a change for the worse, though we know of one or two great men of this age who took pains with the moral as well as the intellectual training of their boys. For a people controlling the Mediterranean world it was necessary to educate the mental faculties, and more especially to teach a boy to speak and read Greek, which was the language of half the civilized world, and the language of commerce everywhere. Now Rome could not supply teachers for this kind of education; Romans were not competent, nor would they have condescended to such work. The Greeks were the one people who could undertake what we call the higher education, and they were now beginning to swarm in Rome. Some Greek teachers were free men, but the greater number were slaves captured in the wars; and thus the first requisite in a school-master, that he should be looked up to and willingly obeyed, was too often absent in this new education. It is men, not methods, that really tell in education. In his heart, as we know from many striking passages in Roman literature, the grown-up Roman despised the Greek, and we may be sure that the Roman boy did too. Greek literature and rhetoric, now fast becoming the staple of the higher education, could never make up for the lack of moral discipline. If we find a spirit of lawlessness in the coming age, and a want of self-restraint in dealing with enemies or opponents, we shall not be far wrong in ascribing it in great part to the loss of the wholesome home influence, and to the introduction of an education outside the home, which entirely failed to make up for the decay of the simple old training in duty and discipline.

The fact is that the Romans were now coming under the influence of a new idea of life, in which the individual played a more important part than ever before at Rome. The Roman of the past had grown up modelled on a type and fixed in a group, so that the individual had little chance of asserting himself; but now we find him asserting himself in every direction, and in every class of society. To think for oneself, even in matters of religion; to speak from personal motives in the senate or law-courts; to aim at one's own advancement in position or wealth – all this seemed natural and inevitable to the men of that day. And so by degrees the individual became the mainspring of action instead of the State. There were some noble exceptions, but most of the leading men played their own game, and often won it at the expense of the State. Many a general hurried on operations towards the close of his command so as not to be superseded before he could earn a triumph, and pass in splendid procession up to the temple on the Capitol, with chained captives following his chariot. And the small men became more and more unwilling to serve as soldiers in distant lands, and more and more rebellious against discipline. In little more than half a century after Hannibal had left Italy the Roman armies were beginning to be incapable of their work.

Along with this too rapid growth of the individual, we have to take account of the sudden incoming of wealth and growth of capital. The old Roman family group had no capital except its land and stock. But now, as the result of plunder and extortion in the provinces, most men of the upper classes had some capital in money, and this was almost always invested in public works and State undertakings of all kinds, *e.g.* the raising of taxes and the fitting out of fleets and armies. These things were all done by contract, and the contracts were taken by companies, in which every man was a shareholder who had anything to invest. Thus the inflow of wealth brought with it the desire of making money, and the forum of Rome became a kind of stock-exchange in which the buying and selling of shares was always going on, and where every man was trying to outwit his neighbour. Of a really productive use of capital in industry or commerce we hear very little; and it would seem that the Roman of that day had no idea of using his means or opportunities in ways likely to produce well-being in the world.

If we turn to rural Italy, the prospect is hardly less dreary. Incalculable damage had been done to agriculture in the great war, and agriculture, in the broad sense of the word, was almost the only Italian industry. Corn, wine, oil, wool and leather had formerly been produced in sufficient quantities to keep the inhabitants in food and clothing, each community growing what it needed, as in mediaeval England. But this simple form of agricultural economy must have suffered a severe shock, not only from the ravages of armies, but from the decrease of the working population owing to war and pestilence.

In order to restore a decaying industry you must have the men to work it. Depopulation as the result mainly of war was a disease epidemic in the Mediterranean in this age; and in Italy we know for certain how rife it was, for we have the records of the census of the body of Roman citizens, which show a steady falling-off in this period, and we must suppose that the same causes were at work among the non-Roman population of the peninsula. There was, indeed, a remedy, but it was almost worse than the disease – I mean the vast numbers of slaves now available for labour. The unskilled slaves, captured or kidnapped in Spain, Gaul, Epirus, Thrace or Asia Minor, were cheap in the Roman market, and would do well enough to run a farm with, especially if that farm were chiefly a pastoral one, with flocks and herds needing no great experience or skill to look after. This cheapness, and the physical conditions of rural life in a mountainous country, made cattle-running and sheep-tending a profitable industry. Large districts of Italy, especially in the centre and south, became covered in this period with huge estates owned by capitalists, and worked by rough and often savage slaves, who were locked up at night in underground prisons and treated simply as "living tools." No ray of hope ever broke in on these miserable beings; no free citizen gave a thought either to their condition or the economic danger of the system; philanthropy and political economy were unknown in the Roman world, for imagination and reflection were alike foreign to the Roman mental habit

Even on the estates of moderate size which were not entirely pastoral, slave-labour was the rule. We know something of such a farm from the treatise on agriculture written by Cato at this time, which has come down to us entire; and it is plain from what he says that though free labour might be employed at certain seasons, *e.g.* at harvest, the economic basis of the business was slave-labour. There is no doubt that all over Italy the small farm and the free cultivator were fast disappearing, with the rapid growth of capital and the cheapness of slaves. In the city of Rome, now beginning to harbour a vast population of many races, the number of domestic slaves tended constantly to increase; they were employed in every capacity by men of wealth and business. Many of them were cultivated men, Greeks for example, who could act as clerks, secretaries or teachers, and these had a fair chance of earning their freedom in time; but great numbers were low and vicious beings, who had no moral standard but that of obedience to a master, no moral sanction except punishment.

Thus, though the shrinkage of the free population was evil enough, the remedy for it was even worse. The slave, plucked up by the roots from the soil in which he had flourished in his native land, deprived of family, property, religion, must in the majority of cases become a demoralized and hopeless being. In the plays of Plautus, which date from this period, the slave is a liar and a thief, and apparently without a conscience. For the slave-owner, too, the moral results were bad enough, though not so obvious at first sight. A man who is served by scores of fellow creatures who are absolutely at his mercy is liable to have his sense of duty gradually paralysed. Towards them he has no obligations, only rights; and thus his sense of duty towards his free fellow citizens is apt to be paralysed too. A habit of mind acquired in dealing with one set of men naturally extends itself and affects all human relations. And so the Roman character, naturally hard enough, came in the later days of the Republic to be harder than ever. In our next two chapters we shall meet with unmistakable proofs of this. Incredible cruelty, recklessness of human life, callousness in dealing with the vanquished and the subject peoples, meet us at every turn in that dark age of Mediterranean history. Under the baleful influence of slavery the hard Roman nature had become brutalized; and we have to wait for the Christian era before we find any sign of sympathy with that vast mass of suffering humanity with which the Roman dominion was populated.

We must glance in the last place at the change brought about by the wars in another department of Roman life, viz. in the working of the constitution. The reader will remember that in early Rome the salient feature in that constitution was the *imperium* of the magistrate, just as in private life the salient feature was the discipline of the family under the rule of the head of the household. The man who held the *imperium* was irresistible so long as he held it, though a wise custom made it necessary for him to seek the advice of his council, the Senate, in all questions of grave importance. But now the long wars took the consul and his *imperium* away from the city for long periods, and as the Empire began to grow up and include provinces beyond sea, those periods became longer and longer. There were, indeed, always two magistrates with *imperium* in Rome, the praetors, who for long past had been elected yearly to help the consuls in judicial business; but the prestige of their *imperium* never reached the level of that of the consuls. And even when a consul returned home, though the majesty of the *imperium* was present in his person as ever, it was not his hand that was really on the helm. The decision of great questions did not lie with him, but with his Council, whose knowledge of affairs and whose 'courage never to submit or yield,' had carried Rome safely through a long series of unexampled trials.

Paramount Power: The Roman Senate

In the period after the war with Hannibal, the Senate, not the *imperium*, is clearly the paramount power in the working of the constitutional machinery. To take a single instance: when the people declined to sanction the war with Philip of Macedon, the Senate directed the consul to convince them that they were wrong, and both consul and people bowed to its will. They had other agents in the tribunes of the people, if the consuls failed them, and would now and then even coerce a consul by means of the power of the tribune. But what chiefly gave the Senate its power was the fact that it was the only permanent part of the government. A senator held office for life unless ejected by the Censor for immorality, while all the magistrates were elected for a year only. In the Senate there sat for life every man who had held high office and done the State good service, and as there were some 300 of these, it was almost impossible for the yearly holders of *imperium* to resist their deliberate judgments. And for those judgments the Senate was responsible to no man.

Probably no assembly has ever comprised so much practical wisdom and experience as the Roman Senate of this period; but that wisdom and that experience was limited to the working of the constitution, the control of foreign affairs, and the direction and supply of armies. As has already been hinted, when it came to providing remedies for economic and moral evils such as I have been sketching, the Senators were useless; they had no training in the art of the State physician, and no desire to learn how to diagnose disease. They were almost all men of the same type, and with the same public and private interests. They belonged, in fact, to a few noble families, and new blood was seldom to be found in their ranks; for though they had all at one time or other been elected to office by the people, the choice of the people almost always fell upon members of the old tried families. The principle that the son of a family that has done good service to the State will be likely himself to do such service, seems to have taken firm hold of the mind of the Roman voter; and thus it came about that the Senate, in spite of its great capacity for business, gradually became an *oligarchical* body – the mouthpiece of one class of society. The principle is by no means a bad one in some stages of social growth, but it is sure in the long run to produce the vices as well as the virtues of oligarchy – the dislike of any kind of change, the narrow view of social life, the want of sympathy with other classes and of the desire to understand their needs. We shall see in the next two chapters how these oligarchical weaknesses brought the Senatorial government to an ignominious end. It had saved the State from its deadliest enemy; it had laid the foundations of the Roman Empire; but it failed utterly when called on to do the nobler work of justice and humanity.

The Roman Citizen

This aptly brings us to our last point in this chapter. As the Roman oligarchy stood to the people, so Rome herself stood as an oligarchy to the populations of her Empire. The Roman citizen was the one most highly privileged person in the civilized world of that day. The great prize of his citizenship was not, as we might suppose it would be, the right to vote in the assemblies, to choose magistrates and pass or reject laws, nor the right to hold office if elected, for to that distinction very few could aspire; it was really the legal protection of his person and his property wherever he might be in the

Empire. No one could maltreat his person with impunity; a fact well illustrated in the life of St. Paul (*Acts* 22:25 foll.). He could do business everywhere with the certainty that his sales, purchases, contracts, would be recognized and defended by Roman law, while the non-citizen had no such guarantees for his transactions. No other city in the Mediterranean had a citizenship to compare with this in practical value, for the Roman law was gradually becoming the only system of law with a real force behind it. To live a life of security and prosperity you must be a Roman citizen.

We, in these days of comparative enlightenment, might perhaps imagine that with a gift like this citizenship in their hands the Romans would have been quick to reward their faithful Italian allies, who had served in their armies all through these wars, by lifting them to their own level of social and political privilege. But if so, we should be ascribing to the human nature of Roman times a degree of generosity and sympathy which was, in fact, almost unknown. We might fancy that they would have grasped the fact that their old city-state had outgrown its cradle, that Italy and not the city of Rome now really supplied the force with which the world was ruled, and that they would put the Italians on the same level of advantage as themselves, at least as regards the protection of person and property. But after the war with Hannibal the tendency was rather in the other direction. All allied Italian cities continued to have to supply contingents to Roman armies and fleets; yet Rome offered them no privileges to make up for these burdens, and her magistrates got more and more into the habit of treating them as inferiors. The Latins, too, that is the old cities of the Latin league, and the colonies with Latin *right*, as it was now called, who already had some of the privileges of citizenship, were carefully prevented from acquiring more, from becoming full citizens of Rome. In this exclusive policy, which seems to us mean and ungrateful, the Roman government undoubtedly lost a great chance, and had to pay dearly later on for her negligence.

The fact was that the imperial idea had taken hold of the governing Romans with force. They were so busy governing, negotiating, arbitrating and making money, that the condition and claims of their own city and country failed to attract the attention of any but a very few among the educated aristocracy. Depopulation, decline of agriculture, slavery and its accompanying evils, injustice to the Italian allies and the ever-growing discontent occasioned by it, misgovernment and plunder in the provinces, all these sources of mischief were now accumulating force, and were before long to bring the whole Roman system to the brink of ruin. But Rome on the brink of ruin meant civilization in imminent danger; for no other power could any longer withstand the barbarians of northern Europe, who were even now beginning to press down into sunny southern lands. So it is that the story of the succeeding century, the last before the Christian era, is one of the most thrilling interest. How did Rome survive and overcome these dangers with renewed strength, and succeed in organizing an Empire on the firm foundations of law and justice, destined to hold the barbarians at bay long enough to inspire them with profound respect for the civilization they were attacking? This question we will try to answer in the remaining chapters of this book.

VI
THE REVOLUTION: ACT I

The Age of Strong Men

Enough was said in the last chapter to show that the age we are now coming to, the last century before Christ, was one full of great issues – not only for Rome, but for all western civilization. The perils threatening, both internal and external, were so real as to call for statesmen and soldiers of the highest quality; and as we shall see, this call was answered. It was this century that produced most of the famous Romans whose names are familiar to us: the two Gracchi, Marius, Sulla, Pompeius, Cicero, Caesar, and finally Augustus, all of whom helped in various ways to save Italy and the Empire from premature dissolution. It was, in fact, an age of great personalities, and one, too, in which personal character became as deeply interesting to the men of the time as it is even now to us. For as the disciplinary force of the State waned, the individual was left freer to make his own force felt; and so great was that force at times, that we are tempted to fix our attention on the man, and to forget the complicated motives and interests of the world in which he was acting. Undoubtedly we should be wrong in doing so; for a very small acquaintance with the facts would show us these great men struggling incessantly with difficulties, and carried out of their own natural course by adverse currents. But nonetheless it is true that hardly any other period of history shows so much, for good and evil alike, depending on individual character. So as the last chapter dealt mainly with perils and problems, our next two will be occupied with the efforts of these famous men to meet the perils and solve the problems.

The Gracchi Brothers

Depopulation and the decline of agriculture were the first of the perils to be considered seriously. This was done in the year 133 BCE, not by the Senate, whose business it really was, but by a young and enthusiastic noble, in some ways one of the finest characters in Roman history. Tiberius Gracchus had the right instinct of the old Roman for duty, and for a Roman he had an unusually tender and generous nature; but he had not the experience and knowledge necessary for one who would take this difficult problem in hand, which in our day would be prepared for legislation by careful inquiry about facts, conducted by authorized experts. His education had been mainly Greek, and a study of hard facts did not form a part of it.

Still, he was able to enlist the help of some capable men, and produced and finally carried a bill which may be called a Small Holdings Act. No one was henceforward to hold more than 500 *jugera* (about 300 acres) of *public land*, or if he had sons, 250 more for each of two. Public land was land owned by the State, but occupied by private men who paid (or ought to have paid) rent for it in some form. Land owned as well as occupied by private men could not be touched; but there was abundance of the other, for the State had retained its hold on a large part of the land of Italy acquired by Rome. This land was now to be divided up in allotments, the State retaining its ownership and forbidding sale, a futile attempt to keep the settlers on the land, even against their will. This courageous plan for bringing the people back to the land was put in action at once, and we still have a few of the inscribed boundary stones set up by the commissioners chosen to carry it out. And there is reason to believe that it did some good in regard both to depopulation and agriculture. The Senate made no serious attempt to interfere with it when once it was passed, and it continued in force for many years.

But unluckily the Senate had done all it could to prevent the bill passing; they would have nothing to say to it, and they put up a tribune to veto it. The veto of the tribune of the plebs was an essential part of the constitution, and could not be disregarded; but Gracchus, also a tribune, had but one year of office, and if he could not get his bill through during that year, he must give up the attempt for a long while. Enthusiasm got the better of prudence; he deliberately broke with law and usage; he defied the Senate and its prerogative, and he carried a bill deposing the tribune who acted for the Senate. He also proposed to offer himself as a candidate for re-election, contrary to the custom if not the law of the constitution. With the highest motives he thus laid himself open to the charge of making himself master of the State, by violating the custom of its forefathers (*mos maiorum*). It had always been a maxim of Roman law that the man who aimed at tyranny might be slain by anyone; and now that even the best aristocrats believed Gracchus guilty, this was the fate that overtook him. He was killed on the Capitol, and the cowardly rabble made no attempt to save him.

The story is perhaps the saddest in Roman history. A little more patience and practical wisdom, a little more of the spirit of compromise on either side, might have saved the situation. The old Roman discipline had avoided violence, and got over constitutional difficulties by consent; now Gracchus laid a violent hand on the constitution, and was repaid with violence by its unworthy defenders. Intending only reform, he ended with starting revolution.

There was another enemy within the gates beside depopulation, one not less to be feared, but less easy to realize as an enemy; I mean slave-labour. Gracchus may be pardoned for making no direct attempt to attack it, though just before his tribunate there had been a rising of slaves in Sicily which showed the military as well as the economic danger of the situation. It is said that 200,000 slaves were in rebellion there at one time, and the war was only ended after a long struggle. These risings, more of which followed at intervals, and finally a most formidable one in Italy 60 years later, were symptoms of a disease calling for a very skilful physician; but no physician was to be found until Caesar tried to make a beginning. As yet the Romans had not had time to realize this danger; living in an atmosphere of slave-labour, they believed that they throve on it. And as this was in one sense true, owing to the decrease of the free labouring population, the evil was too subtle for an uncritical people to discern. In spite of all these dangerous risings, there is no sign in the copious literature of this last century of the Republic of any consciousness of the poison at work.

Nine years after the murder of Tiberius Gracchus, his younger brother Gaius, elected tribune, took up his work and went far beyond his designs. In this most interesting and able man we come at last upon a Roman statesman of the highest order; a practical man, no mere idealist of the new Greek school, and yet a man of genius and a born leader of men. We possess a picture of him, evidently drawn from the life by one who knew him, which shows these gifts at a glance. When he was at the height of his activity, busy with a multitude of details, he seems to have given that eyewitness the impression that he was almost a monarch. But a close study of all we are told about him seems to prove that he was in reality one of those rare men, like Caesar later on, who profoundly believe that they can do the work needed by the State better than any other man, and who are justified in that belief. He would see to the carrying out of his own measures with astonishing speed, sparing no pains, amazing even his enemies by the unflagging energy with which he worked, and by the way he contrived to get work out of others. Perhaps the secret was that he was a gentleman in the best and noblest sense of that word; for Plutarch says that in his dealings with men he was *always dignified, yet always courteous*, invariably giving to every man his due.

In fact, the personality of this man is the real explanation of his work. If it had been possible for him to retain that personal influence which Plutarch emphasizes, and to keep his legislative power even for a few years, as a modern statesman may expect to keep it, it is quite possible that Rome might have escaped an era of danger and degeneracy. But that could not be. A triple-headed Cerberus was guarding the path that led to effectual reform: the forms of the old constitution, out of date many of them, and unsuited to the needs of a great empire: the narrow spirit of the oligarchical faction, opposed, for self-regarding reasons, to all change: and lastly, the mean and fickle temper of the mongrel city populace, whose power was sovereign in legislation and elections. In the effort to overcome this Cerberus Gracchus lost his precious personal influence, and found his original designs warped from their true bearing. He survived through two tribunates, in the course of which he did much valuable work, but in the third year he was brutally and needlessly slain by his political enemies. Already Rome had put to death two of the most valuable men she ever produced, and in the coming century she was to put to death many more.

He had begun his work by a noble effort so to mend the constitution that a reformer might be able to pass his laws without breaking it, as Tiberius had been tempted to do. He tried to increase the numbers of the Senate, so as to leaven that great council, which he rightly looked on as the working centre of the constitution, with new ideas and wider interests. And he sought, too, to solve the great problem of citizenship, by giving the Italians some effectual share in it, and so at least the chance of making their voice heard in Roman politics. But for such measures of real progress neither Senate nor people were ready: the Senate was the stronghold of old prejudices, and the People were not pleased to admit Italians to its privileges. Both these great projects, which show how far-reaching Gracchus's views as a statesman were, proved complete failures.

To conciliate the Senate became more and more hopeless as Gracchus lost his personal influence, and he gave up the attempt. Instead, he dealt the senatorial oligarchy a heavy blow by depriving senators of the right to sit in judgment on ex-provincial governors accused of extortion (a crime now becoming only too common), and giving it to the class below, the Equites, or men of business. Thus he made a split between the two upper classes of society, which had very unfortunate results. Not less unhappy was another measure, meant to conciliate the hungry free population of the city, on which he must depend for the passing of his laws. There had long been a difficulty in feeding this population: for its number had increased beyond all expectation, the corn supply was not properly organized, and the price of grain was constantly fluctuating. Recognizing the fact that any legislator was in peril who could not make it impossible that the price should rise suddenly, he fixed a permanent price, more than half below the normal, to be maintained at State cost, whether or no the State were a loser. But here he went too far and gave later and less scrupulous demagogues the chance of making still more serious mischief. No doubt he thought that the State need not be a loser, if production, transport, warehousing and finance were organized as he meant to organize them; but there is also little doubt that he was mistaken, and that henceforward the "people" were really being fed largely at the expense of the State, and lapsing into a condition of semi-pauperism.

I have said enough to show how sad was the failure of the first real statesman produced by Rome. Yet Gracchus was able to do some useful work which survived. Under his auspices was passed a great law, of the text of which we still possess about one third, for the trial of provincial governors accused of extortion: and we know of another, bearing his own name, which regulated the succession to these governorships with justice and wisdom. Also he took up his brother's land bill, and carried it on with that practical persistency which is reflected, as we saw, in Plutarch's life of him. But in spite of high aims and some successes, his story is a sad one; and the loss to Italy and the Empire at that moment of a man of righteous aims and practical genius was simply incalculable.

Caius Marius

Whatever else the Gracchi did, or failed to do, they undoubtedly succeeded, both in their lives and in their deaths, in shaking the power and prestige of the senatorial government; and nothing had been put in its place, nor had it even been reformed. Henceforward for a long period there was no constitution that could claim an honest man's loyalty or devotion; the idea of the State was growing dim, and the result was inefficiency in every department. The governing class was corrupt and the army undisciplined, and this at a time when there was coming upon Rome, and upon the civilized world, a period of extreme peril from foreign enemies. This corruption and inefficiency became obvious a few years after the death of the younger Gracchus in a long struggle with a Numidian chief in the province of Africa, who contrived to outwit and defy Roman envoys and Roman armies, by taking advantage of the corruptibility of the one and the indiscipline of the other. Luckily for Rome this war produced a great soldier in Caius Marius, a 'new man' (*novus homo*) of Italian birth, and another in L. Cornelius Sulla, a man of high patrician family; and these two, though destined to be the bitterest foes, brought the war to a successful end.

But a far greater peril was threatening Italy herself. As we look at the map of Italy, or better still (if we have the chance) as we look up at the huge rampart of the Alps from the plain of the Po, we are tempted to think of this great barrier as impenetrable. But mountain ranges are always weak lines of defence, and history, ancient and modern alike, has abundantly proved that Italy is open to invasion from the north. Hannibal and his brother had pierced the western flank of the range, where later on there were regular thoroughfares between Rome and her western provinces; and at the eastern end, where the passes gradually lessen in height, access was easy into Italy from the north-east. Beyond this mountain barrier, at the time we have now reached, there was much disturbance going on: hungry masses of population were moving about in search of fertile land to settle in, themselves pressed on by other peoples in the same restless condition. In 113 BCE a great migrating host, apparently of Germans, but probably gathering other peoples as it advanced, seemed to threaten the weak point of the eastern Alps.

A consul with an army was in Illyria, and tried to stop them in the country now called Carinthia, but was badly beaten. If there had been a man of genius at their head, the enemy might have penetrated into Italy; as happened again just a century later, there was nothing to stop them between the Alps and Rome. But the great host was not tempted, and pursued its way westward. In 109 BCE they suddenly appeared beyond the western Alps, where they destroyed another consular army, and yet another fell before the Gauls of that region. Then in 105, at Orange, in Roman territory, while trying to cover the road to Massilia and so into Italy, the Romans experienced a defeat almost as terrible as that of Cannae and half the Empire lay open to the victors. But once again they left their prey untouched, and passed westwards in search of easier conquests.

Rome had a breathing time of nearly three years, and she also had the right man to save her. Marius remodelled the army, revolutionizing it in equipment, tactics, and discipline. For material he was driven hard, and had to find recruits as best he could, drawing them from all parts of the Empire: but he had time to drill them into fine soldiers, and to lay the foundation of a marvellously perfect human defence for Mediterranean civilization. The result was one great victory near Marseilles, and another at the eastern end of north Italy, into which the barbarians had at last penetrated: and Italy was once more secure.

The Army of Roman Citizens and Italians

Now we have to see how this peril, or rather the effort made to escape it, led to changes of the most far-reaching character in the Roman power and polity. Italy had not been saved by Roman armies or the Roman government, but by Marius and the army which he had created. For five successive years Marius was consul, contrary to all precedent, away from Rome; and the army he created looked to him, not to Rome, for pay, promotion, and discharge. We may call that host of his a Mediterranean army under the command of an Italian. It was far more like Hannibal's army than like the old Roman citizen armies that had won the supremacy in Italy; it was a professional army devoted to its general, but with little thought of the Roman State whose servant he was. And henceforward, until Augustus restored the sense of duty to the State, the Roman armies, excellent now as fighting machines, and destined to secure effective frontiers for the Empire, were the men of Marius, Sulla, Pompeius, Caesar, and a constant source of anxiety and danger for the State whom they were supposed to serve.

This 'long-service army' brought Rome face to face with another difficulty, and led indirectly to another great peril. When the soldiers returned home after many years of service in distant regions, what was to be done with them? Many, perhaps most of them, had no homes to go to. The veterans might naturally demand some permanent settlement, but the Senate showed no sign of appreciating the problem, and in this matter the general was helpless without the Senate. So it happened that many of them lapsed into the crowded city, to pick up a living we know not how, with the help of the distribution of cheap corn. Among them were beyond doubt numbers of non-citizens, who could not legally vote in elections or legislation, and were inadequately protected in regard to person and property, in spite of all the long service they had gone through. These men began to offer themselves as voters, and to exercise the rights of citizenship illegally; yet the confusion of the registers was such that they could not be detected. At last the adulteration of the Roman citizen body became so obvious that the consuls of 95 BCE passed a law with the object of making it clear who was a citizen and who was not, and of eliminating those who were not really privileged.

But it was now too late to take such a step. News of it spread over all Italy, and it was construed as a deliberate attempt to exclude Italians from the citizenship. Five years later another vain attempt was made by a noble tribune to do as Gracchus had wished to do, to extend the citizenship and to enlarge the

Senate: but he was assassinated before his laws were passed, and then at last there followed the inevitable outbreak, perhaps long meditated. The social war, as it is called, in reality a civil war, was a crisis in the history of European development. When it was over, the ancient city-state of the Greeks and Italians had vanished in Italy, and in its place arose a new form of polity, for which there was then no name.

The sturdy peoples of central Italy entered on the desperate venture of setting up a rival power against Rome; a plan which, if successful, would have paralysed Rome's work in the world whether for good or evil. They chose the city of Corfinium, in the heart of the Apennines, some 100 miles east of Rome, gave it the new significant name Italica, and made it, as Washington is now, the city-centre of a federation, where deputies from the various members should meet and deliberate under the presidency of consuls. But now was seen the value of the strategical position of Rome. She could strike in any direction from inner lines, while safe from attack or blockade by sea; but Corfinium had no such natural strategic advantage, nor any unifying power. Yet the Italians were for some time successful in the field, and Rome was for a whole year in the utmost peril. At the end of that year (90 BCE) the Etruscans and Umbrians to north and east joined the confederates, and then for the first time Rome was likely to be put on the defensive, with enemies on her left flank, as well as on her right and in front. So a law was hastily passed giving the precious citizenship to all who had not taken up arms; and this was the beginning of a process by which, in some few years, the whole of Italy became Roman in the eye of the law, while, on the other hand, it might be said not untruly that Rome became

Italian. Henceforward we have to think of the whole peninsula as forming the material support of Mediterranean civilization.

Sulla

With this great change one might have expected that peace and harmony would return to Italy. But, on the contrary, she is now about to enter on the most terrible time that she has ever known; even her miserable feuds of the late Middle Ages never quite reached the horror of those of Marius and Sulla. It is hard to explain this; but looking back at what was said in the last chapter about the causes of demoralization, it is possible to make a guess. We have to think of a vast slave State, worn out in the struggle with dangers within and without, enfeebled by constant warfare, and now given over into the hands of powerful military masters, with hosts of veterans at their beck and call. The State seemed to have lost its claim to loyalty, even to consideration: and in its place were rival generals, leaders also of political factions – in these years two, Marius the self-seeking champion of the Italians and the Roman plebs, and Sulla the self-seeking champion of the old aristocracy. All principles were lost on either side in the intensely bitter hatred of the parties and the personal rivalry of the leading men. It happened that a war was threatening in the East, of which we shall hear more in the next chapter; and the command in this war, the great prize of the moment, became a bone of contention outweighing all interest of the State.

The prize fell to Sulla; but no sooner was his back turned on Italy than the Marian faction fell on their political enemies and sought to destroy them by wholesale murder. Compromise was utterly forgotten; all the brutality of unbridled human nature was let loose. And when Sulla returned from the East, after driving the enemy out of Roman territory, the massacres were revenged by more massacres. The loss to Italy of many thousands of her best men, and among them scores who might have done good work in the world, was a calamity never to be repaired.

Where, one may ask, was the old Roman *gravitas* and *pietas*, the self-restraint and sense of duty that had won an empire? It would seem as if the capacity for discipline were entirely lost, except in the long-service army. But the mere fact that in the army this survived is one not to be neglected, even if it were exercised less on behalf of the State than in the interest of the individual commander. For if there could be found a statesman-soldier who could identify himself with the true interest of the State, and so bring back not only the army, but the people to a right idea of Rome's position and duty in the world, the Empire and civilization might yet be saved. Without the army these could not be defended; and the one thing wanting was to make the army loyal to the State as well as to its general. Only the general himself could secure this loyalty, by making himself the true servant of the State.

But the man into whose hands Rome had now fallen was one who could not possibly identify himself with the best interests of the State, because an unsympathetic nature had denied him the power of discerning what those interests were. Sulla has been compared to Napoleon Bonaparte, and in one or two points the comparison holds good; but the two were utterly unlike in the main point, the power of sympathetic discernment. Napoleon, cruel and unscrupulous as he often was, showed plainly, when he organized the institutions of

France, or Switzerland, or Egypt, that he understood the needs of those nations: he divined what would enable them to advance out of stagnation to some better form of life, social and political. But Sulla, though he saw that the call of the moment was for order at almost any price, for peace, strong government, and reform, went about his work in a way which proved that he did not delight in it, or care for the people for whom he was legislating. He did what was necessary for the moment, but did it with force ill-concealed under constitutional forms. So no wise man rejoiced in his work, and the Roman people as a whole felt no loyalty towards him. He provided in many State departments an excellent machinery, but not the motive force to work it.

Nothing in history shows better how much in remedial legislation depends on the spirit in which it is undertaken. Sulla saw that the great council, the Senate, must be the central point and pivot of government, unless indeed there were a master at hand, like himself, to undertake it; that the popular assemblies, untrained in discussion and affairs, could not do the work of administration. Though the theory of the constitution had always been that the people were sovereign, he contrived that the Senate, which had so long practically governed under an unwritten constitution, should now rule without let or hindrance on a basis of statute law; and here we see an unwritten constitution growing into a written one, as with us Britons at this moment. By a great law of treason, the first on the Roman statute book, he made it almost impossible to defy the Senate without the risk of political effacement.

This may be called reactionary, but under the circumstances it was not a reaction to be complained of. The pity was that this master legislator had really none to be grateful or loyal to him but his own army and followers. His constitutional legislation was for the most part swept away soon after his death, and there was no one to lament. On the other hand, all that he did that was not strictly political, and in particular his reorganization of what we may call the civil service, and of the criminal law and procedure, was so obviously progressive and valuable that no one ever attempted to destroy it; and some of his laws of this kind held good throughout Roman history.

Sulla attained his power in 81 BCE, resigned it in 79, and died next year at his villa on the warm Campanian coast, where he had gone to enjoy himself in self-indulgence and literary dilettantism. Here he wrote that autobiography of which some few fragments have come down to us in Plutarch's *Life* of him – a life which will repay the reader, even in translation. One of these fragments has always seemed to me to throw real light on the man's strange nature, and on the imperfection of his work. 'All my most happy resolutions,' he wrote, 'have been the result, not of reasoning, but of momentary inspiration.' In other words, Sulla did not believe in thinking over a problem, and herein he was a true Roman. He hoped to do the right thing on the spur of the moment. Thus it was that no one ever knew what he would do; no one could trust him nor believe in him. Like so many in that and succeeding ages he believed profoundly in Fortune: he called himself Sulla the Fortunate, and gave like names to his two children. What exactly he meant by Fortuna we cannot say; but we may be sure that it was no such conception of a power ruling the world as might guide a statesman's feet out of the path of self-seeking into a more bracing region of high endeavour.

VII
THE REVOLUTION: ACT II

The Unfinished Revolution

With the death of Sulla ends what we may call the first act of the Roman Revolution. We are now in the middle of a revolution in more than one sense of that word. The constitution and the government of Rome are being slowly but surely changed, and at the same time the era of the free and independent city-state of the Graeco-Roman world is being brought to an end. Both these changes, as we can see now, were inevitable; without them the civilized world could not have been defended against barbarian invasion, or Italy united into a contented whole possessed of Roman citizenship. In the first act, as I have called it, the immediate danger of invasion was checked, both in north and east, and Italy had become Roman, enjoying perfect equality with Rome under the great body of Roman law now being rapidly developed.

But, in truth, this inevitable work of change was not as yet half done. It was soon found that both in north and east some definite system of frontier must be fixed, or the Empire would be in continual peril from without. It was also found that Sulla's constitution would not work, and that to defend the frontiers of civilization effectively there must be a government of sterner force, whatever form that force might take. Thus in the second act of the Revolution we have two main points to attend to: first, the settlement of the frontiers against Oriental despots and wandering hordes of Germans: secondly, the acquisition of power by a great soldier-statesman,

Julius Caesar, and the abandonment, as a working power, of the ancient polity of Senate and people. And inasmuch as this period of revolution was also the age of the best and purest bloom of Latin literature, I must find space for a few words about Cicero, Lucretius, and Catullus.

War with Mithradates

I said in the last chapter that there was a very dangerous enemy threatening the eastern or Greek part of the Empire. This was Mithradates, king of Pontus, that part of Asia Minor which borders on the Euxine (Black Sea) eastwards: a man of genius and ambition, and by no means to be reckoned a barbarian. It is curious that he began his great career by protecting Greek cities against their enemies, and one is tempted to ask whether he might not have been at least as beneficent a champion and master for the Greek world as Rome herself. But we must look at things with Roman eyes if we are to understand the work of Rome in the world; we must think of Mithradates as the Romans then did, as the deadly enemy alike of Greek freedom and of Roman interests.

His armies had invaded Greece in 87 BCE and had even occupied Athens, while the Greek cities of Asia Minor had willingly submitted to him: the whole Hellenic world was fast coming under his sway. Then Sulla had expelled his generals from Greece proper, and had forced him to accept such conditions of peace as kept him quiet for a few years. But when Sulla was dead he started on a fresh career of conquest, and once more the Roman protectorate of Greek civilization was broken down. For a time it looked as if no power could restore it. The sea was swarming with pirates from Cilicia, who constantly harassed the Roman fleets, and ventured even as far as Italy, snapping up prisoners for sale as slaves in the great slave-market at Delos. And behind Mithradates and these pirates there was another power even more formidable. Tigranes, king of Armenia, had also been extending his dominions southward, and was even in possession of Syria and Judaea at the time of which we are now speaking, 75 BCE. Should the two kings unite their forces and policy, it would be all but impossible for Rome to remain the mistress of the eastern Mediterranean and the Hellenic world. It was another example of Rome's wonderful good fortune that this alliance was never solidly effected till too late.

The Senate, left by Sulla to govern the world, soon showed that it was incapable of grasping the necessity of vigorous action in the East. It was not till 74 BCE, four years after Sulla's death, that they sent out a really capable general with an adequate force. Lucullus, whose name has become a by-word for wealth and luxury, was in his prime a soldier of great ability, and he soon broke the power of Mithradates, who immediately fled for refuge to Tigranes. This made it absolutely necessary to deal with that king also; and Lucullus invaded Armenia and captured the king's new capital, Tigranocerta. Unluckily, he had not that supreme gift of a great commander which enables him, as it afterwards enabled Caesar, to lead his men where and when he will; the army mutinied, refusing to go farther into the wild Armenian mountains, the most distant and formidable region a Roman army had as yet penetrated. Lucullus had to retreat.

Establishing Frontiers: Pompeius Magnus

Then, under pressure from the men of business who were losing money by the instability of Roman dominion in Asia, Senate and people agreed to supersede Lucullus by a younger man, reckoned the best soldier of the day, and a military pupil of Sulla. This was the famous Cnaeus Pompeius Magnus, known to us familiarly as Pompey the Great. In 67 BCE he had been commissioned to clear the sea of pirates, and did it effectually. Now, with a combination of civil and military power such as no Roman had yet enjoyed, he took over Lucullus's army, made short work of Mithradates, and utterly broke up the empire of Tigranes. He overran Syria, the region between the Mediterranean and the desert stretching to the Euphrates, penetrated to Judaea and took Jerusalem. This famous event is the first in the long and sad story of the relations of Rome with Judaea. At Jericho, before he reached the holy city, he received the dispatch which told him of the death of Mithradates, the removal from the scene of one who had been for 30 years Rome's most dangerous enemy.

The result of the efforts of Lucullus and Pompeius was the establishment of a frontier system in the East which may be said to have held good for the rest of Roman history. The principle of it is not easy to explain; but if the reader will take a map and trace the river Euphrates from its sources in western Armenia to the Arabian desert, and then make it clear to himself that all within that line was to be either Roman or under Roman suzerainty, he will be able to form some idea of its importance in history. There were to be three new Roman provinces: Pontus with Bithynia in the north of Asia Minor,

Cilicia on its south-eastern coast, and Syria, the coast region from Cilicia southwards to the frontier of Egypt. But between these and the Euphrates there were two kingdoms, Cappadocia and Galatia, and other smaller ones, which formed *a Roman sphere of influence* where Rome herself could not as yet be constantly present. Imperfect as this system seems, it was quite strong enough to spread the prestige of the Roman Empire far and wide in the East, and the great king of Parthia, beyond the Euphrates, might well begin to be alarmed for his own safety.

Now in settling this frontier system Pompeius had, of course, to attend to an infinite number of details, and to make decisions, convey privileges, negotiate treaties, and grant charters, in dealing with those cities new and old which formed a most important part of his plan of settlement and defence. All this had to be done on his own responsibility, but would need the sanction of the Senate to be recognized as legally valid. When he returned home in 62 BCE he expected that the Senate would give this sanction, especially as he had just disbanded his army, with which he might, if he had chosen, have enforced his claims. But the Senatorial government was reduced to such a state of imbecility that the majority would have nothing to do with Pompeius's invaluable work: they were jealous, they were lazy, and, above all, they were ignorant. So he had to fall back after a year or two on the consul of 59, C. Julius Caesar, who undertook to get the necessary sanction from the people if not from the Senate. In return Pompeius was to help him to get a long command in Gaul, so that the work of frontier defence there begun by Marius might be resumed and completed. At this very moment a German people, the Suebi, whose name still survives in the modern Swabia, were threatening the rich plains of what is now eastern France: and then, just as a peace had been patched up with them, a Gallic tribe, the Helvetii, suddenly issuing from its home in (modern) Switzerland in search of new settlements, or pressed on by other tribes beyond it, was about to break into the Roman province of Transalpine Gaul. But Caesar had now done his part by Pompeius, though not, indeed, without straining the constitution; and moving with the wonderful swiftness that afterwards became characteristic of him as a general, he reached Geneva just in time to stop them, and soon afterwards beat them in a great battle and forced them back to their homes.

Pushing Boundaries: Julius Caesar

This was the beginning of a career of conquest which made the glorious country we know as France into the most valuable part of the Roman Empire. What motives inspired Caesar in all he did during the nine years he spent there we need not ask, for we can only guess the answer; though he has left us his own story of his campaigns in simple straightforward Latin, he has not chosen to tell us what was all along at the back of his mind. Ambition, says the superficial historian; the desire to make himself in due time tyrant of Rome and the Empire. But we may take it as certain that Caesar, a man whose health was never strong, would not have exposed himself to constant peril of his life for nine successive years had he really all the time been nursing a secret ambition which death or serious illness might at any time destroy. What he really seems to have loved, like C. Gracchus, was work – steady, hard work with no one to hinder him, and with a definite practical object before him. Doubtless further hopes or fears were in his mind, but this great practical genius, with an intellect characteristically Roman, though more scientific in its tendency than that of any other Roman known to us, was always bent on the work immediately in front of him, and never rested till it was completed to his satisfaction.

When Caesar hurried up to check the Helvetii in 58 BCE there was but one Roman province in Gaul, the south-eastern part of modern France (which still teems with Roman remains and inscriptions), together with a considerable district to the west of it at the foot of the Pyrenees. When he finally left Gaul at the end of 50, the whole of modern France and Belgium had been added to the Empire, though not as yet organized into provinces. He did not take long to reach our Channel and to subdue the tribes on the coast; he began the written history of our island by invading it twice, and recording such information as he could gain about its geography and inhabitants. He crossed the Rhine into Germany by a bridge constructed for him by his engineers: and the method of building this bridge survives in his book to puzzle the ingenuity of scholars as well as schoolboys. The Gauls were doubtless amazed at these performances, as he meant them to be; and, after one heroic effort to save themselves from becoming an appendage of a Mediterranean empire, they had to submit. While we can feel with these noble efforts for freedom, or blame Caesar for what sometimes seems unnecessary cruelty, we must remember that from this time forward the country from the Rhine to the ocean becomes a great factor in European civilization.

There was still, indeed, a gap in the line of frontier; how was the eastern end of the Alps to be protected from invasion? There, as we saw, the great rampart was lowest, and beyond it the barbarians were an unknown quantity. Here the river Danube eventually became the frontier, and was carefully connected with that of the Rhine; but this completion of the great work had to wait for half a century, and in the meantime luckily no inroad was made or threatened. It was Tiberius, afterwards emperor, another great soldier, with an army almost as devoted to its general as that of Caesar who after long steady effort planted the Roman power firmly in this region. From a military point of view the Roman Empire, and therefore Western civilization as a whole, owed its very existence for centuries to Pompeius, Caesar and Tiberius, with their splendidly trained armies and their skilful engineers.

All this work of conquest and settlement was not the work of the State, or due to the old civic sense of duty and discipline; it was the work of the armies, due to their good discipline, and to their loyalty to their leaders. This being so, it was of course only natural that the armies and their leaders should claim to control the action and policy of an enfeebled State, as Sulla had already claimed it. This is really, put in a very few words, the secret of the Roman imperial system that was to come. But the question of the moment was whether the commander of one of these Roman armies could so identify himself and his soldiers with the State and its true interests, as to become the means of establishing a sound and efficient government for the Mediterranean world. Sulla had failed so to identify himself: he had neither knowledge enough nor sympathy enough. The chance had been open to Pompeius when he returned from the East in 62, but he had disbanded his army and declined it; he was in many ways a valuable man, but he was not the stuff that real statesmen are made of. After the long war in Gaul the chance was open to Caesar, and he accepted it without hesitation.

He accepted it, but in truth he had to fight for it. For years his operations in Gaul had been looked on at Rome with suspicion, especially by a clique of personal enemies led by the famous Cato, a descendant of the old Cato whom we met in the previous century. These men looked on Caesar as dangerous to the State – and dangerous indeed he was, to that old form of State which neither they nor he could make vigorous and efficient. They clung to the worn-out machinery of the constitution, to the checks, the vetoes, the short tenure of office, to the exclusive right of the Senate to deal with the ever-increasing administrative business of the Empire. Knowing, or guessing, that Caesar, like Caius Gracchus, would force his personal will on the State if he judged it necessary, they were determined to prevent his becoming a political power, and they brought Pompeius to the same view, and armed him with military force to be used against Caesar – against the man, that is, who had spent the best years of his life in indefatigable work for the Empire and civilization. The result was civil war once more; civil war that might unquestionably have been averted by a wider outlook, a more generous feeling, a spirit of compromise, on the part of the high aristocrats who, like Cato, believed themselves to be struggling for liberty. The liberty they were struggling for was in reality the liberty to misgovern the Empire, and to talk without acting efficiently.

Civil War to Caesar's Murder

It is plain, as we may learn from the abundant correspondence of the time, that they did not know the man they had to deal with. Caesar took them completely by surprise; in a few weeks he had cleared Pompeius and Senate and their army out of Italy, had provided for the government, and gone off to Spain to secure the West by turning the Pompeian armies out of that peninsula also. After a brilliant campaign of six weeks, admirably described by himself in his work on the Civil War, he forced those armies to surrender and then let them go, as he had done just before in Italy. His clemency took the world by surprise as much as his generalship.

But the worst was not over for him. Pompeius was gathering all the resources of the East against him, and concentrating them in Epirus with a view to the re-conquest of Italy. Again Caesar's rapidity saved him; he was just in time to strike the first blow by crossing the sea from Brindisi – a rash expedient – and hampering Pompeius before his concentration was effected. Here, however, in his eagerness to bring the campaign to an issue, he made a serious blunder, and had to pay for it by defeat and a retreat to the corn-growing plain of Thessaly. Pompeius unwisely followed him, instead of invading Italy; and here, in August 48 BCE, was utterly beaten at the battle of Pharsalia. The worn-out old soldier fled to Egypt, where he was treacherously murdered by one of the king's generals. He was an estimable man with many excellent qualities, and in a more tranquil age might have well become what Cicero wished to make him, the presiding genius of the Roman State.

Caesar had yet much war before him – war in Egypt, in Asia Minor, in Africa and in Spain, against the supporters of the old régime, for nothing he could do in the way of conciliation would persuade them to forgive him the crime of seeking to identify himself with the State. In doing so they deprived him of the time which he might have spent to far better purpose at Rome on the work of efficient government. As it was, he had been able to spend but a few months in all at home, when on March 15, 44 BCE, he was murdered at a meeting of the Senate, at the feet of Pompeius's statue, by a small group of assassins, some of whom were intimate friends of his own. They thought he was on the point of assuming a visible despotism, and they had some justification for the suspicion, though it was probably a delusion. To kill a tyrant, they thought, was to do a noble work in true old Roman fashion. So did the murderers of the Gracchi.

Caesar's Policy Agenda

From what little we know about such work of reform as Caesar had time for, we may take it as certain that these deluded assassins made a sad blunder. Caesar's legislative work was fragmentary, but every item of it shows intelligence and political insight. He did not attempt to turn out a new constitution in black and white; he did the work of government mainly himself for the time being, and we do not know how he meant to provide for it after his death. In the most important matter of all, the adjustment of the Empire to the home government, and especially the subordination of the provincial governors to a central authority, he forestalled the imperial system of the future: he made himself the central authority, to whom the governors were to be responsible. The other most important question of government, that of the power and composition of the Senate, he answered by raising the number of Senators to 900, as Caius Gracchus had wished to do, and thus destroying the power of the old narrow oligarchical cliques. But perhaps his practical wisdom is best seen in his economic legislation for Rome and Italy. He was the first statesman to try to check the over-abundance of slave labour; the first, too, to lay the foundation of a reasonable bankruptcy law. He regulated the corn supply in the city, and brought down the number of recipients of corn doles to less than one half of what it had lately been. Again, he laid down general rules for the qualification of candidates for municipal office in Italy, and arranged for the taking of a census in all the cities every five years, the records of which were to be deposited at Rome. It would seem as if he meant to work out the enfranchisement of Italy to its natural conclusion: for he not only completed it by extending it to the Alps, which had never yet been done, but went beyond the bounds of Italy, offering the citizenship freely both to Gauls and Sicilians.

Attempts have been made to depict Caesar as almost more than human; and of late again there has been a reaction against him of no less absurdity, holding him up to contempt as a weak but lucky opportunist. As we have his own military writings, a life by Plutarch, a few letters written by or addressed to him, and innumerable allusions to him in contemporary literature, we ought to be able to form some just idea of him. As one who has been familiar with all these materials, and many others of less value, during the greater part of a lifetime, I say without hesitation that Caesar was the one man of his time really gifted with *scientific intelligence* – with the power of seeing the facts before him and adjusting his action to them. This intelligence, combined with great strength of will, made him master of the Roman Empire; and though his character was by no means perfect, he seems to have used his mastership, not like a capricious Oriental despot, but with a real sense of responsibility. A man who combines the qualities of an intelligent statesman in bad times with a generous temper, good taste and good scholarship, surely deserves to be thought of as one altogether out of the common. In William Shakespeare's picture of him, derived from Plutarch's biography, and representing only the last two days of his life, he seems weak in body and overweening in spirit, and is probably meant to seem so by the dramatist for his own purposes. But no sooner have the murderers done with him than the true greatness of the man begins to make itself felt, and is impressed on us in page after page to the end of the play, of which the action may be said to be pivoted on the idea of the horror and the uselessness of their deed.

The Golden Age of Roman Literature

So far in this chapter and the last I have been treating of this age as one of action. It is indeed filled full of human activity, in spite of the laziness of the governing class as a whole. But this activity was shown not only in war and politics; this is also an age of great poets and real men of letters. I must say a word about the two greatest poets, Lucretius and Catullus; but among the men of letters there stands out one far above the rest whose life and genius it would take a long chapter to explain. Cicero's pre-eminence is not easy to understand even after long study of his voluminous works: yet I must try to make it clear that he was, in fact, one of the greatest of all Romans.

Of Lucretius it is our fate to know nothing except his poem in six books on *The Nature of Things*. But his name is Roman, and the poem has the true Roman characteristic of being essentially practical in its object. That object will seem a singular one to those who are unacquainted with the Greek and Roman culture of this age. What roused a poet's passion in this man's mind was simply the desire to free others, as he had freed himself, from the fetters of superstition, or, as he calls it, *religion*; to make them abandon the delusive dream of a life after death, to repudiate the old stories of torment in Hades, and all foolish legends of the gods, who in his view took no interest whatever in human life. All this was, of course, derived from Greek philosophy, the doctrine of the Epicurean school, but no Greek had ever put such passion into a creed as Lucretius. His poetry at times almost reminds us of the grandeur and authority of the Hebrew prophets, so ardently did he believe in his own creed, and in his mission to enforce it on others. Uncouth and dry as much of it is – for he has to explain that Epicurean theory of the universe known still to science as the atomic theory – he breaks out now and again into strains of magnificent verse which reveal a mind all burning within. Here is a specimen:

Mortal, what hast thou of such grave concern
That thou indulgest in too sickly plaints?
Why this bemoaning and beweeping death?
For if thy life aforetime and behind
To thee was grateful, and not all thy good
Was heaped as in sieve to flow away
And perish unavailingly, why not,
Even like a banqueter, depart the halls,
Laden with life? why not with mind content
Take now, thou fool, thy unafflicted rest?
But if whatever thou enjoyed hath been
Lavished and lost, and life is now offence,
Why seekest more to add – which in its turn
Will perish foully and fall out in vain?
O why not rather make an end of life,
Of labour?

Lucretius, *On the Nature of Things* 3.933–948
(William Ellery Leonard's translation)

The other poet, Catullus, was not of Roman birth, but, like so many literary men of this and the following age, an Italian from the basin of the Po. He had no practical aim in writing poetry: he simply wrote because he could not help it, about himself and his friends and his loves. It was his own self that inspired him chiefly, and it is still himself that interests us. According to his own mood, now fresh with the happiness of an artist, now darkened by anger or self-indulgence, his poems are exquisite or repulsive; but they are always true and honest lyrics, and interesting because they are so full of life and passion. Catullus is one of the world's best lyric poets. Here is one of his gems:

Calvus, if anything pleasing or welcome from our grief
can have an effect on silent graves,
then with its longing we renew old loves
and weep friendships once lost,
surely Quintilia does not mourn her premature death
as much as she rejoices in your love.

Catullus, *Poems* 96 (Leonard C. Smithers's translation)

Lastly, we come to the man of letters who has given his name to this period of literature, which indeed draws more than half its interest from him and from his works. Marcus Tullius Cicero was an Italian, and had little of the Roman character in his make; he came from the town of Arpinum, among the foothills of the Apennines some 60 miles southeast of Rome. He made his way into Roman society by his social and conversational powers, and by his capacity for friendship, and into the field of politics by his great gift of oratory, which was now indispensable for public men. As a *novus homo* he never was really at home with the high aristocracy, but he was a man of many friends for all that, and reckoned among them all the great men of his time, including both Caesar and Pompeius. His best and truest friend, who worked for him all his life with unsparing care, was a man of business who stood outside of politics, Pomponius Atticus; and of Cicero's letters to this faithful friend and adviser nearly 400 survive to prove the reality of that lifelong devotion. Some 500 letters to and from other correspondents are also extant, and the whole collection forms the most fascinating record of a great man's life and thoughts that has come down to us from classical antiquity.

Since Theodor Mommsen wrote his famous *History of Rome*, in which he was almost ignored, Cicero has often been treated with contempt as a shallow thinker, deriving all his inspiration from Greek originals, and as a feeble statesman, brilliant only as an orator. It is true that there is a want of *grit* in much that Cicero wrote: he was the child of his age, never tired of writing and talking, little used to profound thinking, and rarely acting with independent vigour. But he has two claims on the gratitude of posterity which should never be forgotten. First, he made Latin into the most perfect language of prose that the world as yet has known. The echoes of his beautiful style can be heard centuries afterwards in the Latin fathers of Christianity, especially St. Augustine and Lactantius, and they are still audible in the best French and Italian prose writers of today. Secondly, of all Romans Cicero is the one best known to us as an individual human being: and few indeed who have had the chance to become really familiar with him can fail to love him as his own friends loved him. He was not the stuff of which strong statesmen are made; he was too dependent on the support and approval of others to inspire men with zeal for a cause – especially for a losing cause. His own consulship was brilliant, for he was able to combine the best elements in the State in the cause of order as against anarchy – anarchy which threatened the very existence of Rome as a city; and at the end of his life he showed the same ability to use a strong combination to good purpose in the political field. But he was not of such strong growth as to mark out a line of his own, and at some unhappy moments of his life his weakness is apt to move our pity, if not our contempt.

But with all his weak points Cicero is one of the best and greatest of all Romans. His gifts were rich, and he used them well. We know him as a man of pure life in an impure age, and as one who never used his gifts or opportunities to do harm to others, whether political enemies or helpless provincials. We know him, too, as a faithful husband and a devoted father. And lastly, we know that he was not lacking in courage when the assassin overtook him – the last of a long list of great men of that age to die a violent death.

VIII
AUGUSTUS AND THE REVIVAL OF THE ROMAN SPIRIT

Poet for the New Age: Virgil

The death of Julius Caesar seemed to plunge the world once more into darkness. We have evidence enough of the general feeling of horror and despair – a despair hard to realize in our days, when settled and orderly government saves us from all serious anxiety about our lives and property. Power fell into the hands of a far more unscrupulous man than Caesar, the Mark Antony of Shakespeare's play; but he had a rival in Caesar's nephew and adopted son, afterwards known as Augustus. Civil war, of course, followed: first, war between these two and the murderers of Julius, and then war between the two victors. Antony, who had in a division of the Empire taken the eastern half, and married Cleopatra, the beautiful queen of Egypt, was crushed at the naval Battle of Actium: the Empire became once more united, and hope began to spring up afresh.

Instead of following the melancholy history of these years (44 to 31 BCE) let us try to realize the need of a complete change in men's minds and in the ways of government, if the Roman Empire was to be preserved, and Mediterranean civilization with it. We can best do this by learning something of the two men who more than all others brought about the change: Virgil, the greatest of Roman poets, and Augustus, the most fortunate and discerning of Roman statesmen. Augustus began a new system of government, based, no doubt, on the ideas of Julius, which lasted, gradually developing itself, till the fifth century of our era. Virgil, the poet of the new Roman spirit, kept that spirit alive into the Middle Ages, and rightly read, he keeps it still before us.

If Virgil had lived in an ordinary age, when the flow of events was smooth and unruffled, he might have been a great poet, but hardly one of the world's greatest. But he lived in a crisis of the history of civilization, and he was called to do his part in it. For a century before he wrote, the one great fact in the world was the marvellous growth of the Roman dominion. When he was born, 70 years before the Christian era, Rome was the only great civilized power left, and a few years later it looked as if she had not even a barbarian rival to menace her, except the Parthians far away in the East. The Roman was everywhere, fighting, trading, ruling; nothing of importance could be done without the thought – What will Rome say to it?

Yet just as Virgil was growing to manhood it became obvious, as we have seen, that this great power was in reality on the verge of breaking up. She had abandoned justice and duty, and given herself to greed and pleasure. Her government was rapacious: she was sucking the life-blood of the nations. She had lost her old virtues of self-sacrifice, purity of family life, reverence for the divine. The rulers of the world had lost the sense of duty and discipline; they were divided into jarring political factions, and had felt the bitterness of civil war, in which men killed each other in cold blood almost for the sake of killing. But with Julius Caesar's strong hand and generous temper it must have seemed to many that a better time was coming, and among these was the young poet from Mantua under the rampart of the Alps.

No one who knows Virgil's poems well can have any doubt that all his hopes for himself and his family, for Italy and the Empire, were bound up with the family of the Caesars. The sub-alpine region in which he was born and bred had been for 10 years of his boyhood and youth under the personal rule of the great Julius, and had supplied him with the flower of that famous army that had conquered first Gaul and then the world. It is possible that the poet owed his position as a Roman citizen to the enlightened policy of Caesar. Even now we cannot read without a thrill of horror the splendid lines in which he records the eclipse of the sun and the mourning of all nature when the great man was murdered by so-called patriots. With such patriots, with the rapacious republican oligarchy, he could have had no sympathy, and there is not a trace of it in his poems. When, during the civil wars that followed the murder, he was turned out of his ancestral farm near Mantua to make room for veteran soldiers, he owed the recovery of it to the master of those soldiers, the second Caesar, whom henceforward he regarded not only as his own protector and friend, but as the one hope of the Empire.

The Second Caesar and Virgil's *Aeneid*

Now this younger Caesar, nephew and adopted son of Julius, though not a great soldier or a hero in any sense, was yet one of those rare men who learn wisdom in adversity, and use it to overcome passion and violence in themselves and others. He came gradually to see that Italy and the world could not be rescued from misery and despair by war and strong government alone. He grasped the fact, which Sulla had missed, that the one thing wanting was loyalty – loyalty to himself and belief in his mission: loyalty to Rome and Italy, and belief in their mission in the world. Confidence in him, and in the destiny of Rome, might create in men's minds a hope for the future, a new self-respect, almost a new faith. Divided and depressed as they were, he wanted to set new ideals before them, and to get them to help him loyally towards the realization of those ideals. Economically, morally, religiously, Italy was to rise to new life in an era of peace and justice.

This may seem too grand an ideal for a man like Augustus Caesar, who (as I have said) was no hero, and who certainly was no philosopher. But it is nonetheless true that he understood that 'peace hath her victories no less renowned than war': and that his own conviction, based, perhaps, on shrewd political reasonings, inspired his poets and historians to hail a new age of peace and prosperity. In one way or another they all fell in with his ideas. Their themes are the glory and beauty of Italy, the greatness of Rome, the divine power which had given her the right to rule the world, and the story of the way in which she had come to exercise that right. But as Virgil is the greatest figure in the group, so is his *Aeneid* the greatest work in which those ideas are immortalized. The Roman Empire has vanished, the ancient city, which rose in fresh magnificence under Augustus, has crumbled away; but the *Aeneid* remains the one enduring monument of that age of new hope.

It is said that Augustus himself suggested to the poet the subject of the *Aeneid*. If so, it was characteristic of a man who used every chance of extending his own fame and influence without forcing them on the attention of his people. If a poem was to be written on the great theme of the revival of Rome and Italy, Augustus himself could not of course be the hero of it, nor even Julius: political and artistic feeling alike forbade. But a hero it must have, and he must be placed, not in the burning light of the politics of the day, but in the dim distance of the past. Such a hero was found in the mythical ancestor of the Julian family, Aeneas, son of Venus and Anchises. A legend, familiar to educated Romans, told how this Trojan hero, whose personality appears in Homer, wandered over the seas after the fall of Troy, and landed at last in Italy; how he subdued the wild tribes then dwelling in Latium, brought peace and order and civilization, and was under the hand of destiny the founder of the great career of Rome. His son Iulus, whose name the Julii believed themselves to bear, was in the legend the founder of the city from which Rome herself was founded; and thus the family of the Caesars, the rescue of Italy from barbarism, and the foundation of the Eternal City, might all be brought into connection with the story of Aeneas the Trojan. Here, then, was the hero, the type of which the antitype was to be found in Augustus.

And this is how the *Aeneid* became a great national and a great imperial poem. It created a national hero, and endowed him with the best characteristics of his race, and especially with that sense of duty which the Romans called *pietas*: this is why it became a great national poem. It connected him with the famous stories of Greece and of Troy, and made him prophetically the ancestor of the man who was rescuing the Empire from ruin: this is why it became a great imperial poem. The idea was a noble one, and Virgil rose to his subject. Though the *Aeneid* has drawbacks which for a modern reader detract from the general effect, yet whenever the poet comes upon his great theme the tone is that of a full organ. Even in a translation, though he cannot feel the witchery of Virgil's magic touch, the reader may recognize and welcome the recurrence of that great theme, and so learn how its treatment made the poem the world's second great epic. It instantly took a firm hold on the Roman mind; It came to be looked on almost as a sacred book, loved and honoured as much by Christian Fathers as by pagan scholars. Italy has given the world two of the greatest poems ever written: the *Aeneid* of Virgil, and the *Divina Commedia* of Dante, in which the younger poet took the imaginary figure of his predecessor as his guide and teacher in his travel through the scenes of the nether world.

Augustus and the Imperial System

But we must now leave poetry for fact and action, and try to gain some idea of that work of Augustus which laid the solid foundation of a new imperial system; a system of which we moderns not only see the relics still around us, but feel unconsciously the influence in many ways. Augustus had found time to discover, since the death of Julius, that the work to be done would fall mainly into two great departments:

(1) Rome and Italy must be loyal, contented, and at peace; and

(2) the rest of the Empire must be governed justly and efficiently.

To this we must add that the whole must contribute, each part in due proportion, to its own defence and government, both by paying taxes and by military service.

On the first condition, the city of Rome, with a population of perhaps half a million, of all races and degrees, had been a constant anxiety to Augustus so far, and had exercised far more power in the Empire than such a mixed and idle population was entitled to. He saw that this population must be well policed, and induced to keep itself in order as far as possible; that it must be made quite comfortable, run no risk of starvation, have confidence in the good-will of its gods, and enjoy plenty of amusement. Above all, it must believe in himself, in order to be loyal to his policy. When he returned to Rome after crushing Marcus Antonius and Cleopatra, the Romans were already disposed to believe in him, and he did all he could to make them permanently and freely loyal. He divided the city into new sections for police purposes, and recruited corps of 'watchmen' (*vigiles*) from the free population; he restored temples and priesthoods, erected many pleasant and convenient public buildings (thus incidentally giving plenty of employment), organized the supply of corn and of water, and encouraged public amusements by his own presence at them. He took care that no one should starve, or become so uncomfortable as to murmur or rebel.

But, on the other hand, he did not mean this motley population to continue to have undue influence on the affairs of the Empire. True, he gave them back their Free State (*res publica*), and you might see magistrates, Senate, and assemblies in the city, just as under the Republic. But the people of the city had henceforth little political power. The consuls and Senate were indeed far from idle, but the assemblies for election and legislation soon ceased to be realities. In elections no money was now to be gained by a vote, and in legislation the "people" were quite content with sanctioning the wisdom of Augustus and his advisers. At the beginning of the next reign it was possible to put nearly the whole of this business into the hands of the Senate, and the Roman people made no objection. Seeing that they were only a fraction of the free population of the Empire, it was as well that this should be so; the rest of the citizen body could not use their votes at a distance from Rome, and the Senate and the *princeps* (as Augustus and his immediate successors were called) represented the interests of the Empire far better than the crowd of voters.

Of the work of Augustus in Italy we unluckily know very little, but what we do know shows that he worked on much the same principles as in the city. Italy was made safe and comfortable, and was now free from all warlike disturbance for a long period. Brigandage was suppressed: roads were repaired: agriculture and country life were encouraged in all possible ways. A book on agriculture written even in Augustus's earlier years boasts of the prosperity of rural Italy, and Virgil's poem on husbandry is full of the love and praise of Italian life and scenery. Here is a specimen:

> But no, not Medeland with its wealth of woods,
> Fair Ganges, Hermus thick with golden silt,
> Can match the praise of Italy [...]
> Here blooms perpetual spring, and summer here
> In months that are not summer's; twice teem the flocks:
> Twice does the tree yield service of her fruit. [...]
> Mark too her cities, so many and so proud,
> Of mighty toil the achievement, town on town
> Up rugged precipices heaved and reared,
> And rivers gliding under ancient walls.

Virgil, *Georgics* 2.136–163 (James Rhoades's version)

On the second condition, the peaceful state of Rome and Italy made it possible for Augustus to undertake, in person to a great extent, the more important work of organizing the rest of the Empire. He found it in a state of chaos. He left it a strongly compacted union of provinces and dependent kingdoms grouped around the Mediterranean, which for a long time to come served two valuable purposes. First, it protected Mediterranean civilization against barbarian attack, the most valuable thing done for us (as I said in my first chapter) by Roman organization. Secondly, it gave free opportunity for the growth of that enlightened system of law which has been the other chief gift of Rome to modern civilization. And also, though without any purpose on the part of the government – nay, in spite of its strenuous opposition – it made possible the rapid growth of Christianity, during the next half-century, which seized on the great towns and the main lines of communication to spread itself among the masses of the people.

Augustus was able to do all this work beyond Italy quite legally, and as a servant of the State. He had succeeded in identifying himself, his family, and all his interests, with the State and its interests, in a way of which Sulla had never dreamt, and which had not been possible for Julius Caesar. When he restored the Free State he divided the work of government with the Senate and the magistrates, and in this division he took care that the whole range of what we should call imperial and foreign affairs should fall to himself, with the sole command of the army. Thus he became supreme ruler of all provinces on or near the frontiers, appointed their governors, and kept them responsible to himself. If there was war on a frontier, it was carried through by his lieutenants, under his *imperium* and his auspices. For a governor to wage war on his own account was no longer possible, for it was made high treason under a new and stringent law. The safety of the Empire, and especially of the frontier provinces, depended on the army, and the army was now identified once more in interest through Augustus with the State.

But of course a system like this would not work of itself; it needed constant looking after. Augustus knew this well, and knew also that he could not by himself either set it going or continue to look after it. It was part of his good fortune that he found a really capable and loyal helper in Marcus Agrippa, a tried soldier and organizer, who till his death in 12 BCE, during the most prosperous years of Augustus's power, was able to identify his own interests with those of his friend and the State. The two worked admirably together, and between them found time to travel over the whole Empire, working hard at settlements of all kinds, and conducting military operations where they were absolutely necessary. It was the same kind of work, but on a far larger scale, as that of Pompeius after his conquests in the East: founding new cities, and settling the status of old ones: making treaties with kings and chieftains: arranging the details of finance, land tenure, and so on. Let us notice two important points in all this work of organization, which will help to show how greatly in earnest Augustus was in his task of welding the Empire into real unity, and ruling it on rational principles.

First, he instituted for the first time (though Julius is said to have contemplated it) a complete survey, or *census* as the Romans called it, of all the material resources of the Empire, in order to ascertain what taxes all its free inhabitants ought to pay for purposes of government. Under the Republic there had never been such a survey, and the result was that abundant opportunity had been found for unfair taxation, and for extortion by corrupt officials. Now every house, field, and wood was duly valued by responsible officials, so that unjust exactions could be easily detected. By accurate keeping of accounts the government was able to tell what sums it ought to receive, and how much it had to spend; and we know that Augustus's foreign policy was greatly influenced by such financial considerations. He kept a kind of yearly balance-sheet himself, and his successor found the affairs of the Empire in perfect order.

Secondly, each province was now for the first time given a kind of corporate existence, and became something more than the military command of a Roman magistrate. A council of the province met once a year at its chief town, and transacted a certain amount of business. True, this did not give the province any measure of real self-government, but it had some useful results, and it is not impossible that Augustus may have intended that more should eventually follow. This meeting of a provincial council brought each province into direct touch with the home government, and in particular enabled it to make complaint of its governor if he had been unpopular and oppressive. And one most interesting feature of these councils was that they had a worship of their own, meant, no doubt, to dim the lustre of local and tribal worships, and to keep the idea of Rome and her rulers constantly before the minds of the provincials. For the divine objects of worship were Augustus himself or his Genius, in combination with the new goddess Roma. The most famous example of this worship is found at Lugdunum (now Lyons), where there was an altar dedicated to Rome and Augustus, at the junction of Rhône and Saone, which served as a religious centre for the three provinces into which Augustus now divided the great area of the Gallic conquests of Julius Caesar.

Though his object was undoubtedly peace, Augustus could not, of course, entirely escape war on his frontiers. He could not have finally settled the frontier on the line of the Danube, which was far the most valuable military work of his time, without wars which were both long and dangerous. It was absolutely necessary to cover Italy on the northeast, where the passes over the Alps are low and comparatively easy, and also to shield the Greek peninsula from attack by the wild tribes to the north of it. I have already alluded to the great work of Tiberius (the stepson of Augustus) in this quarter, which marks him as the third of the great generals who saved the civilization of the Mediterranean for us. At one time Augustus thought of advancing the frontier from the Rhine to the Elbe, and so of connecting Elbe and Danube in one continuous line of defence. But this plan made it necessary to enclose all Germany west of the Elbe in the Roman Empire, and it was soon found that the Germans were not to be made into Roman provincials without a prolonged struggle for which Augustus had neither money nor inclination. So the frontier came back to the Rhine, and the Rhine and the sea marked the Roman frontier on north and west, until Claudius, the third successor of Augustus, added Britain, or rather the southern part of it, to the Empire, in 43 CE.

In the East Augustus contrived to do without war, trusting, and rightly trusting, to the enormous prestige he had won by overcoming Antonius and Cleopatra, and annexing the ancient kingdom of Egypt. His fame spread to India, and probably even to China, with the caravans of merchants who then as now passed along fixed routes from Syria and Egypt to the Far East. Augustus contrived on the strength of his prestige (*auctoritas*) to keep an honourable peace with the Parthians and Armenians who bordered on the Empire along the line of the Euphrates, and his successors would have kept it too had they always followed out his policy. Tiberius, his faithful pupil and successor, did follow out that policy, and showed consummate skill in handling it.

The *Princeps* and the Imperial Succession

The mention of Tiberius, who succeeded to the position of Augustus at the end of his long life, suggests a few words about a weak point in the new system, which was to give some trouble in the future. How was the succession to be effected? Augustus had not made a new constitution; he had only engrafted his own position of authority on the old republican constitution. So at least he wished his position to be understood, and so he was careful to describe it in the record of his deeds which he left behind him, engraved on the walls of the great tomb which he built for himself and his family. In dignity and consequence he wished to be considered the first citizen; and this he expressed by the word *Princeps*, *i.e.* the first man in the State: by the name Augustus, which suggested to a Roman ear something in the nature of religious sanctity: by the honorary title *Pater Patriae* ('Father of his Country'), and in other ways. The real power in his hands had its basis and guarantee in the army, of which his *imperium* made him (as we should say) commander-in-chief; but the army was on the frontiers doing duty for the Empire, all but invisible to the Roman and Italian. Thus his *imperium*, though it might be legally used in Italy, was primarily a military power indispensable for the guardian of the frontiers. To the Italians it might well seem that the Free State was still maintained, and that no new permanent power had been established; though Greeks and foreigners might be, and indeed were, more discerning as to what had really happened.

But when Augustus died, in 14 CE, how was a succession to be effected? Or was there to be a succession at all – would it not be better to let the State pass back again into the hands of the Senate and people? This last was the only logical way, and it was the plan actually adopted in form. A position like that of Augustus could not pass to a successor, unless the State in its old constitutional form chose to appoint such a successor with the same authority as that of Augustus. To this, however, we must add (and it well shows the real change that had been effected by the long revolution) that no choice of Senate and people could hold good unless the consent of the army could be had.

Of course, Augustus had considered all this, and had made his own plans. He would choose a member of his own family, one, that is, who inherited the name and fame of Caesar by blood or adoption, would adopt him as a son (for he had no son of his own), make him his heir, associate him as far as possible in his own dignity and authority, and thus mark him out as the natural heir to the principate. This would make it difficult for Senate or army to refuse him; beyond that Augustus knew that he could not go. He was unlucky in losing one after another the youths whom he thus destined to succeed him, and eventually had to fall back on his stepson Tiberius: a great soldier, as we have seen, and a man of integrity and ability, but of reserved and even morose temper, and one with whom the shrewd and genial Augustus had little in common.

When Augustus died there was an anxious moment. There was no reason why the principate should be confined to the family of the Caesars, nor any reason but expediency for having a *princeps* at all. But, after all, the will of the dead ruler prevailed, and Tiberius slipped into his place without opposition; the Senate accepted him as plainly marked out by Augustus, and the army raised no difficulty, though his nephew Germanicus Caesar was young, popular, and in actual command of the army on the Rhine. Some mocking voices were heard, and throughout his principate of 23 years Tiberius had to endure continual annoyance from the old republican families, but there was no real attempt to quarrel with the principate as an institution of the Roman State.

I have dwelt on this point at some length in order to show what a singular creation this principate of Augustus was. To proclaim monarchy outright would probably have been fatal; to take the whole work on himself would be to leave the old governing families idle and discontented; on the other hand, to do the necessary work as a yearly elected magistrate, according to the old practice, was plainly impossible. Election by the people of the Roman city would have little force in the eyes of the Empire, and it was this Empire as a whole that Augustus wished to represent. The course he took shows him a shrewd, observant, tactical diplomatist, if ever there was one. He is not a man on whose character we dwell with sympathy or enthusiasm; he does not kindle our admiration like C. Gracchus or Caesar; but he was essentially the man for the hour.

To him we owe in large measure the glories of the 'Augustan Age', with its poets, historians, and artists; it was the 'Augustan Peace' (*Pax Augusta*), and the encouragement and patronage of Augustus, that enable Horace to write his perfect lyrics and his good-natured comments on human life, Ovid to pour forth his abundant stream of beautiful versification, Tibullus and Propertius to sing of the Italian country and its deities and festivals, and Livy, the greatest of Roman historians, to do in noble prose what Virgil had done in noble verse – to inspire Romans and Italians with enthusiasm for the great deeds of their ancestors. But the world owes Augustus a still greater debt than this; for he laid securely the foundations of an imperial system strong enough to save for us, through centuries of danger, the priceless treasures of Graeco-Roman civilization.

IX
LIFE IN THE ROMAN EMPIRE

Romanization through Urbanization

Now that we have seen the Empire made comparatively secure by Augustus, and set in the way of development on what seem to be rational principles, let us pause and try to gain some idea of the social life going on within it: excluding that of the city of Rome, which is no longer of the old paramount importance. How did the inhabitants of the Empire live and occupy themselves during the first two centuries of our era?

The first point to make quite sure of is that this life was in the main a life in towns. Roman policy had always favoured the maintenance of existing towns, except in the very rare cases where they were deemed too dangerous. Carthage and Corinth had been destroyed by Rome on this pretext, but they had been founded afresh by Julius Caesar, and were now beginning a long and vigorous city life. In the East, where city-states abounded, Rome retained and adorned them, or built new ones, as Pompeius did after crushing Mithradates and Tigranes. In the West, in Gaul and Spain, where they did not exist at all, she founded some, and by a wonderfully wise policy favoured the natural growth of others. The people of these western provinces lived chiefly in some kind of villages, scattered over a district which we may call a canton, often, perhaps, as big as an English county of today. The Roman policy was either to found a city to serve as the centre of the canton, and to endow it with magistrates and senate on the Roman model: or to give the canton its senate and magistrates, and leave it to develop its own town centre.

This policy shows extremely well the genius of Rome for *civitas* – civilizing, or Romanizing, without destroying the grouping and the habits of the people to be civilized, or Romanized. The old tribal (or cantonal) system remained, and its officers were the chiefs of the old population; but they now bore Roman names, *duoviri*, *quaestores*, and so on, and sat in an assembly called *ordo* – i.e. senate. If a town were not founded at once, in which the business of the canton could be carried on, it was certain to grow of itself. A purely rural region, where the people live in villages only, was contrary to Roman interests and traditions; it was inconvenient for raising taxes, and it did not give those opportunities of culture and amusement which the Roman looked for when he travelled or settled in a province. The provincials, too, were in this way made more happy and contented; town life greatly helped in civilizing them, attracting the better or richer people from the villages.

Instinctively the Romans perceived that if a province were to be Romanized, the process could not be set going in villages; and where there were only villages, they gave the districts the opportunity of developing towns in their midst. The opportunity, we may reasonably suppose, was rarely missed for, at all times in their history, the Romans had a wonderful power of making their subjects eager to imitate their own institutions. Thus Spain, Gaul, and even Britain, became rich in towns after the Roman model – towns which served to humanize the people, while making them obedient subjects.

An Empire of Cities

Let us now see, with the help of a few striking examples, how, by the second century of our era, the Empire was covered with towns. For Italy and Greece we do not need illustrations – we are already well aware of the fact. But even far away in the East, in regions where the Greeks had never settled, if the Romans came to stay they left cities behind them. Look, for example, at a map of Syria or Palestine, and note the great caravan route leading from Damascus southwards on the east side of the Jordan, a road important to Rome because it carried the merchandise of the Far East to Damascus and the Mediterranean by way of the Persian Gulf and Petra. Before the traveller of today has gone far south from Damascus he will come on the splendid ruins of two successive cities built by the Romans in this period, Gerasa and Philadelphia, where the sheep now graze among the ruins of temples, theatres, and baths. A famous English traveller wrote of them long ago that they enabled him to form some conception of the grandeur and might of the Roman Empire: 'That cities so far removed from the capital, and built almost in the desert, should have been adorned with so many splendid monuments, afforded one of the most striking proofs of the marvellous energy and splendid enterprise of that great people who had subjected the world.'

The mention of Damascus may remind us of a traveller of the first century CE whose journeys are fortunately recorded and admirably illustrate the fact that in Asia Minor and Greece the life of the people was centred in the great cities. St. Paul went from city to city, choosing by preference for his missionary work the most populous ones, such as Antioch, Ephesus, Thessalonica, Corinth and Athens.

Passing westwards, and leaving out of account the many cities of Egypt, we shall find that what has been so far said holds good of the Roman province of Africa. This province eventually became one of the most highly cultured as well as populous, mainly owing to its numerous towns. Of many of these the remains still astonish the traveller. A photograph lies before me of one of them which still stands almost in the desert, silent and abandoned, with temples, streets, and all the belongings of a great city as perfect as at the excavated Pompeii, which was overwhelmed in this period by the great eruption of Vesuvius (79 CE). An inscription tells us that Thamugadi was founded in the year 100 CE and built with the help of a legion of Roman soldiers to guard civilization against the marauders of the desert. Another of these towns is a good example of the way in which the army contributed to the policy of creating town centres; Lambæsis, now called Djebel-Aures, was the permanent station of a military force, round which there grew up a civil population of traders and camp-followers. Great roads, here as everywhere in the Empire, connected these towns with each other and with the capital of the province, in this case Carthage.

If we cross the sea from Africa to Gaul or Spain we shall find the same process going on. Spain we must pass by; but in Gaul we land at the ancient Greek city of Massilia, which, as Marseilles, is still the great port of southern France. A little to the north, *Nîmes* (ancient Nemausus) was formed into a city by Augustus out of a rural population; its vast Roman amphitheatre and an exquisitely beautiful temple belong to the second century, and still stand in the middle of the modern city. Lyons was also founded by Augustus, as we saw in the last chapter, with a special purpose. Farther north the cities on the great roads were gradually formed, out of tribal populations living in villages, and many of them still bear the names of those tribes: Paris is the town centre of the Parisii, Rheims of the Remisii, Soissons of the Suessiones, Trier of the Treveri. This last city, on the Moselle, now a German one, can boast of more imposing Roman work than any north of Italy, and is within comparatively easy reach of visitors from our shores.

Britain, which was invaded and made the province of Britannia in the reign of Claudius, was never so fully Romanized as other provinces, partly owing to the wild and stubborn nature of its inhabitants; but even in our midst the Roman has left obvious traces of his belief in town life. London was a trading centre before the coming of the Romans, and they maintained it as such; but nearly all their other towns had a more directly military origin and object. The oldest of them is Colchester, a *colonia*, which still has its Roman walls. Then came London (Londinium), St. Albans (Verulamium), Gloucester (Glevum), Chester (Deva), Lincoln (Lindum) and York (Eboracum), strategical points of importance, where populous cities still stand. In a few cases towns have disappeared, and have only been recovered by excavation, *e.g.* Calleva (Silchester, near Basingstoke), the town centre of the Atrebates; but many of our country towns, besides those just mentioned, still stand on ancient Roman sites, and even without much excavation have yielded traces of their Roman inhabitants. One, and one only, Dorchester (Durnovaria), still boasts of a complete little amphitheatre, which stands just outside the town between the Great Western and South Western railways, and has been used by Thomas Hardy for a scene in one of his novels. All our towns and villages of which the names contain the word *chester* or *cester* are Roman in origin, though they may not have been large cities like Gloucester; for *chester* is only our English form of *castra*, the Latin for a military encampment.

Life in the Provincial Cities

If it is now quite clear that the town is the unit of civilization in the Empire, what was the social and political life of the town? Of this we know now much more than we used to do, for it is mirrored in the many thousands of inscriptions from every Roman province, which have now at last been collected and correctly published under the direction of the famous Theodor Mommsen, whose name cannot be omitted entirely, even in such an unpretending book about Rome as this. In records on stone there is, indeed, something lacking that can only be supplied by literature, which reports more elaborately and earnestly the thoughts and feelings of men; and in the Empire, apart from Italy and Rome, there is but little literature to help us out. But the inscriptions supply us with the necessary facts.

First, of the political condition of these innumerable towns we may say that it shows diversity in unity. There were several grades of privilege among them. Some were nominally independent of the Roman government, and in alliance with it, but these were few; Athens is the most famous example. Others were communities of Roman citizens; and many had the Latin right, *i.e.* inferior privilege. Lastly, there were great numbers of cities – a majority of the whole number – whose inhabitants were not Roman citizens at all, but directly under the control of the governor of their province, who was limited in his authority over the more privileged and independent towns. So much for diversity.

But all the cities were in reality governed and organized in much the same way. In each there was a constitution closely resembling that of Rome, and in most instances modelled directly upon it. As at Rome, they had yearly elected magistrates, who, after holding office, passed into a senate of advisers and councillors; and these magistrates were elected by the *populus*, or the whole body of citizens. Here was plenty of useful work to do, as we can guess from our own experience of local self-government. Plutarch, writing in this period of his own little town of Chaeronea in Greece, realizes this to the full, and urges that the work of the magistrate is honourable work, and the more so as it is combined with the sense of citizenship in a great empire.

'Bread and Circuses'

There was, however, a tendency in these provincial towns, as in the city of Rome itself, for the magistrate, who must be a man of substance, to undertake the expense of amusing the people; a tendency to make the people dependent on the rich for their comforts rather than on their own industry and exertion. The magistrate, besides paying a large fee on his accession to office, was expected to give public games, to feast the people, or to give them a present of money all round. And he would wish, too, to distinguish his magistracy by erecting some public buildings – a bath, aqueduct, or theatre; or to endow a school. So it came to pass in course of time that his burdens were heavier than he could bear, and that the whole class to which he belonged, the senatorial one, was involved in the same difficulties. This class could not be recruited from the common people, who rarely had the means, or, indeed, the energy, to rise to affluence; and the tendency as time went on was to draw the line ever more sharply between the dignity of the various classes. But the ruin of the senatorial class, or *curiales*, lies outside our limits.

The lower class was engaged in industry, either on the land, or in the town itself. This industry was not to any large extent employed by capital, nor was it in competition with slave-labour, of which in provincial towns we do not hear much. The members of the various trades and callings worked on their own account, but were almost invariably grouped together in gilds or associations, and these are one of the most interesting features in the life of this period. Each of these gilds was licensed, or should have been licensed, by the central government at Rome – a good example of the way in which the long arm of that government reached to every provincial town through the agency of the provincial governor and his officials. Illegal association was a serious crime, and this was one of the reasons why the small Christian communities were looked on with suspicion by the government.

What was the object of these associations? The question has often been asked whether they were in any sense provident societies like our friendly societies, and, on the whole, the conclusion of investigators has been that they were not. If we had more literature dealing with provincial life, or such a correspondence as that of Cicero and his friends, we could give a more certain answer.

But in one sense at least they may be called provident societies. All, or nearly all, of them had as one main object the assurance of a proper tomb and decent funeral for the members. This object can only be fully appreciated after some real study of the social life and religion of that and the preceding age, but when it is understood it is inexpressibly touching. It would seem that the life of the working man of that day was by no means an unhappy one, that he was not driven or enslaved by an employer nor forced to live in grimy and unwholesome surroundings. So far as we can tell he had little anxiety in this life, and worshipped his gods, and performed his vows to them, with genuine gratitude. But that he should be utterly neglected and forgotten after death, thrown into some common grave to moulder away unnoticed, 'where no hand would bring the annual offering of wine and flowers' – this seems to have been the shadow ever hanging over his life. We may doubt whether the hope of immortality had, as a rule, anything to do with this anxiety. It was rather an inherited instinct than a faith or creed that moved these poor people. Originally it had been the desire not to have to wander as a ghost for want of due burial; now it is rather the fear that they might be forgotten by those left behind, or, indeed, by future generations.

The instinct of association is common to man, and in a vast empire, where the tendency was, and long had been, to obliterate the old social grouping of kinship, real or supposed, it would be some consolation to belong to a club of friends with common interests, accustomed to share the joys and perils of life, and bent on decent burial when death should overtake them. Even in this life they would meet from time to time to eat, drink and enjoy themselves.

On the whole, we may conclude that this life of the towns was a happy one, so long as the frontiers were well guarded and no sudden raid or invasion by an enemy was likely; so long, too, as person and property were securely protected under Roman law administered without corruption, and amusements and conveniences were to be had for little or nothing. But undoubtedly something was wanting; there was mischief in the social system somewhere, though it was not easy to lay finger upon it. The sap was running in the plant too feebly; there was a lack of keen industrial energy and of the instinct of self-help. As time went on, the central government grew too paternal, interfered too much in the life of these towns, and so encouraged the tendency to 'slackness'. And more and more, as pressure came on the Empire from without, the play of life in these once happy cities became an automatic movement of machinery, the central wheel of which was the Caesar at Rome.

Another aspect of the life of the provincial towns must be mentioned here, which suggests that the trend of the time was not entirely healthy. I said at the beginning of this book that the great monuments left behind her by Rome were mainly of a useful and practical kind, *e.g.* roads, aqueducts, places of business. This is true, but it is now necessary to add that some of the most imposing of these fabrics were, in the period we have now reached, entirely devoted to amusement, and amusement of a kind neither educating nor humane. The taste had long been growing at Rome for spectacles of bloodshed – combats of gladiators, and the hunting of wild beasts in a confined space; and from Rome this degraded taste passed only too rapidly into the provinces. Most large provincial towns had their amphitheatre, in imitation of the huge one at Rome, which we know as the Coliseum; and the more fully Romanized a province was, the more of these homes of inhumanity were to be found in it. The most magnificent one still standing outside Italy, that at *Nîmes*, dates, strange to say, from the mild and enlightened age of the Antonines, to which we are coming in the next chapter. The Greeks, indeed, never took much interest in such shows; but in the western provinces, where the best and most virile populations of the Empire were now to be found, their effect was beyond doubt pernicious, for they encouraged not only inhumanity, but idleness. Day after day the greater part of the population of a city might sit and watch lazily these bloody entertainments, on which, perhaps, some wealthy citizen was wasting his capital to his own ruin.

As may, perhaps, be said of ourselves in this present age, the Romans of the Empire were being encouraged to live too much in the enjoyment of the present, without anxiety for the future. So, too, the cultured classes gradually came to look back at the past, to the great achievements of Rome in war and literature, as all in all to them, and lost the desire to strike out new lines, to make new discoveries, to try new experiments.

X
THE EMPIRE UNDER THE ANTONINES

A Civilized State Surrounded by Barbarism

The chief work of Rome in the world, as has often been said in this little book, was the defence of Mediterranean civilization against external enemies. That work was of a double nature. It could not be done simply by marking out and holding lines of frontier; it was also necessary so to organize the Empire within its frontiers that the whole should contribute to the common object, with men, money and public spirit. The last two chapters will have shown that from the time of Julius and Augustus Roman rulers fully recognized this twofold nature of their task. Augustus in particular, while gradually settling the frontiers on a system well thought out, and adapted to his means and experience, also spent much time and pains on internal organization. He found the Empire a loose collection of subject territories, each governed, well or ill as it might happen, by an officer almost independent of the central authority; he left it, at the end of his long life, in the way of becoming a well-compacted whole, in which every part felt more or less the force of a just central government; a civilized State 'standing out in clear relief against the surrounding barbarism.'

In such an empire there must, of course, be differences of race and language – differences, too, of habits, feelings, modes of thought; but under just and wise rule such differences need be no hindrance to the political unity of the whole. There is a book of this period, within the reach of everyone, which illustrates better than any other this unity in diversity of the Roman Empire – I mean the Acts of the Apostles. It should be studied carefully, with maps and such other helps as may be available, down to the last chapter, where it leaves St. Paul at Rome, living in his own hired house, in the centre of Mediterranean life and government.

Under the immediate successors of Augustus, Tiberius, Claudius and Nero, his policy was, on the whole, maintained with good faith and discretion; and at the close of the first century CE Vespasian and his two sons, Titus and Domitian, did little more than improve the working of the machinery of his government. More and more, it is true, the constitution became a real monarchy; the part played in it by the Senate of the free State was getting steadily narrowed; but this was all in the interest of efficiency, and, so far as we can see, it was necessary to the internal development of the Empire. The Caesars of the first century must have the credit of ruling wisely, with the help of their advisers, on the Augustan principles. True, the great literary genius of the age, the historian Tacitus, by drawing brilliant and lurid portraits of some of them, has diverted our attention from their work as agents of a great system; but to tell their story as Tacitus has told it is neither possible nor necessary here. I may pass them over and go on to the second century and the age of the Antonines, which has rightly been judged by historians to be the most brilliant and the happiest in all Roman history.

Zenith of the Roman Empire: Trajan

That four men of what seems to us 'right judgment in all things' should succeed each other in power at this critical time, is one more example of the wonderful good fortune of Rome. All were men of capacity and education, hard workers and conscientious, and they seem to have communicated their good qualities to their subordinates, for they never wanted for loyal helpers. The Senate, indeed, was now of little avail for actual work, and the greater part of the business had long been done by Caesar and his own 'servants', freedmen for the most part, often ambitious and unscrupulous Greeks; but in this period, as we shall see directly, the civil service, as we may call it, was placed on a sound and honourable basis. It would seem as if the ideas of duty and discipline were once more to prevail throughout the Roman official world.

The first of the four rulers, Marcus Ulpius Trajanus, known to us all as Trajan, was not of Roman or even Italian birth, but came from the province of Hispania Beatica: a fact which marks the growth of the idea that every part of the Empire may now be turned to account for the common good. Trajan was a soldier by breeding and disposition, and his contribution to the work of this period was mainly a military one. The frontier along the Danube, the last (as we have seen) to be settled, had always been the weakest; and yet here henceforward was to be the most dangerous point in the Empire's line of defence. Along the whole length of the lower Danube a great mass of barbarian tribes was already pressing, pressed themselves from behind by others to north and east. And here, to the north of the river, a great kingdom had been founded by a king of the Dacian people, which corresponds roughly with the modern Romania. A glance at a map of the Empire will show that such a kingdom would be a standing menace to Italy, to Greece, and even to the peninsula of Asia Minor, and from the Roman point of view Trajan was quite justified in his determination to conquer and annex it. He carried out this policy in two successive wars, with consummate daring and skill. Dacia became a Roman province, and lasted as such long enough (about 200 years) to be an effectual help to imperial defence in this quarter. The story of the two wars is told in the marvellous series of sculptures forming a spiral round the column of Trajan, which stood and still stands at Rome in the forum built by him and called by his name.

Towards the end of his life Trajan embarked on a new policy in the East, and failed to carry it out. The shrewd Augustus, as we saw, had trusted here to his prestige, knowing that war in this region was both perilous and expensive. Since then both peril and expense had been incurred here under Nero, and no definite results had been gained. Trajan, however, provoked by a move of the Parthian king, made up his mind to seize Armenia, the old bone of contention between Rome and Parthia, and not only did this, but added by conquest two other provinces, Mesopotamia and Assyria. Some historians have thought his judgment as good here as it was on the Danube. The best way of deciding the question is to look carefully at a map of the Empire and then to ask oneself whether these territories were really needed for the protection of Mediterranean civilization. For myself I unhesitatingly answer in the negative; but there is no need to dispute the point here, as Trajan died before he had made his conquests secure. The Jews dispersed all over these regions, urged by their implacable hatred of Rome, stirred up rebellion in Trajan's rear with alarming ferocity, and in the middle of this turmoil he died on his way back to Rome. His successor Hadrian at once renounced any attempt to keep the new provinces.

It would be unjust to the memory of a great man if we were to think of Trajan as a soldier only. He was a strenuous man, unsparing of himself in any part of his duty. He pursued a policy of public benefit in Italy, striving, like Augustus, to encourage agriculture and population, and carrying out a plan of his predecessor Nerva for providing a fund for the education of poor children. This last institution became an important one, and shows well how really benevolent – perhaps even to excess – how anxious for the well-being of Italy, were the Caesars of the second century. Money was lent by the State to the Italian farmers in need of it, and the interest, at five per cent, was appropriated to the education of boys up to 18 and girls up to 14 years of age.

Trajan bestowed the same minute care on the provinces. In most of these there was no trouble, but in one case, Bithynia, which had been under Senatorial governors, he had to send out a special commissioner to repair neglect and mischief. Luckily for us it happened that this commissioner was Pliny the Younger, nephew of the great encyclopedist Pliny the Elder; and Pliny was so prominent a figure of the time that his correspondence has been preserved. That part of it which contains his letters to Trajan, and Trajan's brief and pithy answers, is one of the most precious treasures that have survived from ancient literature. Pliny consults him on a variety of details, some of them almost ludicrously petty, some of them of general importance, such as a famous one about his policy towards the Christians; and the answers show us Trajan as a shrewd and sensible man, fully aware that in such a unity as the Roman Empire there must needs be diversity, and that governors must learn to adapt themselves to such diversity without losing hold of the principles of justice and equity. Before we leave this subject it may be as well to mention that this constant interchange of letters between persons more than 1,000 miles apart need astonish no one. In the interest of imperialism the public posts had been thoroughly organized by Augustus; the roads were excellent, the shipping well seen to, and travelling was at least as easy and rapid as it was in England less than a century ago.

Trajan's strong and rather rugged features, familiar to all students of the Empire, are in striking contrast to those of his three successors. He was clean shaven, but his next successor, Hadrian, introduced the practice of wearing his beard, and this was adhered to. All the imperial portraits of this age, as preserved on coins and sculptures, are perfectly authentic, and the likenesses are consistent. In the British Museum the reader may see the features of these great Caesars as faithfully reproduced as those of British statesmen in the National Portrait Gallery.

Hadrian

Trajan was succeeded by his cousin Hadrian, beyond doubt one of the most capable and efficient men who ever wielded great power. No one can study his reign without feeling that it was better in this age, if an efficient man could be found, that his hand alone should be at the helm. Probably Hadrian was only one of many who might have done as well as he did, for there was now a spirit abroad of intelligent industry directed to the good of the State; yet it is almost certain that the Empire was the better for not having the sovereignty put into commission. It has been well said of Hadrian that he desired 'to see himself all that was to be seen, to know all that was to be known, to do all that was to be done'; and subsequent events proved that this intelligent industry could hardly have been carried all through the imperial work with equal effect, had it been shared with others.

Hadrian accomplished his work by two long periods of travel, each lasting some four years. Without any pomp or state he made himself acquainted with all parts of the Empire and their needs, as no ruler had done since Augustus and Agrippa shared such a task between them. The more immediate object was to inspect the frontiers and secure them, and as Hadrian was a trained soldier, with much experience under Trajan, this was to him familiar work. But he was so full of curiosity, so anxious to see all that the Empire had to show him, that while he practised his indefatigable industry he could also gratify his intelligence. In this he was more like Julius Caesar than any other Roman we know of, though in most traits of character he was very different from that great man. It is not possible here to describe Hadrian's frontier work in detail, but a specimen of it shall be given which should be interesting to British readers.

Britain had been invaded by Claudius in the previous century, and the southern part of the island had been made into a Roman province. Since then the frontier had been pushed farther north, and the frontier strongholds were no longer Colchester and Gloucester, but Lincoln, Chester and York. Hadrian spent several months here in the course of his first journey, and his visit had a remarkable result which we can see with our eyes at this moment. He must have noted two facts: first, the unsettled and rebellious condition of the natives of Yorkshire and Northumberland (Brigantes): and secondly, the narrow waist of the island between the Solway Firth and the mouth of the Tyne. He must have reasoned that if Roman forces could be permanently established on a fortified line between the two seas, this line would serve as a check on the Brigantes, and also as a base of operations for further advance northwards.

Thus it is that Hadrian's Wall remains as the most striking of all Roman works in our island. It is about 70 miles long, and consisted eventually (for we cannot be sure that it was completed by Hadrian) of a stone wall on the northern side, 20 feet high, an earthen rampart on the southern side, and a military road between them. At intervals there were fortified stations, 17 in all, including the two which connected the lines with the sea; of these two the eastern one, near Newcastle, now famous for its collieries, is still known as *Wallsend*. The Wall enabled the Romans to advance northwards, and soon another fortification was built on a smaller scale between the Forth and Clyde. The conquest of the Scottish Highlands was never, indeed, carried out; but Hadrian's great work had an immense moral effect on the population to the south of it, and Britain became very substantially Romanized. Towns and country houses (*villae*) sprang up in abundance along or near the military roads. As I write these lines in North Oxfordshire, I have the remains of several of these *villae* within easy reach, and can visit, each in a day, at least four considerable Roman towns, *viz.* Cirencester, Gloucester, Silchester, and last, but not least, Bath (Aquae Sulis), where the Romans found and used, as they always did in such spots, the magnificent hot springs, building noble baths about them which may be seen to this day.

Hadrian's care for the good working of the civil government was as great as his zeal for frontier defence. Two forward steps were taken by him in this department, both of which helped on that consolidation of the Empire which was his constant aim.

First, he organized and dignified the Civil Service, on which the actual good working of the whole system depended. Caesar's share in this work had steadily been increasing while that of the Senate diminished; yet Caesar had so far done his part, as we saw just now, with the help only of his own personal 'servants', who were mostly freedmen, *i.e.* slaves by origin, and many of them Greeks. Hadrian now established a public imperial civil service, of which the members must be Roman knights, *i.e.* men of a certain consequence in regard to birth and property. These new civil servants were excused all military service, and could thus be trained to the work without interruption, during their earlier years.

Secondly, we may date from Hadrian's reign the beginning of the consolidation of Roman law, and the rise of a school of great lawyers such as the world has never known since. Apart from the defence of Mediterranean civilization, to which, indeed, its indirect contribution was not small, this was the most valuable legacy of Rome to modern Europe. Law had originally consisted mainly of the old legal rules of the city-state of Rome, embodied in the Twelve Tables, and a few statutes; but, in course of time, through the need of interpreting these, and adjusting them to the customs of other peoples in the Empire, an immense body of what we may call *judge-made law* had arisen in the form of edicts or public notices of magistrates, issued both in Italy and the provinces. As these customs were now well known, and as the Empire had reached its limits, it was possible to close and consolidate this huge body of official decisions and precedents; and this was done under Hadrian's direction. The other two sources of law were still to grow largely before they could be welded into the great 'Body of Law' (*Corpus Juris*) compiled under the orders of Justinian in the sixth century CE, which is still the chief European textbook of legal studies. These two sources were the delivered opinions of wise lawyers on points of law, and the decisions of the Caesars in various forms, all of which had the force of law.

Antoninus Pius

The death of Hadrian in 138 CE brings us to the third of the great Caesars of this age, Titus Antoninus, a man who, at 52, had already done excellent work for the Empire. He is known to history as Antoninus Pius, and this last name, given him apparently on his accession, may be a reminiscence of Virgil's epithet for his hero, and may be due to the strong sense of duty which marked his whole life, public and private. He seems, indeed, vividly to recall the ideal of the Roman character as we traced it in the third chapter of this book; yet he was not Italian by birth. His family belonged to *Nîmes* in southern Gaul, and that ancient city still honours him with a 'Place Antonin', in which his statue stands. His features, as they appear on portrait busts, entirely confirm the account of him left us by his nephew and successor. Grave and wise, gentle yet firm, religious in the true old Roman sense, pure in life, and simple in all his needs and pleasures, he ruled over a peaceful and contented empire, devoting himself to the work of humanizing and softening the life and lot of his subjects.

Let us glance, for example, at his attitude towards slavery, which, when we last noticed it, was threatening to become a deadly poison in the Roman system. During the first century of the Empire, chiefly under the influence of the Stoic philosophy, as later on under that of Christianity, there had been growing up a feeling that a slave was, after all, a human being, and had some claim to be treated as such under the Roman law, beneficent in its dealings with all other human beings. Antoninus followed out this new idea both in legislation and in his private life, as did his successor also, who adored his memory. They limited the right of a master over his slaves in several ways; ordaining that if cruelty were proved against a master, he should be compelled to sell the slave he had ill-treated. It is noteworthy, too, that the philosopher in whom they most delighted, Epictetus, had himself originally been a slave. There is no better way of realizing the spirit of humanity which actuated Antoninus and his successor than by making some acquaintance with the moral philosophy of Epictetus, and the *Meditations* of Marcus Aurelius.

Hadrian had left the Empire well-guarded, and it does not seem to have occurred to Antoninus to see for himself that Hadrian's vigilance was maintained. This was the one weak point of his reign, and it cost his successors dear. He only once left Italy, and his mind was never occupied with wars or rumours of wars; he lived tranquilly, and died peacefully, without trouble or anxiety. But we know that even before his death clouds were beginning to gather on the northern frontier; and we cannot but feel that the beautiful tranquillity of Antoninus's life was hardly compatible with the duty of an imperial guardian.

Marcus Aurelius

Marcus Aurelius, the author of the *Meditations*, succeeded his uncle and adoptive father in 161 CE. Though not the greatest of the four as a ruler, he was the most remarkable as a man, and holds a higher place than the others in the world's esteem. We may find parallels in history to Trajan, less easily, perhaps, to Hadrian and Antoninus; but there is no monarch like Marcus, not even in the history of the Jews. It is, indeed, astonishing that Rome, Rome of the hard practical temperament, should have produced a ruler who was a philosopher and almost a saint, and yet capable of government. It is the last striking manifestation of the old Roman spirit of duty and discipline, now kindled into a real ethical emotion by the teaching of the Stoics, far the most inspiring creed then available for a man of action. Without any aid from Christianity, which, indeed, he could not understand and occasionally persecuted, Marcus learnt not only how to make his own life pure, but how to live and work for the world of his day.

It is, perhaps, true that the mind of Marcus was more active, and found greater satisfaction, in questioning itself than in anxious inquiry into the state of the Empire. He was not one of those of whom our poet says that they do Duty's work *and know it not*; and, as a consequence, his days were not serene and bright. He had a tendency to be morbid, and, like all morbid men, he was serious even to sadness. It has been well said of him that he is always insisting on his faith in a universe in which, nevertheless, he can find nothing but disappointment.

His sensitiveness about his duty sometimes warped his judgment and blunted his discernment of character. At the outset he made a bad blunder in dividing the imperial power with his brother by adoption, Lucius Verus, who had little principle and much leaning to pleasure. To him he committed the charge of a war with Parthia which became inevitable, and though the Roman arms were successful, this was not due to the skill or energy of either Marcus or Verus. Had a strong scientific mind been in command, it might have been possible to avert or mitigate a calamity which now fell on the Mediterranean world, and had a share, perhaps a large one, in the decay and fall of the Empire. The legions brought back with them from the East one of the most terrible plagues known to history, which can only be compared for its effects with the Black Death in the fourteenth century.

Not only in the East, but nearer home, Marcus had to meet formidable foes who broke through the frontiers with which Hadrian had taken such pains. Pushed forward by pressure from the rear, German tribes unwillingly made their way into Roman territory, overran the new province of Dacia, crossed the Danube, and even passed over the Alps into Italy. Marcus's difficulties were great, but he met them with patience and courage. The pestilence had so greatly thinned the population that both men and money were wanting for the war, and the struggle to drive back the unwilling invaders was prolonged for 13 years. It was still going on when Marcus died of fever in camp at Vienna. As he closed his eyes in his tent he must have felt that he had spent himself in vain, and that evil days were in store for the Empire. He left a worthless son, Commodus, who failed to understand the danger, and let things go.

The Legacy of Rome

We need not follow the Empire in its downward course. We have seen what the work of Rome in the world was to be, and how at last she accomplished it in spite of constant peril and frequent disaster. From Marcus Aurelius onwards the strain of self-defence was too great to allow of progress in any social or political sense. The monarchy became more absolute, the machinery of government more complicated; the masses were over taxed, and the middle classes ruined. Depopulation again set in, and attempts to remedy it by settling barbarian invaders within the frontiers had some bad results. In less than a century from the death of Marcus the Empire had been divided into two halves of east and west, with a new capital for the eastern half at Byzantium (Constantinople). This, like all the changes of the later Empire, was meant strictly for the purpose of resisting the invaders; but, nonetheless, they broke at last through all barriers.

Yet this did not happen before the name and fame of Rome had made such deep impression on their minds that they sought to deserve the inheritance which had thus fallen to them; despising, indeed, the degenerate provincials who struck no blow in their own defence, but full of respect for the majestic power which had for so many centuries confronted and instructed them. They never swept away the civilization of the Mediterranean; from Julius Caesar onwards the Roman rulers had done so much to defend it, had raised its prestige so high, had so thoroughly organized its internal life, that uncivilized peoples neither could nor would destroy it.

We still enjoy its best fruits – the art, science and literature of Hellas, the genius of Rome for law – for 'the just interference of the State in the interests and passions of humanity' (Mommsen's definition of Law). We may be apt at the present day, when science has opened out for us so many new paths of knowledge, and inspired us with such enthusiasm in pursuing them, to forget the value of the inheritance which Rome preserved for us. But this is merely a passing phase of feeling; it is really quite inconsistent with the character of an age which recognizes the doctrine of evolution as its great discovery. It is natural to civilized man to go back upon his past, and to be grateful for all profit he can gain from the study of his own development. So we may be certain that the claim of Greece and Rome to our eternal gratitude will never cease to be asserted, and their right to teach us still what we could have learnt nowhere else, will never be successfully disputed.

PART TWO

THE ROMANS IN THEIR OWN WORDS

The Romans were a literate people. Not only did they carve inscriptions in stone on public buildings and private funerary monuments, but they also painted advertisements and scribbled graffiti on walls, scratched notes on to pieces of pottery or incised them on wax tablets, wrote financial accounts, letters and reports with pen and ink on thin sheets of trimmed wood and even copied entire books by hand on to scrolls made of papyrus. While a fraction – perhaps less than one per cent – of the works that were written during the Republic and Empire survive, what has come down to us provides extraordinary insights into the issues that concerned and fascinated the Romans themselves.

The Romans wrote in Latin and Greek, the two official languages of the Empire, about all aspects of life. They wrote plays and poems (as examples from Catullus, Lucretius and Virgil cited in Part One illustrate). The origins of their people and how they created an empire were written about in annals, chronicles and histories, such as those by Livy, Appian, Tacitus, Cassius Dio, Ammianus Marcellinus and Orosius. The personal stories of notable Romans were documented by biographers, such as Plutarch and Suetonius. The State's institutions and their functions, for example the way in which the Senate and People's Assemblies worked together, were described by Polybius; the intricate workings of Rome's water distribution system were explained by Julius Frontinus; the training of new army recruits was the subject of a treatise by Vegetius; and the universe itself and everything in it was recorded in great detail in encyclopedias, such as the one written by Pliny the Elder. The Romans celebrated their own individual achievements too, in books of collected speeches (like those of Cicero), or in letters (like those of Pliny the Younger) or in official accounts of military campaigns (like those of Julius Caesar or his adopted son Caesar Augustus).

The extracts in translation included here in Part Two illuminate over 1,000 years of Roman civilization – from its legendary beginnings in the eighth century BCE, through the height of its power in the second century CE, to its Christianization in the fourth century CE.

FROM LIVY'S
FROM THE FOUNDATION OF THE CITY

Livy (Titus Livius, 59 BCE–17 CE) is the most important source of information about the early history of Rome. His epic work, the Latin title of which translates as *From the Foundation of the City* (the city being Rome), covers the period 753–9 BCE. It is an erudite weaving together of stories, both tales derived from legend and traditional interpretations and facts gleaned from chronicles and official reports. Of the 142 books making up the complete work, just 35 survive in part or in whole.

Preface
Livy on Writing about the Past

Whether the task I have undertaken of writing a complete history of the Roman People from the very commencement of its existence will reward me for the labour spent on it, I neither know for certain, nor if I did know would I venture to say.

For I see that this is an old-established and a common practice, each fresh writer being invariably persuaded that he will either attain greater certainty in the materials of his narrative or surpass the rudeness of antiquity in the excellence of his style. However this may be, it will still be a great satisfaction to me to have taken my part, too, in investing, to the utmost of my abilities, the annals of the foremost nation in the world with a deeper interest; and if in such a crowd of writers my own reputation is thrown into the shade, I would console myself with the renown and greatness of those who eclipse my fame. The subject, moreover, is one that demands immense labour. It goes back beyond 700 years and, after starting from small and humble beginnings, has grown to such dimensions that it begins to be overburdened by its greatness. I have very little doubt, too, that for the majority of my readers the earliest times and those immediately succeeding, will possess little attraction; they will hurry on to these modern days in which the might of a long paramount nation is wasting by internal decay. I, on the other hand, shall look for a further reward of my labours in being able to close my eyes to the evils which our generation has witnessed for so many years; so long, at least, as I am devoting all my thoughts to retracing those pristine records, free from all the anxiety which can disturb the historian of his own times even if it cannot warp him from the truth.

The traditions of what happened prior to the foundation of the City or whilst it was being built, are more fitted to adorn the creations of the poet than the authentic records of the historian, and I have no intention of establishing either their truth or their falsehood. This much licence is conceded to the ancients, that by intermingling human actions with divine they may confer a more august dignity on the origins of states. Now, if any nation ought to be allowed to claim a sacred origin and point back to a divine paternity that nation is Rome. For such is her renown in war that when she chooses to represent Mars as her own and her founder's father, the nations of the world accept the statement with the same equanimity with which they accept her dominion. But whatever opinions may be formed, or criticizms passed upon these and similar traditions, I regard them as of small importance. The subjects to which I would ask each of my readers to devote his earnest attention are these – the life and morals of the community; the men and the qualities by which through domestic policy and foreign war dominion was won and extended. Then as the standard of morality gradually lowers, let him follow the decay of the national character, observing how at first it slowly sinks, then slips downward more and more rapidly, and finally begins to plunge into headlong ruin, until he reaches these days, in which we can bear neither our diseases nor their remedies.

There is this exceptionally beneficial and fruitful advantage to be derived from the study of the past, that you see, set in the clear light of historical truth, examples of every possible type. From these you may select for yourself and your country what to imitate and also what, as being mischievous in its inception and disastrous in its issues, you are to avoid. Unless, however, I am misled by affection for my undertaking, there has never existed any commonwealth greater in power, with a purer morality, or more fertile in good examples; or any state in which avarice and luxury have been so late in making their inroads, or poverty and frugality so highly and continuously honoured, showing so clearly that the less wealth men possessed the less they coveted. In these latter years, wealth has brought avarice in its train, and the unlimited command of pleasure has created in men a passion for ruining themselves and everything else through self-indulgence and licentiousness. But criticizms, which will be unwelcome, even when perhaps necessary, must not appear in the commencement at all events of this extensive work. We should much prefer to start with favourable omens, and if we could have adopted the poets' custom, it would have been much pleasanter to commence with prayers and supplications to gods and goddesses that they would grant a favourable and successful issue to the great task before us.

Book I, Chapter 4
The Story of Romulus

But the Fates had, I believe, already decreed the origin of this great city and the foundation of the mightiest empire under heaven. The Vestal was forcibly violated and gave birth to twins. She named Mars as their father, either because she really believed it, or because the fault might appear less heinous if a deity were the cause of it. But neither gods nor men sheltered her or her babies from the king's cruelty; the priestess was thrown into prison, the boys were ordered to be thrown into the river. By a heaven-sent chance it happened that the Tiber was then overflowing its banks and stretches of standing water prevented any approach to the main channel. Those who were carrying the children expected that this stagnant water would be sufficient to drown them, so under the impression that they were carrying out the king's orders they exposed the boys at the nearest point of the overflow, where the *Ficus Ruminalis* (said to have been formerly called Romularis) now stands. The locality was then a wild solitude. The tradition goes on to say that after the floating cradle in which the boys had been exposed had been left by the retreating water on dry land, a thirsty she-wolf from the surrounding hills, attracted by the crying of the children, came to them, gave them her teats to suck and was so gentle towards them that the king's flock-master found her licking the boys with her tongue. According to the story his name was Faustulus. He took the children to his hut and gave them to his wife Larentia to bring up. Some writers think that Larentia, from her unchaste life, had got the nickname of 'She-wolf' amongst the shepherds, and that this was the origin of the marvellous story.

As soon as the boys, thus born and thus brought up, grew to be young men they did not neglect their pastoral duties, but their special delight was roaming through the woods on hunting expeditions. As their strength and courage were thus developed, they used not only to lie in wait for fierce beasts of prey, but they even attacked brigands when loaded with plunder. They distributed what they took amongst the shepherds, with whom, surrounded by a continually increasing body of young men, they associated themselves in their serious undertakings and in their sports and pastimes.

Book I, Chapter 5
Romulus Recognized, Amulius Killed

It is said that the festival of the Lupercalia, which is still observed, was even in those days celebrated on the Palatine Hill This hill was originally called *Pallantium* from a city of the same name in Arcadia; the name was afterwards changed to *Palatium*. Evander, an Arcadian, had held that territory many ages before, and had introduced an annual festival from Arcadia in which young men ran about naked for sport and wantonness, in honour of the Lycaean Pan, whom the Romans afterwards called Inuus. The existence of this festival was widely recognized, and it was while the two brothers were engaged in it that the brigands, enraged at losing their plunder, ambushed them. Romulus successfully defended himself, but Remus was taken prisoner and brought before Amulius, his captors impudently accusing him of their own crimes. The principal charge brought against them was that of invading Numitor's lands with a body of young men whom they had got together and carrying off plunder as though in regular warfare. Remus accordingly was handed over to Numitor for punishment.

Faustulus had from the beginning suspected that it was royal offspring that he was bringing up, for he was aware that the boys had been exposed at the king's command and the time at which he had taken them away exactly corresponded with that of their exposure. He had, however, refused to divulge the matter prematurely, until either a fitting opportunity occurred, or necessity demanded its disclosure. The necessity came first. Alarmed for the safety of Remus he revealed the state of the case to Romulus. It so happened that Numitor also, who had Remus in his custody, on hearing that he and his brother were twins, and comparing their ages, and the character and bearing so unlike that of one in a servile condition, began to recall the memory of his grandchildren, and further inquiries brought him to the same conclusion as Faustulus; nothing was wanting to the recognition of Remus. So the king Amulius was being enmeshed on all sides by hostile purposes.

Romulus shrank from a direct attack with his body of shepherds, for he was no match for the king in open fight. They were instructed to approach the palace by different routes and meet there at a given time, whilst from Numitor's house Remus lent his assistance with a second band he had collected. The attack succeeded and the king was killed.

Book I, Chapter 6
The Foundation of Rome (21st April 753 BCE)

After the government of Alba was thus transferred to Numitor, Romulus and Remus were seized with the desire of building a city in the locality where they had been exposed. There was the superfluous population of the Alban and Latin towns, to these were added the shepherds: it was natural to hope that with all these Alba would be small and Lavinium small in comparison with the city which was to be founded. These pleasant anticipations were disturbed by the ancestral curse – ambition – which led to a deplorable quarrel over what was at first a trivial matter. As they were twins and no claim to precedence could be based on seniority, they decided to consult the tutelary deities of the place by means of augury as to who was to give his name to the new city, and who was to rule it after it had been founded. Romulus accordingly selected the Palatine Hill as his station for observation, Remus the Aventine Hill.

Book I, Chapter 7
The Death of Remus

Remus is said to have been the first to receive an omen: six vultures appeared to him. The augury had just been announced to Romulus when double the number appeared to him. Each was saluted as king by his own party. The one side based their claim on the priority of the appearance, the other on the number of the birds. Then followed an angry altercation; heated passions led to bloodshed; in the tumult Remus was killed. The more common report is that Remus contemptuously jumped over the newly raised walls and was forthwith killed by the enraged Romulus, who exclaimed, 'So shall it be henceforth with everyone who leaps over my walls!' Romulus thus became sole ruler, and the city was called after him, its founder.

His first work was to fortify the Palatine Hill where he had been brought up.

Book I, Chapter 8
The Political Constitution

After the claims of religion had been duly acknowledged, Romulus called his people to a council. As nothing could unite them into one political body but the observance of common laws and customs, he gave them a body of laws, which he thought would only be respected by a rude and uncivilized race of men if he inspired them with awe by assuming the outward symbols of power. He surrounded himself with greater state and, in particular, he called into his service 12 lictors. Some think that he fixed upon this number from the number of the birds who foretold his sovereignty; but I am inclined to agree with those who think that as this class of public officers was borrowed from the same people from whom the *sella curulis* [foldable chair] and the *toga praetexta* [*toga* with a broad purple border] were adopted – their neighbours, the Etruscans – so the number itself also was taken from them. Its use amongst the Etruscans is traced to the custom of the 12 sovereign cities of Etruria, when jointly electing a king furnishing him each with one lictor.

Meantime, the City was growing by the extension of its walls in various directions an increase due rather to the anticipation of its future population than to any present overcrowding. His next care was to secure an addition to the population that the size of the City might not be a source of weakness. It had been the ancient policy of the founders of cities to get together a multitude of people of obscure and low origin and then to spread the fiction that they were the children of the soil. In accordance with this policy, Romulus opened a place of refuge on the spot where, as you go down from the Capitol, you find an enclosed space between two groves. A promiscuous crowd of freemen and slaves, eager for change, fled thither from the neighbouring states. This was the first accession of strength to the nascent greatness of the City.

When he was satisfied as to its strength, his next step was to provide for that strength being wisely directed. He created 100 senators; either, because that number was adequate, or because there were only 100 heads of houses who could be created. In any case they were called the *Patres* ['Fathers'] in virtue of their rank, and their descendants were called 'Patricians.'

Book I, Chapter 9
The Rape of the Sabine Women

The *Res Romana* [Roman State] had now become so strong that it was a match for any of its neighbours in war, but its greatness threatened to last for only one generation, since through the absence of women there was no hope of offspring, and there was no right of intermarriage with their neighbours. Acting on the advice of the Senate, Romulus sent envoys amongst the surrounding nations to ask for alliance and the right of intermarriage on behalf of his new community. It was represented that cities, like everything else, sprang from the humblest beginnings, and those who were helped on by their own courage and the favour of heaven won for themselves great power and great renown. As to the origin of Rome, it was well known that whilst it had received divine assistance, courage and self-reliance were not wanting. There should, therefore, be no reluctance for men to mingle their blood with their fellowmen.

Nowhere did the envoys meet with a favourable reception. Whilst their proposals were treated with contumely, there was at the same time a general feeling of alarm at the power so rapidly growing in their midst. Usually, they were dismissed with the question, 'whether they had opened an asylum for women, for nothing short of that would secure for them intermarriage on equal terms.' The Roman youth could ill brook such insults, and matters began to look like an appeal to force.

To secure a favourable place and time for such an attempt, Romulus, disguising his resentment, made elaborate preparations for the celebration of games in honour of 'Equestrian Neptune', which he called *Consualia*. He ordered public notice of the spectacle to be given amongst the adjoining cities, and his people supported him in making the celebration as magnificent as their knowledge and resources allowed, so that expectations were raised to the highest pitch. There was a great gathering; people were eager to see the new City, all their nearest neighbours – the people of Caenina, Antemnae, and Crustumerium – were there, and the whole Sabine population came, with their wives and families. They were invited to accept hospitality at the different houses, and after examining the situation of the City, its walls and the large number of dwelling-houses it included, they were astonished at the rapidity with which the Roman State had grown.

When the hour for the games had come, and their eyes and minds were alike riveted on the spectacle before them, the preconcerted signal was given and the Roman youth dashed in all directions to carry off the maidens who were present. The larger part were carried off indiscriminately, but some particularly beautiful girls who had been marked out for the leading patricians were carried to their houses by plebeians told off for the task. One, conspicuous amongst them all for grace and beauty, is reported to have been carried off by a group led by a certain Talassius, and to the many inquiries as to whom she was intended for, the invariable answer was given, 'For Talassius'. Hence the use of this word in the marriage rites. Alarm and consternation broke up the games, and the parents of the maidens fled, distracted with grief, uttering bitter reproaches on the violators of the laws of hospitality and appealing to the god to whose solemn games they had come, only to be the victims of impious perfidy.

The abducted maidens were quite as despondent and indignant. Romulus, however, went round in person, and pointed out to them that it was all owing to the pride of their parents in denying right of intermarriage to their neighbours. They would live in honourable wedlock, and share all their property and civil rights, and – dearest of all to human nature – would be the mothers of freemen. He begged them to lay aside their feelings of resentment and give their affections to those whom fortune had made masters of their persons. An injury had often led to reconciliation and love; they would find their husbands all the more affectionate because each would do his utmost, so far as in him lay to make up for the loss of parents and country. These arguments were reinforced by the endearments of their husbands who excused their conduct by pleading the irresistible force of their passion – a plea effective beyond all others in appealing to a woman's nature.

Book I, Chapter 10
The First Wars

The feelings of the abducted maidens were now pretty completely appeased, but not so those of their parents. They went about in mourning garb and tried by their tearful complaints to rouse their countrymen to action. Nor did they confine their remonstrances to their own cities; they flocked from all sides to Titus Tatius, the king of the Sabines, and sent formal deputations to him, for his was the most influential name in those parts. The people of Caenina, Crustumerium, and Antemnae were the greatest sufferers; they thought Tatius and his Sabines were too slow in moving, so these three cities prepared to make war conjointly. Such, however, were the impatience and anger of the Caeninensians that even the Crustuminians and Antemnates did not display enough energy for them, so the men of Caenina made an attack upon Roman territory on their own account. Whilst they were scattered far and wide, pillaging and destroying, Romulus came upon them with an army, and after a brief encounter taught them that anger is futile without strength. He put them to a hasty flight, and following them up, killed their king and despoiled his body; then after slaying their leader took their city at the first assault. He was no less anxious to display his achievements than he had been great in performing them, so, after leading his victorious army home, he mounted to the Capitol with the spoils of his dead foe borne before him on a frame constructed for the purpose. He hung them there on an oak, which the shepherds looked upon as a sacred tree, and at the same time marked out the site for the Temple of Jupiter, and addressing the god by a new title, uttered the following invocation:

'Jupiter Feretrius! These arms taken from a king, I, Romulus a king and conqueror, bring to thee, and on this

domain, whose bounds I have in will and purpose traced,
I dedicate a temple to receive the spolia opima *['rich*
spoils'] which posterity following my example shall bear
hither, taken from the kings and generals of our foes slain
in battle.'

Such was the origin of the first temple dedicated in
Rome. And the gods decreed that though its founder did
not utter idle words in declaring that posterity would thither
bear their spoils, still the splendour of that offering should
not be dimmed by the number of those who have rivalled
his achievement. For after so many years have elapsed and
so many wars been waged, only twice have the *spolia opima*
been offered. So seldom has Fortune granted that glory
to men.

Book I, Chapter 55
The First Public Works in Rome

After the acquisition of Gabii, Tarquinius made peace
with the Aequi and renewed the treaty with the Etruscans.
Then he turned his attention to the business of the City.
The first thing was the Temple of Jupiter on the Tarpeian
Mount, which he was anxious to leave behind as a memorial
of his reign and name, both the Tarquinii were concerned
in it, the father had vowed it, the son completed it. That
the whole of the area which the Temple of Jupiter was to
occupy might be wholly devoted to that deity, he decided
to deconsecrate the *fanes* [sanctuaries] and chapels, some of
which had been originally vowed by King Tatius at the crisis

of his battle with Romulus, and subsequently consecrated and inaugurated.

Tradition records that at the commencement of this work the gods sent a divine intimation of the future vastness of the empire, for whilst the omens were favourable for the deconsecration of all the other shrines, they were unfavourable for that of the fane of Terminus. This was interpreted to mean that as the abode of Terminus was not moved and he alone of all the deities was not called forth from his consecrated borders, so all would be firm and immovable in the future empire.

This augury of lasting dominion was followed by a prodigy, which portended the greatness of the empire. It is said that whilst they were digging the foundations of the temple, a human head came to light with the face perfect; this appearance unmistakably portended that the spot would be the stronghold of empire and the head of all the world. This was the interpretation given by the soothsayers in the City, as well as by those who had been called into council from Etruria. The king's designs were now much more extensive; so much so that his share of the spoils of Pometia, which had been set apart to complete the work, now hardly met the cost of the foundations. This makes me inclined to trust Fabius – who, moreover, is the older authority – when he says that the amount was only 40 talents, rather than Piso, who states that 40,000 pounds of silver were set apart for that object. For not only is such a sum more than could be expected from the spoils of any single city at that time, but it would more than suffice for the foundations of the most magnificent building of the present day.

Book I, Chapter 56
The Mission to Delphi

Determined to finish his temple, he sent for workmen from all parts of Etruria, and not only used the public treasury to defray the cost, but also compelled the plebeians to take their share of the work. This was in addition to their military service and was anything but a light burden. Still, they felt it less of a hardship to build the temples of the gods with their own hands, than they did afterwards when they were transferred to other tasks less imposing but involving greater toil – the construction of the *fori* in the Circus and that of the *Cloaca Maxima*, a subterranean tunnel to receive all the sewage of the City. The magnificence of these two works could hardly be equalled by anything in the present day. When the plebeians were no longer required for these works, he considered that such a multitude of unemployed would prove a burden to the State, and as he wished the frontiers of the empire to be more widely colonized, he sent colonizts to Signia and Circeii to serve as a protection to the City by land and sea.

While he was carrying out these undertakings a frightful portent appeared; a snake gliding out of a wooden column created confusion and panic in the palace. The king himself was not so much terrified as filled with anxious forebodings. The Etruscan soothsayers were only employed to interpret prodigies which affected the State; but this one concerned him and his house personally, so he decided to send to the world-famed oracle of Delphi. Fearing to entrust the oracular response to anyone else, he sent two of his sons to Greece, through lands at that time unknown and overseas still less known. Titus and Arruns started on their journey.

They had as a travelling companion Lucius Junius Brutus, the son of the king's sister, Tarquinia, a young man of a very different character from that which he had assumed. When he heard of the massacre of the chiefs of the State, amongst them his own brother, by his uncle's orders, he determined that his intelligence should give the king no cause for alarm nor his fortune any provocation to his avarice, and that as the laws afforded no protection, he would seek safety in obscurity and neglect. Accordingly, he carefully kept up the appearance and conduct of an idiot, leaving the king to do what he liked with his person and property, and did not even protest against his nickname of 'Brutus'; for under the protection of that nickname the soul which was one day to liberate Rome was awaiting its destined hour.

The story goes that, when brought to Delphi by the Tarquinii, more as a butt for their sport than as a companion, he had with him a golden staff enclosed in a hollow one of cornel wood, which he offered to Apollo as a mystical emblem of his own character. After executing their father's commission, the young men were desirous of ascertaining to which of them the kingdom of Rome would come. A voice came from the lowest depths of the cavern: 'Whichever of you, young men, shall be the first to kiss his mother, he shall hold supreme sway in Rome.' Sextus had remained behind in Rome and to keep him in ignorance of this oracle and so deprive him of any chance of coming to the throne, the two Tarquinii insisted upon absolute silence being kept on the subject. They drew lots to decide which of them should be the first to kiss his mother. On their return to Rome, Brutus, thinking that the oracular utterance had another meaning, pretended to stumble, and as he fell kissed the ground, for the earth is of course the common mother of us all.

Then they returned to Rome, where preparations were being energetically pushed forward for a war with the Rutulians.

Book I, Chapter 57
The Story of Lucretia (509 BCE)

This people who were at that time in possession of Ardea, were, considering the nature of their country and the age in which they lived, exceptionally wealthy. This circumstance really originated the war, for the Roman king was anxious to repair his own fortune, which had been exhausted by the magnificent scale of his public works, and also to conciliate his subjects by a distribution of the spoils of war. His tyranny had already produced disaffection but what moved their special resentment was the way they had been so long kept by the king at manual and even servile labour.

An attempt was made to take Ardea by assault; when that failed recourse was had to a regular investment to starve the enemy out. When troops are stationary, as is the case in a protracted more than in an active campaign, furloughs are easily granted, more so to the men of rank however, than to the common soldiers. The royal princes sometimes spent their leisure hours in feasting and entertainments, and at a wine party given by Sextus Tarquinius at which Collatinus, the son of Egerius, was present, the conversation happened to turn upon their wives, and each began to speak of his own in terms of extraordinarily high praise.

As the dispute became warm Collatinus said that there was no need of words, it could in a few hours be ascertained how far his Lucretia was superior to all the rest. 'Why do we not,' he exclaimed, 'if we have any youthful vigour about us mount our horses and pay your wives a visit and find out their characters on the spot? What we see of the behaviour, of each on the unexpected arrival of her husband, let that be the surest test.' They were heated with wine, and all shouted, 'Good! Come on!' Setting spur to their horses they galloped off to Rome, where they arrived as darkness was beginning to close in.

Thence they proceeded to Collatia, where they found Lucretia very differently employed from the king's daughters-in-law, whom they had seen passing their time in feasting and luxury with their acquaintances. She was sitting at her wool work in the hall, late at night, with her, maids busy round her. The palm in this competition of wifely virtue was awarded to Lucretia. She welcomed the arrival of her husband and the Tarquinii, whilst her victorious spouse courteously invited the royal princes to remain as his guests. Sextus Tarquinius, inflamed by the beauty and exemplary purity of Lucretia, formed the vile project of effecting her dishonour. After their youthful frolic they returned for the time to camp.

Book I, Chapter 58
Sextus Tarquinius Threatens Lucretia

A few days afterwards, Sextus Tarquinius went, unknown to Collatinus, with one companion to Collatia. He was hospitably received by the household, who suspected nothing, and after supper was conducted to the bedroom set apart for guests. When all around seemed safe and everybody fast asleep, he went in the frenzy of his passion with a naked sword to the sleeping Lucretia, and placing his left hand on her breast, said, 'Silence, Lucretia! I am Sextus Tarquinius, and I have a sword in my hand; if you utter a word, you shall die.' When the woman, terrified out of her sleep, saw that no help was near, and instant death threatening her, Tarquinius began to confess his passion, pleaded, used threats as well as entreaties, and employed every argument likely to influence a female heart. When he saw that she was inflexible and not moved even by the fear of death, he threatened to disgrace her, declaring that he would lay the naked corpse of the slave by her dead body, so that it might be said that she had been slain in foul adultery. By this awful threat, his lust triumphed over her inflexible chastity, and Tarquinius went off exulting in having successfully attacked her honour.

Lucretia, overwhelmed with grief at such a frightful outrage, sent a messenger to her father at Rome and to her husband at Ardea, asking them to come to her, each accompanied by one faithful friend; it was necessary to act, and to act promptly; a horrible thing had happened. Spurius Lucretius came with Publius Valerius, the son of Volesus; Collatinus with Lucius Junius Brutus, with whom he happened to be returning to Rome when he was met by his wife's messenger. They found Lucretia sitting in her room prostrate with grief.

As they entered, she burst into tears, and to her husband's inquiry whether all was well, replied, 'No! What can be well with a woman when her honour is lost? The marks of a stranger Collatinus are in your bed. But it is only the body that has been violated; the soul is pure; death shall bear witness to that. But pledge me your solemn word that the adulterer shall not go unpunished. It is Sextus Tarquinius, who, coming as an enemy instead of a guest forced from me last night by brutal violence a pleasure fatal to me, and, if you are men, fatal to him.' They all successively pledged their word, and tried to console the distracted woman, by turning the guilt from the victim of the outrage to the perpetrator and urging that it is the mind that sins not the body, and where there has been no consent there is no guilt.

'It is for you,' she said, 'to see that he gets his deserts: although I acquit myself of the sin, I do not free myself from the penalty; no unchaste woman shall henceforth live and plead Lucretia's example.'

Book I, Chapter 59
The Expulsion of the Tarquinii from Rome

Whilst they were absorbed in grief, Brutus drew the knife from Lucretia's wound and holding it, dripping with blood, in front of him, said, 'By this blood – most pure before the outrage wrought by the king's son – I swear, and you, O gods, I call to witness that I will drive hence Lucius Tarquinius Superbus, together with his cursed wife and his whole brood, with fire and sword and every means in my power, and I will not suffer them or anyone else to reign in Rome.' Then he handed the knife to Collatinus and then to Lucretius and Valerius, who were all astounded at the marvel of the thing, wondering whence Brutus had acquired this new character.

They swore as they were directed; all their grief changed to wrath, and they followed the lead of Brutus, who summoned them to abolish the monarchy forthwith. They carried the body of Lucretia from her home down to the Forum [the public space that would become the Forum Romanum], where, owing to the unheard-of atrocity of the crime, they at once collected a crowd. Each had his own complaint to make of the wickedness and violence of the royal house. Whilst all were moved by the father's deep distress, Brutus bade them stop their tears and idle laments, and urged them to act as men and Romans and take up arms against their insolent foes. All the high-spirited amongst the younger men came forward as armed volunteers, the rest followed their example. A portion of this body was left to hold Collatia, and guards were stationed at the gates to prevent any news of the movement from reaching the king; the rest marched in arms to Rome with Brutus in command.

On their arrival, the sight of so many men in arms spread panic and confusion wherever they marched, but when again the people saw that the foremost men of the State were leading the way, they realized that whatever the movement was it was a serious one. The terrible occurrence created no less excitement in Rome than it had done in Collatia; there was a rush from all quarters of the City to the *Forum*.

When they had gathered there, the herald summoned them to attend the 'Tribune of the Celeres'; this was the office which Brutus happened at the time to be holding. He made a speech quite out of keeping with the character and temper he had up to that day assumed. He dwelt upon the brutality and licentiousness of Sextus Tarquinius, the infamous outrage on Lucretia and her pitiful death, the bereavement sustained by her father, Tricipitinus, to whom the cause of his daughter's death was more shameful and distressing than the actual death itself. Then he dwelt on the tyranny of the king, the toils and sufferings of the plebeians kept underground clearing out ditches and sewers – Roman men, conquerors of all the surrounding nations, turned from warriors into artisans and stonemasons! He reminded them of the shameful murder of Servius Tullius and his daughter driving in her accursed chariot over her father's body, and solemnly invoked the gods as the avengers of murdered parents. By enumerating these and, I believe, other still more atrocious incidents which his keen sense of the present injustice suggested, but which it is not easy to give in detail, he goaded on the incensed multitude to strip the king of his sovereignty and pronounce a sentence of banishment against Tarquin with his wife and children.

With a picked body of the 'Juniors,' who volunteered to follow him, he went off to the camp at Ardea to incite the army against the king, leaving the command in the City to Lucretius, who had previously been made Prefect of the City by the king. During the commotion Tullia fled from the palace amidst the execrations of all whom she met, men and women alike invoking against her father's avenging spirit.

Book I, Chapter 60
Romans Elect their First Consuls (509 BCE)

When the news of these proceedings reached the camp, the king, alarmed at the turn affairs were taking, hurried to Rome to quell the outbreak. Brutus, who was on the same road, had become aware of his approach, and to avoid meeting him took another route, so that he reached Ardea and Tarquinius Rome almost at the same time, though by different ways.

Tarquinius found the gates shut, and a decree of banishment passed against him; the Liberator of the City received a joyous welcome in the camp, and the king's sons were expelled from it. Two of them followed their father, into exile amongst the Etruscans in Caere. Sextus Tarquin proceeded to Gabii, which he looked upon as his kingdom, but was killed in revenge for the old feuds he had kindled by his rapine and murders.

Lucius Tarquinius Superbus reigned 25 years. The whole duration of the regal government from the foundation of the City to its liberation was 244 years. Two consuls were then elected in the assembly of centuries by the prefect of the City, in accordance with the regulations of Servius Tullius. They were Lucius Junius Brutus and Lucius Tarquinius Collatinus.

Book II, Chapter 10
The Story of Horatius Cocles

On the appearance of the enemy the country people fled into the City as best they could. The weak places in the defences were occupied by military posts; elsewhere the walls and the Tiber were deemed sufficient protection. The enemy would have forced their way over the Sublician bridge had it not been for one man, Horatius Cocles. The good fortune of Rome provided him as her bulwark on that memorable day. He happened to be on guard at the bridge when he saw the Janiculum taken by a sudden assault and the enemy rushing down from it to the river, whilst his own men, a panic-struck mob, were deserting their posts and throwing away their arms. He reproached them one after another for their cowardice, tried to stop them, appealed to them in heaven's name to stand, declared that it was in vain for them to seek safety in flight whilst leaving the bridge open behind them, there would very soon be more of the enemy on the Palatine and the Capitol than there were on the Janiculum. So he shouted to them to break down the bridge by sword or fire, or by whatever means they could, he would meet the enemies' attack so far as one man could keep them at bay. He advanced to the head of the bridge.

Amongst the fugitives, whose backs alone were visible to the enemy, he was conspicuous as he fronted them armed for fight at close quarters. The enemy were astounded at his preternatural courage. Two men were kept by a sense of shame from deserting him – Spurius Lartius and Titus Herminius – both of them men of high birth and renowned courage. With them he sustained the first tempestuous shock and wild confused onset, for a brief interval. Then, whilst only a small portion of the bridge remained and those who were cutting it down called upon them to retire, he insisted upon these, too, retreating. Looking round with eyes dark with menace upon the Etruscan chiefs, he challenged them to single combat, and reproached them all with being the slaves of tyrant kings, and whilst unmindful of their own liberty coming to attack that of others.

For some time they hesitated, each looking round upon the others to begin. At length shame roused them to action, and raising a shout they hurled their javelins from all sides on their solitary foe. He caught them on his outstretched shield, and with unshaken resolution kept his place on the bridge with firmly planted foot. They were just attempting to dislodge him by a charge when the crash of the broken bridge and the shout which the Romans raised at seeing the work completed stayed the attack by filling them with sudden panic. Then Cocles said, 'Tiberinus, holy father, I pray thee to receive into thy propitious stream these arms and this thy warrior.' So, fully armed, he leaped into the Tiber, and though many missiles fell over him he swam across in safety to his friends: an act of daring more famous than credible with posterity.

The State showed its gratitude for such courage; his statue was set up in the *Comitium*, and as much land given to him as he could drive the plough round in one day. Besides this public honour, the citizens individually showed their feeling; for, in spite of the great scarcity, each, in proportions to his means, sacrificed what he could from his own store as a gift to Cocles.

FROM APPIAN'S *ROMAN HISTORY*

Appian (Appianus of Alexandria, *c.* 95–*c.* 165 CE) was not a historian like Livy who wrote chronologically. Instead, his work is ethnographical. It explains, by region, the conflicts between peoples in which Roman armies fought, from the very beginning of Roman history to the time of Trajan (r. 98–117 CE). Of the 24 volumes, 11 have survived complete or in part, namely those on the Spanish, Hannibalic, Punic (or Sicilian), Illyrian, Syrian, and Mithridatic Wars, and five books on the Civil Wars. It included a detailed account of their victory in the Second Punic War (218–201 BCE) at Zama against Hannibal Barca of Carthage, which transformed Rome into a Mediterranean superpower.

The Punic Wars, Chapter 7
The Battle of Zama (202 BCE)

The Carthaginian council warmly welcomed the [peace] agreement [offered by Rome] and exhorted the people to adhere to its terms, explaining all their misfortunes and their immediate want of soldiers, money, and provisions. But the people, like a mere mob, behaved like fools. They thought that their generals had made this arrangement for their own private ends, so that, relying upon the Romans, they might hold the power in their own country. They said that Hannibal was doing now what had been done before by Hasdrubal, who had betrayed his camp to the enemy by night, and a little later wanted to surrender to [Publius Cornelius] Scipio, having approached him for that purpose, and was now concealed in the city.

Thereupon there was a great clamour and tumult, and some of them left the assembly and went in search of Hasdrubal. He had anticipated them by taking refuge in his father's tomb, where he destroyed himself with poison. But they pulled his corpse out, cut off his head, put it on a pike, and carried it about the city. Thus was Hasdrubal first banished unjustly, next falsely slandered by Hanno, and then driven to his death by the Carthaginians, and loaded with indignities after his death.

Then the Carthaginians ordered Hannibal to break the truce and begin war against Scipio, and to fight as soon as possible on account of the scarcity of provisions. Accordingly, he sent word that the truce was at an end. Scipio marched immediately and took the great city of Partha and encamped near Hannibal. The latter moved off, but he sent three spies into the Roman camp who were captured by Scipio. The latter did not put them to death, however, according to the custom of dealing with spies, but ordered that they should be taken around and shown the camp, the arsenals, the engines, and the army under review. He then set them free so that they might inform Hannibal concerning all these things. The latter deemed it advisable to have a parley with Scipio, and when it was granted, he said that the Carthaginians had rejected the former treaty on account of the money indemnity. If he would remit that, and if the Romans would content themselves with Sicily, Spain, and the islands they now held, the agreement would be lasting. 'Hannibal's escape from Italy would be a great gain to him,' said Scipio, 'if he could obtain these terms in addition.' He then forbade Hannibal to send any more messages to him. After indulging in some mutual threats, they departed, each to his own camp.

The town of Cilla was in the neighbourhood and near it was a hill well adapted for a camp. Hannibal, perceiving this, sent a detachment forward to seize it and lay out a camp. Then he started and moved forward as though he were already in possession of it. Scipio having anticipated him and seized it beforehand, Hannibal was cut off in the midst of a plain without water and was engaged all night digging wells. His army, by toiling in the sand, with great difficulty obtained a little muddy water to drink, and so they passed the night without food, without care for their bodies, and some of them without removing their arms. Scipio, mindful of these things, moved against them at daylight while they were exhausted with marching, with want of sleep, and want of water. Hannibal was troubled, since he did not wish to join battle in that plight. Yet he saw that if he should remain there his army would suffer severely from want of water, while if he should retreat the enemy would take fresh courage and fall upon his rear. For these reasons it was necessary for him to fight. He speedily put in battle array about 50,000 men and 80 elephants. He placed the elephants in the front line at intervals, in order to strike terror into the enemy's ranks. Next to them he placed the third part of his army, composed of Celts and Ligurians, and mixed with them everywhere Moorish and Balearic archers and slingers. Behind these was his second line, composed of Carthaginians and Africans. The third line consisted of Italians who had followed him from their own country, in whom he placed the greatest confidence, since they had the most to apprehend from defeat. The cavalry was placed on the wings. In this way Hannibal arranged his forces.

Scipio had about 23,000 foot and 1,500 Italian and Roman horse. He had as allies Masinissa with a large number of Numidian horse, and another prince, named Dacamas, with 1,600 horse. He drew up his infantry, like those of Hannibal, in three lines. He placed all his cohorts in straight lines with open spaces so that the cavalry might readily pass between them. In front of each cohort he stationed men armed with heavy stakes two cubits long, mostly shod with iron, for the purpose of assailing the oncoming elephants by hand, as with catapult bolts. He ordered these and the other foot-soldiers to avoid the impetus of these beasts by turning aside and continually hurling javelins at them, and by darting around them to hamstring them whenever they could. In this way Scipio disposed his infantry. He stationed his Numidian horse on his wings because they were accustomed to the sight and smell of elephants. As the Italian horse were not so, he placed them all in the rear, ready to charge through the intervals of the foot-soldiers when the latter should have checked the first onset of the elephants. To each horseman was assigned an attendant armed with plenty of darts with which to ward off the attack of these beasts. In this way was his cavalry disposed. Laelius commanded the right wing and Octavius the left. In the middle both Hannibal and himself took their stations, out of respect for each other, each having a body of horse in order to send reinforcements wherever they might be needed. Of these Hannibal had 4,000 and Scipio 2,000, besides the 300 Italians whom he had armed in Sicily.

When everything was ready each one rode up and down encouraging his soldiers. Scipio, in the presence of his army, invoked the gods, whom the Carthaginians had offended by their frequent violation of treaties. He told the soldiers not to think of the numbers of the enemy but of their own valour, by which aforetime these same enemies, in even greater numbers, had been overcome in this same country. If fear, anxiety, and doubt oppress those who have hitherto been victorious, how much more, he said, must these feelings weigh upon the vanquished. Thus did Scipio encourage his forces and console them for their inferiority in numbers. Hannibal reminded his men of what they had done in Italy, their great and brilliant victories won, not over Numidians, but over those who were all Italians, and throughout Italy. He pointed out, in plain sight, the smallness of the enemy's force, and exhorted them not to show themselves inferior to a less numerous body in their own country. Each general magnified to his own men the consequences of the coming engagement. Hannibal said that the battle would decide the fate of Carthage and all Africa; if vanquished, they would be enslaved forthwith, if victorious, they would have universal supremacy hereafter. Scipio said that there was no safe refuge for his men if they were vanquished, but if victorious there would be a great increase of the Roman power, a rest from their present labours, a speedy return home, and glory for ever after.

Having thus exhorted their men they joined battle. Hannibal ordered the trumpet to sound, and Scipio responded in like manner. The elephants began the fight decked out in fearful panoply and urged on with goads by their riders. The Numidian horse flying around them incessantly thrust darts into them. Being wounded and put to flight and having become unmanageable, their drivers took them out of the combat. This is what happened to the elephants on both wings. Those in the centre trampled down the Roman infantry, who were not accustomed to that kind of fighting and were not able to avoid or to pursue them easily on account of their heavy armour, until Scipio brought up the Italian cavalry, who were in the rear and more lightly armed, and ordered them to dismount from their frightened horses, and run around and stab the elephants. He was himself the first to dismount and wound the front-tramping elephant. The others were encouraged by his example, and they inflicted so many wounds upon the elephants that these also withdrew.

The field being cleared of these beasts the battle was now waged by men and horses only. The Roman right wing, where Laelius commanded, put the opposing Numidians to flight, and Masinissa struck down their prince, Massathes, with a dart, but Hannibal quickly came to their rescue and restored the line of battle. On the left wing, where Octavius commanded and where the hostile Celts and Ligurians were stationed, a doubtful battle was going on. Scipio sent the tribune Thermus thither with a reënforcement of picked men, but Hannibal, after rallying his left wing, flew to the assistance of the Ligurians and Celts, bringing up at the same time his second line of Carthaginians and Africans, Scipio, perceiving this, brought his second line in opposition. When the two greatest generals of the world thus met, in hand-to-hand fight, there was, on the part of the soldiers of each, a brilliant emulation and reverence for their commanders, and no lack of zeal on either side in the way of sharp and vehement fighting and cheering.

As the battle was long and undecided, the two generals had compassion on their tired soldiers, and rushed upon each other in order to bring it to a more speedy decision. They threw their javelins at the same time. Scipio pierced Hannibal's shield. Hannibal hit Scipio's horse. The horse, smarting from the wound, threw Scipio over backwards. He quickly mounted another and again hurled a dart at Hannibal but missed him and struck another horseman near him. At this juncture, Masinissa, hearing of the crisis, came up, and the Romans seeing their general not only serving as a commander but fighting also as a common soldier, fell upon the enemy more vehemently than before, routed them, and pursued them in flight. Nor could Hannibal, who rode by the side of his men and besought them to make a stand and renew the battle, prevail upon them to do so. Therefore, despairing of these, he turned to the Italians who had come with him, and who were still in reserve and not demoralized. These he led into the fight, hoping to fall upon the Romans in disorderly pursuit. But they perceived his intention, and speedily called one another back from the pursuit and restored the line of battle. As their horse were no longer with them and they were destitute of missiles, they now fought sword in hand in close combat. Great slaughter ensued and innumerable wounds, mingled with the shouts of the combatants and the groans of the dying, until, finally, the Romans routed these also and put them to flight. Such was the brilliant issue of this engagement.

Hannibal in his flight seeing a mass of Numidian horse collected together, ran up and besought them not to desert him. Having secured their promise, he led them against the pursuers, hoping still to turn the tide of battle. The first whom he encountered were the Massylians, and now a single combat between Masinissa and Hannibal took place. Rushing fiercely upon each other, Masinissa drove his spear into Hannibal's shield, and Hannibal wounded his antagonist's horse. Masinissa, being thrown, sprang towards Hannibal on foot, and struck and killed a horseman who was advancing towards him in front of the others. At the same time he received in his shield – made of elephant's hide – several darts, one of which he pulled out and hurled at Hannibal; but, as it happened, it struck another horseman who was near and killed him. While he was pulling out another, he was wounded in the arm, and withdrew from the fight for a brief space. When Scipio learned this, he feared for Masinissa and hastened to his relief, but he found that the latter had bound up his wound and returned to the fight on a fresh horse. Thus, the battle continued doubtful and very severe, the soldiers on either side having the utmost reverence for their commanders, until Hannibal, discovering a body of Spanish and Celtic troops on a hill nearby, dashed over to them to bring them into the fight. Those who were still engaged, not knowing the cause of his going, thought that he had fled. Accordingly, they abandoned the fight of their own accord and broke into disorderly rout, not following after Hannibal, but helter-skelter. This band having been dispersed, the Romans thought that the fight was over and pursued them in a disorderly way, not perceiving Hannibal's purpose.

Presently Hannibal returned accompanied by the Spanish and Celtic troops from the hill. Scipio hastened to recall the Romans from the pursuit, and formed a new line of battle much stronger than those who were coming against him, by which means he overcame them without difficulty. When this last effort had failed, Hannibal despaired utterly, and fled in plain sight. Many horsemen pursued him, and among others Masinissa, although suffering from his wound, pressed him hard, striving eagerly to take him prisoner and deliver him to Scipio. But night came to his rescue and under cover of darkness, with 20 horsemen who had alone been able to keep pace with him, he took refuge in a town named Thon. Here he found many Bruttian and Spanish horsemen who had fled after the defeat. Fearing the Iberians because they were fickle barbarians, and apprehending that the Bruttians, as they were Scipio's countrymen, might deliver him up in order to secure pardon for their transgression against Italy, he fled secretly with one horseman in whom he had full confidence. Having accomplished about 3,000 *stades* in two nights and days, he arrived at the seaport of Hadrumetum, where a part of his army had been left to guard his supplies. Here he began to collect forces from the adjacent country and from those who had escaped from the recent engagement, and to prepare arms and engines of war.

The Punic Wars, Chapter 8
Scipio Imposes Terms on the Carthaginians

Now Scipio, having gained this splendid victory, girded himself as for a sacrifice and burned the less valuable spoils of the enemy, as is the custom of the Roman generals. He sent to Rome 10 talents of gold, 2,500 talents of silver, a quantity of carved ivory, and many distinguished captives in ships, and Laelius to carry news of the victory. The remainder of the spoils he sold, and divided the proceeds among the troops. He also made presents for distinguished valour, and crowned Masinissa again. He also sent out expeditions and gathered in more cities. Such was the result of the engagement between Hannibal and Scipio, who here met in combat for the first time. The Roman loss was 2,500 men, that of Masinissa rather more. That of the enemy was 25,000 killed, and 8,500 taken prisoners. Three hundred Iberians deserted to Scipio, and 800 Numidians to Masinissa.

Before the news reached either Carthage or Rome, the former sent word to Mago, who was collecting Gallic mercenaries, to invade Italy if possible, and if not, to set sail with his forces for Africa. These letters being intercepted and brought to Rome, another army, together with horses, ships, and money, was dispatched to Scipio. The latter had already sent Octavius by the land route to Carthage and was going there himself with his fleet. When the Carthaginians learned of Hannibal's defeat, they sent ambassadors to Scipio on a small, fast-sailing ship, of whom the principal ones were Hanno the Great and Hasdrubal Eriphus, who bore a herald's staff aloft on the prow and stretched out their hands toward Scipio in the manner of suppliants. He directed them to come to the camp and, when they had arrived, he attended to their business in high state. They threw themselves on the ground weeping, and when the attendants had lifted them up and bade them say what they wished, Hasdrubal Eriphus spoke as follows:

'For myself, Romans, and for Hanno here, and for all sensible Carthaginians, let me say that we are guiltless of the wrongs which you lay at our door. For when the same men, driven by hunger, did violence to your legates, we rescued them and sent them back to you. You ought not to condemn all the people of Carthage who so recently sought peace, and when it was granted eagerly took the oath to support it. But cities are easily swayed to their hurt because the masses are always controlled by what is pleasing to their ears. We have had experience of these things, having been unable either to persuade or to restrain the multitude by reason of those who slandered us at home and who have prevented us from making ourselves understood by you. Romans, do not judge us by the standard of your own discipline and good counsel. If anyone esteems it a crime to have yielded to the persuasions of these rabble-rousers, consider the hunger and the necessity that was upon us by reason of suffering. For it could not have been a deliberate intention on the part of our people, first to ask for peace, and give such a large sum of money to obtain it, and deliver up all their galleys except a few, and surrender the bulk of their territory, swear to these things, and send an embassy to Rome with the ratifications, and then wantonly to violate the agreement before our embassy had returned. Surely some god misled them and the tempest that drove your supplies into Carthage; and besides the tempest, hunger carried us away, for people who are in want of everything do not form the best judgments respecting other people's property. It would not be reasonable to punish with severity a multitude of men so disorganized and unfortunate.'

'But if you consider us more guilty than unfortunate, we confess our fault and ask pardon for it. Justification belongs to the innocent, entreaty to those who have offended. And much more readily will the fortunate extend pity to others, when they observe the mutability of human affairs, and see people craving mercy today who yesterday were carrying things with a high hand. Such is the condition of Carthage, the greatest and most powerful city of Africa, in ships and money, in elephants, in infantry and cavalry, and in subject peoples, which has flourished 700 years and held sway over all Africa and so many other nations, islands, and seas, standing for the greater part of this time on an equality with yourselves, but which now places her hope of safety not in her dominion of the sea, her ships, her horses, her subjects (all of which have passed over to you), but in you, whom we have heretofore shamefully treated. Contemplating these facts, Romans, it is fit that you should beware of the Nemesis which has come upon them and should use your good fortune mercifully, to do deeds worthy of your own magnanimity and of the former fortunes of Carthage, and to deal with the changes which Providence has ordered in our affairs without reproach, so that your conduct may be blameless before the gods and win the praises of all mankind.'

'There need be no fear that the Carthaginians will change their minds again, after being subjected to such repentance and punishment for their past folly. Wise men are prevented from wrongdoing by their wisdom, the wicked by their suffering and repentance. It is reasonable to suppose that those who have been chastised will be more trusty than those who have not had such experience. Be careful that you do not imitate the cruelty and the sinfulness that you lay at the door of the Carthaginians. The misfortunes of the miserable are the source of fresh transgressions arising from poverty. To the fortunate the opportunity for clemency exists in the abundance of their means. It will be neither to the glory nor to the advantage of your government to destroy so great a city as ours, instead of preserving it. Still, you are the better judges of your own interests. For our safety we rely on these two things: the ancient dignity of the city of Carthage and your well-known moderation, which, together with your arms, has raised you to so great dominion and power. We must accept peace on whatever terms you grant. It is, needless to say, that we place everything in your hands.'

At the conclusion of his speech Eriphus burst into tears.

Then Scipio dismissed them and consulted with his officers a long time. After he had come to a decision, he called the Carthaginian envoys back and addressed them thus: 'You do not deserve pardon, you who have so often violated your treaties with us, and only lately abused our envoys in such a public and heaven-defying manner that you can neither excuse yourselves nor deny that you are worthy of the severest punishment. But what is the use of accusing those who confess? And now you take refuge in prayers, you who would have wiped out the very name of Rome if you had conquered. We did not imitate your bad example. When your ambassadors were at Rome, although you had violated the agreement and maltreated our envoys, the city allowed them to go free, and when they were driven into my camp, although the war had been recommenced, I sent them back to you unharmed. Now that you have condemned yourselves, you may consider whatever terms are granted to you in the light of a gain. I will tell you what my views are, and our Senate will vote upon them as it shall think best.'

'We will yet grant you peace, Carthaginians, on condition that you surrender to the Romans all your warships except ten, all your elephants, the plunder you have lately taken from us, or the value of what has been lost, of which I shall be the judge, all prisoners and deserters and those whom Hannibal led from Italy. These conditions to be fulfilled within 30 days after peace is declared. Mago to depart from Liguria within 60 days, and your garrisons to be withdrawn from all cities beyond the Phoenician trenches and their hostages to be surrendered. You to pay to Rome the sum of 250 Euboïc talents per annum for 50 years. You shall not recruit mercenaries from the Celts or the Ligurians, nor wage war against Masinissa or any other friend of Rome, nor permit any Carthaginians to serve against them with consent of your people. You to retain your city and as much territory inside the Phoenician trenches as you had when I sailed for Africa. You to remain friends of Rome and be her allies on land and sea; all this, if the Senate please, in which case the Romans will evacuate Africa within 150 days. If you desire an armistice until you can send ambassadors to Rome, you shall forthwith give us 150 of your children as hostages whom I shall choose. You shall also give 1,000 talents in addition for the pay of my army, and provisions likewise. When the treaty is ratified, we will release your hostages.'

The Punic Wars, Chapter 9
Hannibal's Last Stand in Africa

When the Carthaginians were continually beaten by Scipio in Africa those of the Bruttians who heard of it revolted from Hannibal, some of them slaying their garrisons and others expelling them. Those who were not able to do either of these things sent messengers to Rome secretly to explain the necessity under which they had acted and to declare their good will. Hannibal came with his army to Petelia, which was not now occupied by the Petelians, as he had expelled them and given the town to the Bruttians. He accused the latter of sending an embassy to Rome. When they denied it, he pretended to believe them, but in order, as he said, that there might be no ground for suspicion, he delivered their principal citizens over to the Numidians, who were ordered to guard each one of them separately. He also disarmed the people, armed the slaves, and stationed them as guards over the city. He did the same to the other cities that he visited. He removed 3,000 citizens of Thurii, who were particularly friendly to the Carthaginians, and 500 others from the country, but gave the goods of the remainder as spoils to his soldiers. Leaving a strong garrison in the city he settled these 3,500 people at Croton, which he found to be well situated for his operations and where he established his magazines and his headquarters against the other towns.

When the Carthaginians summoned him to hasten to the aid of his own country, which was in danger from Scipio, and sent Hasdrubal, their admiral, to him that there might be no delay, he lamented the perfidious and ungrateful conduct of the Carthaginians toward their generals, of which he had had long experience. Moreover, he had apprehensions for himself touching the cause of this great war, which had been begun by himself in Spain. Nevertheless, he recognized the necessity of obeying, and accordingly he built a fleet, for which Italy supplied abundant timber. Despising the cities still allied to him now as foreigners, he resolved to plunder them all, and thus, by enriching his army, render himself secure against his calumniators in Carthage. But being ashamed of such a breach of faith, he sent Hasdrubal, the admiral, about, on pretence of inspecting the garrisons. The latter, as he entered each city, ordered the inhabitants to take what things they and their slaves could carry, and move away. Then he plundered the rest. Some of them, learning of these proceedings before Hasdrubal came, attacked the garrisons, overcoming them in some places and being overcome by them in others. Indiscriminate slaughter, accompanied by the violation of wives and the abduction of virgins, and all the horrors that usually take place when cities are captured, ensued.

Hannibal himself, knowing that the Italians in his army were extremely well-drilled soldiers, sought to persuade them by lavish promises to accompany him to Africa. Those of them who had been guilty of crimes against their own countries willingly expatriated themselves and followed him. Those who had committed no such wrong hesitated. Collecting together those who had decided to remain, as though he wished to say something to them, or to reward them for their services, or to give them some command as to the future, he surrounded them with his army unexpectedly, and directed his soldiers to choose from among them such as they would like to have for slaves. Some made their selections accordingly. Others were ashamed to reduce their comrades in so many engagements to servitude. All the rest Hannibal put to death with darts in order that the Romans might not avail themselves of such a splendid body of men. With them he slaughtered also about 4,000 horses and a large number of pack animals, which he was not able to transport to Africa.

Thereupon he embarked his army and waited for a wind, having left a few garrisons on the land. These the Petalini and other Italians set upon, slew some of them, and then ran away. Hannibal passed over to Africa, having devastated Italy for 16 successive years, and inflicted countless evils upon the inhabitants, and reduced Rome several times to the last extremity, and treated his own subjects and allies with contumely as enemies. For, just as he had made use of them for a time, not from any good will but from necessity, so now that they could be of no further service to him he scorned them and considered them enemies.

When Hannibal had departed from Italy, the Senate pardoned all the Italian peoples who had sided with him and voted a general amnesty except as to the Bruttians, who remained most zealous for him to the end. From these they took away a considerable part of their land, also their arms, if there were any that Hannibal had not taken. They were also forbidden to be enrolled in the military forces thereafter, as being no longer free persons, and they were required to attend as servants upon the consuls and praetors who went about inspecting the affairs of government and the public works of the provinces. Such was the end of Hannibal's invasion of Italy.

FROM POLYBIUS'S *HISTORIES*

Polybius of Megalopolis (*c.* 200–*c.* 118 BCE) was held as a hostage in Rome, serving as a client to the Scipio family. His *Histories*, starting with the year 264 BCE and ending in 146 BCE, focus on the 53 years in which Rome became the international power of his day. Of the 40 books making up the complete work just five exist in part or in whole.

Book VI, Chapters 12–14
The Political System of Rome

The Consuls, previous to leading out their legions, exercise authority in Rome over all public affairs, since all the other magistrates except the tribunes are under them and bound to obey them, and it is they who introduce embassies to the Senate. Besides this it is they who consult the Senate on matters of urgency, they who carry out in detail the provisions of its decrees. Again, as concerns all affairs of state administered by the People it is their duty to take these under their charge, to summon assemblies, to introduce measures, and to preside over the execution of the popular decrees. As for preparation for war and the general conduct of operations in the field, here their power is almost uncontrolled; for they are empowered to make what demands they choose on the allies, to appoint Military Tribunes, to levy soldiers and select those who are fittest for service. They also have the right of inflicting, when on active service, punishment on anyone under their command; and they are authorized to spend any sum they decide upon from the public funds, being accompanied by a Quaestor who faithfully executes their instructions. So that if one looks at this part of the administration alone, one may reasonably pronounce the constitution to be a pure monarchy or kingship. I may remark that any changes in these matters or in others of which I am about to speak that may be made in present or future times do not in any way affect the truth of the views I here state.

To pass to the Senate: in the first place it has the control of the treasury, all revenue and expenditure being regulated by it. For, with the exception of payments made to the Consuls, the Quaestors are not allowed to disburse for any particular object without a decree of the Senate. And even the item of expenditure which is far heavier and more important than any other – the outlay every five years by the Censors on public works, whether constructions or repairs – is under the control of the Senate, which makes a grant to the Censors for the purpose. Similarly, crimes committed in Italy which require a public investigation, such as treason, conspiracy, poisoning, and assassination, are under the jurisdiction of the senate. Also, if any private person or community in Italy is in need of arbitration or indeed claims damages or requires succour or protection, the Senate attends to all such matters.

It also occupies itself with the dispatch of all embassies sent to countries outside of Italy for the purpose either of settling differences, or of offering friendly advice, or indeed of imposing demands, or of receiving submission, or of declaring war; and in like manner with respect to embassies arriving in Rome it decides what reception and what answer should be given to them. All these matters are in the hands of the Senate, nor have the people anything whatever to do with them. So that again to one residing in Rome during the absence of the consuls the constitution appears to be entirely aristocratic; and this is the conviction of many Greek states and many of the kings, as the Senate manages all business connected with them.

After this we are naturally inclined to ask what part in the constitution is left for the People, considering that the Senate controls all the particular matters I mentioned and, what is most important, manages all matters of revenue and expenditure, and considering that the consuls again have uncontrolled authority as regards armaments and operations in the field. But, nevertheless, there is a part and a very important part left for the People. For it is the People which alone has the right to confer honours and inflict punishment, the only bonds by which kingdoms and states and in a word human society in general are held together. For where the distinction between these is overlooked or is observed but ill applied, no affairs can be properly administered. How indeed is this possible when good and evil men are held in equal estimation? It is by the People, then, in many cases the offences punishable by a fine are tried when the accused have held the highest office; and they are the only court which may try on capital charges. As regards the latter they have a practice which is praiseworthy and should be mentioned. Their usage allows those on trial for their lives when found guilty liberty to depart openly, thus inflicting voluntary exile on themselves, if even only one of the tribes that pronounce the verdict has not yet voted. Such exiles enjoy safety in the territories of Naples, Praeneste, Tibur, and other *civitates foederatae* ['allied states']. Again, it is the People who bestow office on the deserving, the noblest regard of virtue in a state; the People have the power of approving or rejecting laws, and what is most important of all, they deliberate on the question of war and peace. Further in the case of alliances, terms of peace, and treaties, it is the People who ratify all these or the reverse. Thus, here again one might plausibly say that the People's share in the government is the greatest, and that the constitution is a democratic one.

FROM PLUTARCH'S *PARALLEL LIVES*

Plutarch (Lucius Mestrius Plutarchus, *c.* 46–after 119 CE) wrote about famous Greeks and Romans in his series of biographical portraits entitled *Parallel Lives*. His subjects included Caius Marius and Lucius Cornelius Sulla, two rival 'strong men' of the first century BCE who were instrumental in for ever changing the *Res Publica*.

Life of Marius, Chapter 3
The Early Life and Career of Marius

Born of parents who were altogether obscure – poor people who lived by the labour of their own hands (Marius was his father's name, Fulcinia that of his mother), it was not until later that he saw the city or got a taste of city ways. In the meantime, he lived at Cirrhaeaton, a village in the territory of Arpinum, in a manner that was quite rude when compared with the polished life of a city, but temperate, and in harmony with the rearing which the ancient Romans gave their children. His first service as a soldier was in a campaign against the Celtiberians, when Scipio Africanus was besieging Numantia, and he attracted the notice of his general by excelling the other young men in bravery, and by his very cheerful acceptance of the changed regimen which Scipio introduced into his army when it was spoiled by luxury and extravagance. It is said, too, that he encountered and laid low an enemy in the sight of his general. Therefore he was advanced by his commander to many honours; and once, when the talk after supper had to do with generals, and one of the company (either because he really wished to know or merely sought to please) asked Scipio where the Roman people would find any such chieftain and leader to follow him, Scipio, gently tapping Marius on the shoulder as he reclined next him, said: 'Here, perhaps.' So gifted by nature were both men; the one in showing himself great while still a young man, and the other in discerning the end from the beginning.

Life of Marius, Chapter 9
Marius Challenges the *Status Quo*

He [Marius] was triumphantly elected, and at once began to levy troops. Contrary to law and custom he enlisted many a poor and insignificant man, although former commanders had not accepted such persons, but bestowed arms, just as they would any other honour, only on those whose property assessment made them worthy to receive these, each soldier being supposed to put his substance in pledge to the state. It was not this, however, that brought most odium upon Marius, but the boldly insolent and arrogant speeches with which he vexed the nobles, crying out that he had carried off the consulship as spoil from the effeminacy of the rich and well-born, and that he had wounds upon his own person with which to vaunt himself before the people, not monuments of the dead nor likenesses of other men. Often, too, he would mention by name the generals in Africa who had been unsuccessful, now Bestia, and now Albinus, men of illustrious houses indeed, but unfortunate themselves, and unwarlike, who had met with disaster through lack of experience; and he would ask his audience if they did not think that the ancestors of these men would have much preferred to leave descendants like himself, since they themselves had been made illustrious, not by their noble birth, but by their valour and noble deeds. Such talk was not mere empty boasting, nor was his desire to make himself hated by the nobility without purpose; indeed, the people, who were delighted to have the senate insulted and always measured the greatness of a man's spirit by the boastfulness of his speech, encouraged him, and incited him not to spare men of high repute if he wished to please the multitude.

Life of Marius, Chapter 10
Enmity Between Marius and Sulla

When he [Marius] had crossed to Africa, Metellus, now become a victim of jealousy, and vexed because, after he had brought the war to an end and had nothing further to do except to seize the person of Jugurtha, Marius was coming to enjoy the crown and the triumph – a man whose ingratitude towards his benefactor had raised him to power – would not consent to meet him, but privately left the country while Rutilius, who had become his legate, handed over the army to Marius. And in the end a retribution fell upon Marius; for Sulla robbed him of the glory of his success, as Marius had robbed Metellus. How this came to pass, I will narrate briefly, since the details are given more at length in my *Life of Sulla*.

Bocchus, the king of the Barbarians in the interior, was a son-in law of Jugurtha, and apparently gave him little or no assistance in his war, alleging his faithlessness as an excuse, and fearing the growth of his power. But when Jugurtha in his flight and wandering felt compelled to make him his last hope and sought haven with him, Bocchus received him, more out of regard for his position as a suppliant than from goodwill and kept him in his hands. So far as his open acts were concerned, Bocchus entreated Marius on behalf of his father-in law, writing that he would not give him up and assuming a bold tone; but secretly he planned to betray him, and sent for Lucius [Cornelius] Sulla, who was quaestor for Marius and had been of some service to Bocchus during the campaign. But when Sulla had come to him in all confidence, the Barbarian experienced a change of heart and felt repentant, and for many days wavered in his plans, deliberating whether to surrender Jugurtha or to hold Sulla also a prisoner. Finally, however, he decided upon his first plan of treachery, and put Jugurtha alive into the hands of Sulla.

This was the first seed of that bitter and incurable hatred between Marius and Sulla, which nearly brought Rome to ruin. For many wished Sulla to have the glory of the affair because they hated Marius, and Sulla himself had a seal-ring made, which he used to wear, on which was engraved the surrender of Jugurtha to him by Bocchus. By constantly using this ring Sulla provoked Marius, who was an ambitious man, loath to share his glory with another, and quarrelsome. And the enemies of Marius gave Sulla most encouragement, by attributing the first and greatest successes of the war to Metellus, but the last, and the termination of it, to Sulla, so that the people might cease admiring Marius and giving him their chief allegiance.

Life of Sulla, Chapter 5
The Start of Sulla's Political Ambitions

Sulla now thought that the reputation which he had won in war was sufficient to justify political activities, and therefore at once exchanged military service for public life, offered himself as a candidate for the city praetorship, and was defeated. The responsibility for his defeat, however, he lays upon the populace. They knew, he says, about his friendship with Bocchus, and expected that if he should be made aedile before his praetorship, he would treat them to splendid hunting scenes and combats of Libyan wild beasts, and therefore appointed others to the praetorship, in order to force him into the aedileship.

But subsequent events would seem to show that Sulla does not confess the real reason for his failure. For, in the following year, he obtained the praetorship, partly because he was subservient to the people, and partly because he used money to win their support. And so it happened that, during his praetorship, when he angrily told Caesar [not the famous Julius Caesar] that he would use his own authority against him, Caesar laughed and said, 'You do well to consider the office your own, for you bought it!'

Life of Sulla, Chapter 6
Sulla's Good Luck

Moreover, Sulla's quarrel with Marius broke out afresh on being supplied with fresh material by the ambition of Bocchus, who, desiring to please the people at Rome, and at the same time to gratify Sulla, dedicated on the Capitol some images bearing trophies, and beside them gilded figures representing Jugurtha being surrendered by Bocchus to Sulla. Thereupon Marius was very angry, and tried to have the figures taken down, but others were minded to aid Sulla in opposing this, and the city was all but in flames with their dispute, when the Social War [91–87 BCE], which had long been smouldering, blazed up against the city and put a stop for the time being to the quarrel.

In this war, which proved of the greatest moment and most varied fortunes and brought innumerable mischiefs and the gravest perils upon the Romans, Marius was unable to render any great service, and proved that military excellence requires a man's highest strength and vigour. Sulla, on the other hand, did much that was memorable, and achieved the reputation of a great leader among his fellow citizens, that of the greatest of leaders among his friends, and that of the most fortunate even among his enemies.

But he did not feel about this as Timotheus the son of Conon did, who, when his adversaries ascribed his successes to Fortune, and had him represented in a painting as lying asleep, while Fortune cast her net about the cities, was rudely angry with those who had done this, because, as he thought, they were robbing him of the glory due to his exploits, and said to the people once, on returning from a campaign in which he was thought to have been successful, 'In this campaign, at least, men of Athens, Fortune has no share.' Upon Timotheus, then, who had shown himself so covetous of honour, the deity is said to have requited his youthful petulance, so from that time on he did nothing brilliant, but miscarried in all his undertakings, gave offence to the people, and was finally banished from the city; whereas Sulla not only accepted with pleasure such felicitations and admiration, but actually joined in magnifying the aid of Heaven in what he did, and gave the credit of it to Fortune, either out of boastfulness, or because he had such a belief in the divine agency. For in his *Memoirs* he writes that, of the undertakings which men thought well-advised, those upon which he had boldly ventured, not after deliberation, but on the spur of the moment, turned out for the better.

And further, from what he says about his being well endowed by nature for Fortune rather than for war, he seems to attribute more to Fortune than to his own excellence, and to make himself entirely the creature of this deity, since he accounts even his concord with Metellus, a man equal in rank, and a relative by marriage, a piece of divine felicity; for whereas he expected much annoyance from him as a colleague in office, he found him most obliging.

And still further, in the dedication of his *Memoirs* to Lucullus, he advises him to deem nothing so secure as what the divine power enjoins upon him in his dreams. And he relates that when he was dispatched with an army to the Social War, a great chasm in the earth opened near Laverna, from which a great quantity of fire burst forth and a bright flame towered up towards the heavens; whereupon the soothsayers declared that a brave man, of rare courage and surpassing appearance, was to take the government in hand and free the city from its present troubles. And Sulla says that he himself was this man, for his golden head of hair gave him a singular appearance, and as for bravery, he was not ashamed to testify in his own behalf, after such great and noble deeds as he had performed. So much, then, regarding his attitude towards the divine powers.

FROM CICERO'S SPEECH AGAINST VERRES

Cicero (Marcus Tullius Cicero, 106–43 BCE) was a statesman (consul in 63 BCE), lawyer, scholar, philosopher, and writer. He began his distinguished career as a court advocate. In 70 BCE, he spoke for the prosecution in the trial of Caius Verres, the infamous governor of Sicily, who had swindled and illegally tortured and executed Roman citizens.

Clauses 61–63
'I am a Roman Citizen!'

For why should I speak of Publius Gavius, a citizen of the municipality of Cosa, O judges? Or with what vigour of language, with what gravity of expression, with what grief of mind shall I mention him? But, indeed, that indignation fails me. I must take more care than usual that what I am going to say be worthy of my subject – worthy of the indignation which I feel. For the charge is of such a nature, that when I was first informed of it, I thought I should not avail myself of it. For although I knew that it was entirely true, still I thought that it would not appear credible. Being compelled by the tears of all the Roman citizens who are living as traders in Sicily, being influenced by the testimonies of the men of Valentia, most honourable men, and by those of all the Rhegians, and of many Roman *equites* ['knights'] who happened at that time to be at Messana, I produced at the previous pleading only just that amount of evidence which might prevent the matter from appearing doubtful to anyone. What shall I do now? When I have been speaking for so many hours of one class of offenses, and of that man's nefarious cruelty – when I have now expended nearly all my treasures of words of such a sort as are worthy of that man's wickedness on other matters, and have omitted to take precautions to keep your attention on the stretch by diversifying my accusations, how am I to deal with an affair of the importance that this is?

There is, I think, but one method, but one line open to me. I will place the matter plainly before you, which is of itself of such importance that there is no need of my eloquence – and eloquence, indeed, I have none, but there is no need of any one's eloquence to excite your feelings.

This Gavius whom I am speaking of, a citizen of Cosa, when he (among that vast number of Roman citizens who had been treated in the same way) had been thrown by Verres into prison, and somehow or other had escaped secretly out of the stone quarries, and had come to Messana, being now almost within sight of Italy and of the walls of Rhegium, and being revived, after that fear of death and that darkness, by the light, as it were, of liberty and of the fragrance of the laws, began to talk at Messana, and to complain that he, a Roman citizen, had been thrown into prison. He said that he was now going straight to Rome, and that he would meet Verres on his arrival there.

The miserable man was not aware that it made no difference whether he said this at Messana, or before the man's face in his own praetorian palace. For, as I have shown you before, that man had selected this city as the assistant in his crimes, the receiver of his thefts, the partner in all his wickedness. Accordingly, Gavius is at once brought before the Mamertine magistrates; and, as it happened, Verres came on that very day to Messana. The matter is brought before him. He is told that the man was a Roman citizen, who was complaining that at Syracuse he had been confined in the stone-quarries, and who, when he was actually embarking on board ship, and uttering violent threats against Verres, had been brought back by them, and reserved in order that he himself might decide what should be done with him. He thanks the men and praises their goodwill and diligence in his behalf. He himself, inflamed with wickedness and frenzy, comes into the forum. His eyes glared; cruelty was visible in his whole countenance. All men waited to see what steps he was going to take – what he was going to do; when all of a sudden he orders the man to be seized, and to be stripped and bound in the middle of the forum, and the rods to be got ready. The miserable man cried out that he was a Roman citizen, a citizen, also, of the municipal town of Cosa – that he had served with Lucius Pretius a most illustrious Roman knight, who was living as a trader at Panormus, and from whom Verres might know that he was speaking the truth. Then Verres says that he has ascertained that he had been sent into Sicily by the leaders of the runaway slaves, in order to act as a spy; a matter as to which there was no witness, no trace, nor even the slightest suspicion in the mind of anyone. Then he orders the man to be most violently scourged on all sides.

In the middle of the forum of Messana a Roman citizen, O judges, was beaten with rods; while in the meantime no groan was heard, no other expression was heard from that wretched man, amid all his pain, and between the sound of the blows, except these words: 'I am a citizen of Rome!' He fancied that by this one statement of his citizenship he could ward off all blows and remove all torture from his person. He not only did not succeed in averting by his entreaties the violence of the rods, but as he kept on repeating his entreaties and the assertion of his citizenship, a cross – a cross, I say! – was got ready for that miserable man, who had never witnessed such a stretch of power.

O the sweet name of Liberty! O the admirable privileges of our citizenship! O Porcian Law! O Sempronian Laws! O power of the tribunes, bitterly regretted by, and at last restored to the Roman people! Have all our rights fallen so far, that in a Province of the Roman People – in a town of our confederate allies – a Roman citizen should be bound in the forum, and beaten with rods by a man who only had the fasces and the axes through the kindness of the Roman people? What shall I say? When fire, and red-hot plates, and other instruments of torture were employed? If the bitter entreaties and the miserable cries of that man had no power to restrain you, were you not moved even by the weeping and loud groans of the Roman citizens who were present at that time? Did you dare to drag anyone, to the cross who said that he was a Roman citizen?

I was unwilling, O judges, to press this point so strongly at the former pleading; I was unwilling to do so. For you saw how the feelings of the multitude were excited against him with indignation, and hatred, and fear of their common danger. I, at that time, fixed a limit to my oration, and checked the eagerness of Caius Numitorius, a Roman knight, a man of the highest character, one of my witnesses. And I rejoiced that Glabrio had acted (and he had acted most wisely) as he did in dismissing that witness immediately, in the middle of the discussion. In fact, he was afraid that the Roman people might seem to have inflicted that punishment on Verres by tumultuary violence, which he was anxious he should only suffer according to the laws and by your judicial sentence.

Now since it is made clear beyond a doubt to everyone, in what state your case is, and what will become of you, I will deal thus with you: I will prove that that Gavius whom you all of a sudden assert to have been a spy, had been confined by you in the stone-quarries at Syracuse; and I will prove that, not only by the registers of the Syracusans – lest you should be able to say that, because there is a man named Gavius mentioned in those documents, I have invented this charge, and picked out this name so as to be able to say that this is the man – but in accordance with your own choice I will produce witnesses, who will state that that identical man was thrown by you into the stone-quarries at Syracuse. I will produce, also, citizens of Cosa, his fellow citizens and relations, who shall teach you (though it is too late), and who shall also teach the judges (for it is not too late for them to know them) that that Publius Gavius whom you crucified was a *Roman citizen*, and a citizen of the municipality of Cosa – not a spy of runaway slaves!

* * *

Cicero's impassioned speech convinced the judges. Found guilty, Verres was ordered to pay an indemnity. The Porcian Laws (*Leges Porciae*) Cicero referred to in his speech ended summary executions of Roman citizens living in the provinces and permitted guilty citizens to evade capital punishment through voluntary self-exile. Verres remained in exile until his death in 43 BCE.

FROM SUETONIUS'S *LIFE OF DIVINE JULIUS*

Suetonius (Caius Suetonius Tranquillus, *c.* 69–after *c.* 122 CE), was a personal secretary to Emperor Hadrian (r. 117–138 CE). He wrote *Lives of the Caesars*, a collection of biographies of the first 12 autocrats who ruled Rome, starting with Julius. Suetonius had special access to the public records archived in Rome. He was able to read works actually penned by Caesar himself, as well as other contemporary documents by other authors. From them, he composed a lively biographical account of the man. Though the first few chapters are missing, what remains tells us a great deal about Caesar's ancestry, his early life, his political and military achievements, as well as his appearance, foibles, peccadilloes, and his death.

Chapter 25
Campaigns in Gaul and Britain (58–50 BCE)

During the nine years of his command this is in substance what he did. All that part of Gaul which is bounded by the Pyrenees, the Alps and the Cévennes, and by the Rhine and Rhône rivers, a circuit of some 3,200 miles, with the exception of some allied states which had rendered him good service, he reduced to the form of a province; and imposed upon it a yearly tribute of 40,000,000 sesterces.

He was the first Roman to build a bridge and attack the Germans beyond the Rhine; and he inflicted heavy losses upon them. He invaded the Britons too, a people unknown before, vanquished them, and exacted moneys and hostages. Amid all these successes he met with adverse fortune but three times in all: in Britannia, where his fleet narrowly escaped destruction in a violent storm; in Gaul, when one of his legions was routed at Gergovia; and on the borders of Germania, when his lieutenants Titurius and Aurunculeius were ambushed and slain.

Chapter 56
Julius Caesar the Writer

He left memoirs too of his deeds in the Gallic War and in the Civil War with Pompeius; for the author of the Alexandrian, African, and Spanish Wars is unknown; some think it was

Oppius, others Hirtius, who also supplied the final book of the Gallic War, which Caesar left unwritten. With regard to Caesar's memoirs Cicero, also in the *Brutus*, speaks in the following terms: 'He wrote memoirs which deserve the highest praise; they are naked in their simplicity, straightforward yet graceful, stripped of all rhetorical adornment, as of a garment; but while his purpose was to supply material to others, on which those who wished to write history might draw, he haply gratified silly folk, who will try to use the curling-irons on his narrative, but he has kept men of any sense from touching the subject.' Of these same memoirs Hirtius uses this emphatic language: 'They are so highly rated in the judgment of all men, that he seems to have deprived writers of an opportunity, rather than given them one; yet our admiration for this feat is greater than that of others; for they know how well and faultlessly he wrote, while we know besides how easily and rapidly he finished his task.' Asinius Pollio thinks that they were put together somewhat carelessly and without strict regard for truth; since in many cases Caesar was too ready to believe the accounts which others gave of their actions, and gave a perverted account of his own, either designedly or perhaps from forgetfulness; and he thinks that he intended to rewrite and revise them.

He left besides a work in two volumes *On Analogy*, the same number of *Speeches Criticizing Cato*, in addition to a poem, entitled *The Journey*. He wrote the first of these works while crossing the Alps and returning to his army from Gallia Citerior, where he had held the assizes; the second about the time of the battle of Munda, and the third in the course of a 24 days' journey from Rome to Hispania Ulterior. Some letters of his to the senate are also preserved, and he seems to have been the first to reduce such documents to pages and the form of a notebook, whereas previously consuls and generals sent their reports written right across the sheet.

There are also letters of his to Cicero, as well as to his intimates on private affairs, and in the latter, if he had anything confidential to say, he wrote it in cipher, that is, by so changing the order of the letters of the alphabet, that not a word could be made out. If anyone wishes to decipher these, and get at their meaning, he must substitute the fourth letter of the alphabet, namely D, for A, and so with the others.

We also have mention of certain writings of his boyhood and early youth, such as the *Praises of Hercules*, a tragedy *Oedipus*, and a *Collected Sayings*; but Augustus forbade the publication of all these minor works in a very brief and frank letter sent to Pompeius Macer, whom he had selected to set his libraries in order.

Chapter 57
Julius Caesar the Military Genius

In the conduct of his campaigns it is a question whether he was more cautious or more daring, for he never led his army where ambuscades were possible without carefully reconnoitring the country, and he did not cross to Britannia without making personal inquiries about the harbours, the course, and the approach to the island. But on the other hand, when news came that his camp in Germania was beleaguered, he made his way to his men through the enemies' pickets, disguised as a Gaul. He crossed from Brundisium to Dyrrachium in winter time, running the blockade of the enemy's fleets; and when the troops which he had ordered to follow him delayed to do so, and he had sent to fetch them many times in vain, at last in secret and alone he boarded a small boat at night with his head muffled up; and he did not reveal who he was, or suffer the helmsman to give way to the gale blowing in their teeth, until he was all but overwhelmed by the waves.

Chapters 78–80
Julius Caesar was 'No King' (45–44 BCE)

But it was the following action in particular that roused deadly hatred against him. When the Senate approached him in a body with many highly honourary decrees, he received them before the temple of Venus Genetrix without rising. Some think that when he attempted to get up, he was held back by Cornelius Balbus; others, that he made no such move at all, but on the contrary frowned angrily on Caius Trebatius when he suggested that he should rise. And this action of his seemed the more intolerable, because when he himself in one of his triumphal processions rode past the benches of the tribunes, he was so incensed because a member of the college, Pontius Aquila, did not rise, that he cried: 'Come then, Aquila, take back the Republic from me, you tribune'; and for several days he would not make a promise to anyone without adding, 'That is, if Pontius Aquila will allow me.'

To an insult which so plainly showed his contempt for the Senate he added an act of even greater insolence; for at the Latin Festival [held in April on the Alban Mount], as he was returning to the city, amid the extravagant and unprecedented demonstrations of the populace, someone in the press placed on his statue a laurel wreath with a white fillet tied to it; and when Epidius Marullus and Caesetius Flavius, tribunes of the commons, gave orders that the ribbon be removed from the wreath and the man taken off to prison, Caesar sharply rebuked and deposed them, either offended that the hint at regal power had been received with so little favour, or, as he asserted, that he had been robbed of the glory of refusing it.

But from that time on he could not rid himself of the odium of having aspired to the title of monarch, although he replied to the commons, when they hailed him as king, 'I am Caesar and no king', and at the Lupercalia [held in February], when the consul [Marcus] Antonius several times attempted to place a crown upon his head as he spoke from the rostra, he put it aside and at last sent it to the Capitol, to be offered to Jupiter Optimus Maximus. Nay, more, the report had spread in various quarters that he intended to move to Ilium [Troy] or Alexandria, taking with him the resources of the state, draining Italy by levies, and leaving the charge of the city to his friends; also that at the next meeting of the Senate Lucius Cotta would announce as the decision of [the Commission of the] Fifteen that, inasmuch as it was written in the books of fate that the Parthians could be conquered only by a king, Caesar should be given that title.

It was this that led the conspirators to hasten in carrying out their designs in order to avoid giving their assent to this proposal.

Chapters 80–81
The Assassination of Julius Caesar
(15th March 44 BCE)

More than 60 joined the conspiracy against him [Julius Caesar], led by Caius Cassius, and Marcus and Decimus Brutus. At first, they hesitated whether to form two divisions at the elections in the *Campus Martius* [Field of Mars], so that while some hurled him from the bridges as he summoned the tribes to vote, the rest might wait below and slay him; or to set upon him in the Sacred Way or at the entrance to the theatre. When, however, a meeting of the Senate was called for the Ides of March in the Hall of Pompeius, they readily gave that time and place the preference.

Now, Caesar's approaching murder was foretold to him by unmistakable signs. A few months before, when the settlers assigned to the colony at Capua by the Julian Law were demolishing some tombs of great antiquity, to build country houses, and plied their work with the greater vigour because as they rummaged about they found a quantity of vases of ancient workmanship, there was discovered in a tomb, which was said to be that of Capys, the founder of Capua, a bronze tablet, inscribed with Greek words and characters to this purport: 'Whenever the bones of Capys shall be moved, it will come to pass that a son of Ilium shall be slain at the hands of his kindred, and presently avenged at heavy cost to Italy.' And let no one think this tale a myth or a lie, for it is vouched for by Cornelius Balbus, an intimate friend of Caesar. Shortly before his death, as he was told, the herds of horses which he had dedicated to the river Rubicon when he crossed it, and had let loose without a keeper, stubbornly refused to graze and wept copiously. Again, when he was offering sacrifice, the soothsayer Spurinna warned him to beware of danger, which would come not later than the Ides of March; and on the day before the Ides of that month a little bird called the king-bird flew into the Hall of Pompeius with a sprig of laurel, pursued by others of various kinds from the grove hard by, which tore it to pieces in the hall. In fact, the very night before his murder he dreamt now that he was flying above the clouds, and now that he was clasping the hand of Jupiter; and his wife Calpurnia thought that the pediment of their house fell, and that her husband was stabbed in her arms; and on a sudden the door of the room flew open of its own accord.

Both for these reasons and because of poor health he hesitated for a long time whether to stay at home and put off what he had planned to do in the senate; but at last, urged by Decimus Brutus not to disappoint the full meeting which had for some time been waiting for him, he went forth almost at the end of the fifth hour; and when a note revealing the plot was handed him by someone on the way, he put it with others which he held in his left hand, intending to read them presently. Then, after several victims had been slain, and he could not get favourable omens, he entered the House in defiance of portents, laughing at Spurinna and calling him a false prophet, because the Ides of March were come without bringing him harm; though Spurinna replied that they had of a truth come, but they had not gone.

As he took his seat, the conspirators gathered about him as if to pay their respects, and straightway Tillius Cimber, who had assumed the lead, came nearer as though to ask something;

and when Caesar with a gesture put him off to another time, Cimber caught his toga by both shoulders; then as Caesar cried, 'Why, this is violence!', one of the Cascas stabbed him from one side just below the throat. Caesar caught Casca's arm and ran it through with his *stylus* [writing pen], but as he tried to leap to his feet, he was stopped by another wound. When he saw that he was beset on every side by drawn daggers, he muffled his head in his robe, and at the same time drew down its lap to his feet with his left hand in order to fall more decently, with the lower part of his body also covered. And in this position he was stabbed with 23 wounds, uttering not a word, but merely a groan at the first stroke, though some have written that when Marcus Brutus rushed at him, he said in Greek: 'You too, my child?'

All the conspirators made off, and he lay there lifeless for some time, and finally three common slaves put him on a litter and carried him home, with one arm hanging down. And of so many wounds none turned out to be mortal, in the opinion of the physician Antistius, except the second one in the breast.

The conspirators had intended after slaying him to drag his body to the Tiber, confiscate his property, and revoke his decrees; but they forebore through fear of Marcus Antonius the consul, and Lepidus, the Master of Horse.

FROM CASSIUS DIO'S *ROMAN HISTORY*

Over **22 years**, Cassius Dio (Lucius Cassius Dio, *c.* 164–*c.* 229/235 CE) wrote *Roman History* spanning the millennium from the foundation of the city (753 BCE) to his own time (around 233 CE). Of the 80 volumes, about a third survive, but large parts of them are only known in Byzantine excerpts. The most complete texts cover the period 69 BCE–46 CE.

Book LIII, Chapter 11
Caesar's Heir Negotiates His Powers and Privileges with the Senate (13th January 27 BCE)

While Caesar [Julius Caesar's adopted son and heir] was reading this address, varied feelings took possession of the senators. A few of them knew his real intention and consequently kept applauding him enthusiastically; of the rest, some were suspicious of his words, while others believed them, and therefore both classes marvelled equally, the one at his cunning and the other at his decision, and both were displeased, the former at his scheming and the latter at his change of mind. For already there were some who abhorred the democratic constitution as a breeder of strife, were pleased at the change in government, and took delight in Caesar.

Consequently, though they were variously affected by his announcement, their views were the same. For, on the one hand, those who believed he had spoken the truth could not show their pleasure – those who wished to do so being restrained by their fear and the others by their hopes – and those, on the other hand, who did not believe it did not dare accuse him and expose his insincerity, some because they were afraid and others because they did not care to do so. Hence, all the doubters either were compelled to believe him or else pretended that they did. As for praising him, some had not the courage and others were unwilling; on the contrary, but while he was reading and afterwards, they kept shouting out, begging for a monarchical government and urging every argument in its favour, until they forced him as it was made to appear, to assume autocratic power.

His very first act was to secure a decree granting to the men who should compose his bodyguard [Praetorian Cohorts] double the pay that was given to the rest of the soldiers [of the legions], so that he might be strictly guarded. When this was done, he was eager to establish the monarchy in very truth.

Book LIII, Chapter 12
Division of the Roman Provinces

In this way he had his supremacy ratified by the senate and by the people as well. But as he wished even so to be thought democratic, while he accepted all the care and oversight of the public business, on the ground that it required some attention on his part, yet he declared he would not personally govern all the provinces, and that in the case of such provinces as he should govern he would not do so indefinitely; and he did, in fact, restore to the Senate the weaker provinces, on the ground that they were peaceful and free from war, while he retained the more powerful, alleging that they were insecure and precarious and either had enemies on their borders or were able on their own account to begin a serious revolt. His professed motive in this was that the Senate might fearlessly enjoy the finest portion of the empire, while he himself had the hardships and the dangers; but his real purpose was that by this arrangement the senators will be unarmed and unprepared for battle, while he alone had arms and maintained soldiers.

Africa, Numidia, Asia, Greece with Epirus, the Dalmatian and Macedonian districts, Sicily, Crete and the Cyrenaic portion of Libya, Bithynia with Pontus which adjoined it, Sardinia and Baetica were held to belong to the People and the Senate; while to Caesar belonged the remainder of Hispania – that is, the district of Tarraco and Lusitania – and all the Gauls – that is, Gallia Narbonensis, Gallia Lugdunensis, Aquitania, and Belgica, both the natives themselves and the aliens among them. For some of the Celts, whom we call Germans, had occupied all the Belgic territory along the Rhine and caused it to be called Germania, the upper portion extending to the sources of that river, and the lower portion reaching to the British Ocean. These provinces, then, together with Coele-Syria, as it is called, Phoenicia, Cilicia, Cyprus and Egypt, fell at that time to Caesar's share; for afterwards he gave Cyprus and Gallia Narbonensis back to the people, and for himself took Dalmatia instead.

This same course was followed subsequently in the case of other provinces also, as the progress of my narrative will show; but I have enumerated these provinces in this way because at the present time each one of them is governed separately, whereas in the beginning and for a long period thereafter they were administered two and three together. The others I have not mentioned because some of them were acquired later, and the rest, even if they were already subjugated, were not being governed by the Romans, but either had been left autonomous or had been attached to some kingdom or other. All of them which came into the Roman Empire after this period were added to the provinces of the one who was emperor at the time.

Book LIII, Chapter 13
Administration of the Provinces

Such, then, was the apportionment of the provinces. And wishing, even then, to lead the Romans a long way from the idea that he was at all monarchical in his purposes, Caesar undertook for only 10 years the government of the provinces assigned him; for he promised to reduce them to order within this period, and boastfully added that, if they should be pacified sooner, he would the sooner restore them, to the senate. Thereupon he first appointed the senators themselves to govern both classes of provinces, except Egypt. This province alone he assigned to a knight [Cornelius Gallus].

Next, he ordained that the governors of senatorial provinces should be annual magistrates, chosen by lot, except when a senator enjoyed a special privilege because of the large number of his children or because of his marriage. These governors were to be sent out by vote of the senate in public meeting; they were to carry no sword at their belt nor to wear military uniform; the name of proconsul was to belong not only to the two ex-consuls but also to the others who had merely served as praetors or who held at least the rank of ex-praetors; both classes were to employ as many lictors as were usual in the capital; and they were to assume the insignia of their office immediately upon leaving the *pomerium* [sacred boundary of the city] and were to wear them constantly until they returned.

The other governors, on the other hand, were to be chosen by the emperor himself and were to be called his envoys and propraetors, even if the men selected were ex-consuls. Thus, of these two titles which had been in vogue so long under the republic, he gave that of praetor to the men chosen by him, on the ground that from very early times it had been associated with warfare, calling them propraetors; and he gave the name of consul to the others, on the ground that their duties were more peaceful, styling them proconsuls. For he reserved the full titles of consul and praetor for Italy and designated all the governors outside of Italy as acting in their stead. So, then, he caused the appointed governors to be known as propraetors and to hold office for as much longer than a year as should please him; he made them wear the military uniform, and a sword, with which they are permitted to execute even soldiers. For no one else, whether proconsul, propraetor, or procurator, has been given the privilege of wearing a sword without also having been accorded the right to put a soldier to death; indeed, this right has been granted, not only to the senators, but also to the knights who are entitled to wear a sword. So much for this.

All the propraetors alike employ five lictors, and, indeed, all of them except those who were ex-consuls at the time of appointment to governorships receive their title from this very number. Both classes alike assume the decorations of their position of authority when they enter their appointed province and lay them aside immediately upon completing their term of office.

Book LIII, Chapter 14
Assigning Governors to the Provinces of the Senate and People

It was thus, and on these conditions, that the custom was established of sending out ex-praetors and ex-consuls respectively as governors of the two classes of provinces.

In the one case, the emperor would commission a governor to any province he wished and when he wished, and many secured provincial commands while still praetors or consuls, as sometimes happens even at the present day.

In the case of the Senatorial Provinces, he assigned Asia and Africa on his own responsibility to the ex-consuls, and all the other provinces to the ex-praetors; but by public decree, applicable to all the senatorial governors, he forbade the allotment of any senator to a governorship before the expiration of five years from the time he had held office in the city. For a time all who fulfilled these requirements, even if they exceeded the number of the provinces, were allotted to governorships; but later, inasmuch as some of them did not govern well, the appointment of these officials, too, was put in the emperor's hands. And thus, it is, in a manner of speaking, the emperor who assigns these governors also to their commands; for he always orders the allotment of precisely the number of governors that there are provinces, and orders to be drawn whomsoever he pleases. Some emperors have sent men of their own choosing to these provinces also and have allowed certain of them to hold office for more than a year; and some have assigned certain provinces to knights instead of to senators.

These were the principles established at that time in regard to the particular class of senators who had the right to inflict the death penalty upon their subjects in the provinces. For it should be stated that there is a class who have not this right – those, namely, who are sent to the provinces styled the 'Provinces of the Senate and People' – I mean those who serve either as quaestors, being designated by lot to this office, or as assessors to those who hold the actual authority. For this would be the correct way for me to style these officials, having regard not to their name, but to their duties as just described, although others in Hellenizing their title call these also 'envoys'. Concerning this title, however enough has been said in what precedes. As to assessors in general, each governor chooses his own, the ex-praetors selecting one from their peers or even from their inferiors, and the ex-consuls three from among those of equal rank, subject to the emperor's approval. For, although a certain change was made in regard to these men also, yet it soon lapsed, and it will be sufficient to mention it at the proper time.

Book LIII, Chapter 15
Assigning Governors and Tax Officers to the Imperial Provinces

This is the system followed in the case of the Provinces of the People. To the others, which are called the 'Imperial Provinces' and have more than one citizen-legion, are sent officials who are to govern them as legates; these are appointed by the emperor himself, generally from the ex-praetors, though also from the ex-quaestors, or men who have held an office between the praetorship and the quaestorship. These positions, then, appertain to the senators.

Passing now to the equestrians ['knights'], the emperor himself selects equestrians to be sent out as military tribunes (both those who are prospective senators and the others; concerning their difference in rank I have already spoken), dispatching some of them to take command of the garrisons of purely citizen-legions, and others of the foreign legions as well. In this matter he follows the custom then instituted by Caesar.

The procurators (for this is the name we give to the men who collect the public revenues and make disbursement according to the instructions given them) he sends out to all the provinces alike, to those of the people as well as to his own, and to this office knights are sometimes appointed and sometimes even freedmen; but the proconsuls may exact the tribute from the people they govern. The emperor gives instructions to the procurators, the proconsuls, and the propraetors, in order that they may be under definite orders when they go out to their provinces. For both this practice and the giving of salaries to them and to the other officials was established at this time. In former times, of course, certain persons had made a business of furnishing the officials with all they needed for the conduct of their office, drawing upon the treasury for the money; but under Caesar these officials now for the first time began to receive a fixed salary. This was not assigned to them all on the same basis, but approximately as their needs required; and the procurators, indeed, get the very title of their rank from the amount of the salaries assigned to them.

The following regulations were laid down for them all alike: they were not to raise levies of soldiers or to exact money beyond the amount appointed, unless the senate should so vote or the emperor so order; and when their successors arrived, they were to leave the province at once, and not to delay on the return journey, but to get back within three months.

Book LIII, Chapter 16
Caesar's Heir Declared 'Augustus'

These regulations were established at that time, to speak generally; for in reality Caesar himself was destined to have absolute control of all matters for all time, because he was not only master of the funds (nominally, to be sure, he had separated the public funds from his own, but as a matter of fact, he always spent the former also as he saw fit), but also commanded the soldiers.

At all events, when his 10-year period came to an end [19 BCE], there was voted to him another five years, then five more, after that ten, and again another ten, and then 10 for the fifth time, so that by the succession of 10-year periods he continued to be sole ruler for life. And it is for this reason that the subsequent emperors, though no longer appointed for a specified period, but for their whole life once for all, nevertheless always held a celebration every 10 years, as if then renewing their sovereignty once more; and this is done even at the present day.

Now Caesar had received many privileges and honours even previously, when the question of declining the sovereignty and that of apportioning the provinces were under discussion. For the right to place the laurel trees in front of the royal residence and to hang the crown of oak above them was then voted him to symbolize that he was always victor over his enemies and the saviour of the citizens. The royal residence is called *Palatium*, not because it was ever decreed that this should be its name, but because Caesar dwelt on the Palatine Hill and had his military headquarters there, though his residence gained a certain degree of fame from the mount as a whole also, because Romulus had once lived there. Hence, even if the emperor resides somewhere else, his dwelling retains the name of *Palatium*.

And when Caesar had actually carried out his promises, the name *Augustus* was at length bestowed upon him by the Senate and by the People or when they wished to call him by some distinctive title, and men were proposing one title and another and urging its selection, Caesar was exceedingly desirous of being called *Romulus*, but when he perceived that this caused him to be suspected of desiring the kingship, he desisted from his efforts to obtain it, and took the title of *Augustus*, signifying that he was more than human; for all the most precious and sacred objects are termed *augusta*. Therefore, they addressed him also in Greek as *Sebastos*, meaning an *august* personage, from the passive of the verb *sebazo*, 'to revere'.

Book LV, Chapter 23–24
Augustus Establishes the Professional Roman Army and Refines Terms and Conditions of Service

The soldiers were sorely displeased at the paltry character of the rewards given them for the wars which had been waged at this time and none of them consented to bear arms for longer than the regular period of his service. It was therefore voted that 20,000 sesterces should be given to members of the Pretorian Cohorts when they had served 16 years, and 12,000 to the other soldiers when they had served 20 years.

Twenty-three, or, as others say, 25, legions of citizen soldiers were being supported at this time [14 CE]. At present [233 CE] only 19 of them still exist, as follows: the Second (*Augusta*), with its winter quarters in Britannia Superior; the three Thirds – the *Gallica* in Phoenicia, the *Cyrenaica* in Arabia, and the *Augusta* in Numidia; the Fourth (*Scythica*) in Syria; the Fifth (*Macedonica*) in Dacia; the two Sixths, of which the one (*Victrix*) is stationed in Britannia Inferior, the other (*Ferrata*) in Judaea; the Seventh (generally called *Claudia*) in Moesia Superior; the Eighth (*Augusta*) in Germania Superior; the two Tenths in Pannonia Superior (*Gemina*) and in Judaea; the Eleventh (*Claudia*) in Moesia Inferior (for two legions were thus named after Claudius because they had not fought against him in the rebellion of Camillus); the Twelfth (*Fulminata*) in Cappadocia; the Thirteenth (*Gemina*) in Dacia; the Fourteenth (*Gemina*) in Pannonia Superior; the Fifteenth (Apollinaris) in Cappadocia; 6 the Twentieth (called both *Valeria* and *Victrix*) in Britannia Superior. These latter, I believe, were the troops which Augustus took over and retained, along with those called the Twenty-second who are quartered in Germania – and this in spite of the fact that they were by no means called Valerians by all and do not use that name any longer. These are the legions that still remain out of those of Augustus; of the rest, some were disbanded altogether, and others were merged with various legions by Augustus himself and by other emperors, in consequence of which such legions have come to bear the name *Gemina*.

Now that I have once been led into giving an account of the legions, I shall speak of the other legions also which exist today [233 CE] and tell of their enlistment by the emperors subsequent to Augustus, my purpose being that, if anyone desires to learn about them, the statement of all the facts in a single portion of my book may provide him easily with the information. Nero organized the First Legion, called the *Italica*, which has its winter quarters in Moesia Inferior; Galba the First (*Adiutrix*), with quarters in Pannonia Inferior, and the Seventh (*Gemina*), in Spain; Vespasian the Second (*Adiutrix*), in Pannonia Inferior, the Fourth (*Flavia*), in Moesia Superior, and the Sixteenth (*Flavia*), in Syria; Domitian the First (Minervia), in Germany Inferior; Trajan the Second (*Aegyptia*) and the Thirtieth (*Germanica*), both of which he also named after himself; Marcus Antoninus [r. 138–161 CE] the Second, in Noricum, and the Third, in Rhaetia, both of which are called *Italica*; and Severus [r. 193–211 CE] the *Parthicae* – the First and Third, quartered in Mesopotamia, and the Second, quartered in Italy. This is at present the number of the legions of regularly enrolled troops, exclusive of the Urban Cohorts and the Praetorian Cohorts; but at that time, in the days of Augustus, those I have mentioned were being maintained, whether the number is 23 or 25, and there were also allied forces of infantry, cavalry, and sailors, whatever their numbers may have been (for I cannot state the exact figures).

Then there were the bodyguards, 10,000 in number and organized in 10 cohorts ['divisions'], and the Watchmen of the city, 6,000 in number and organized in four cohorts; and there were also picked foreign horsemen, who were given the name of Batavians, after the island of Batavia in the Rhine, inasmuch as the Batavians are excellent horsemen. I cannot, however, give their exact number any more than I can that of the *Evocati* ['recalled']. These last-named Augustus began to make a practice of employing from the time when he called again into service against [Marcus] Antonius the troops who had served with his father [Julius Caesar], and he maintained them afterwards; they constitute even now a special corps, and carry rods, like the centurions.

Now Augustus lacked funds for all these troops, and therefore he introduced a proposal in the senate that revenues in sufficient amount and continuing from year to year should be set aside, in order that the soldiers might receive without stint from the taxes levied their maintenance and bonuses without any outside source being put to annoyance. The means for such a fund were accordingly sought. Now when no one showed a willingness to become aedile, some men from the ranks of the ex-quaestors and ex-tribunes were compelled by lot to take the office – a thing which happened on many other occasions.

Book LV, Chapter 25
Augustus Puts Funding for the Roman Army on a Firmer Footing

After this, in the consulship of Aemilius Lepidus and Lucius Arruntius [6 CE], when no revenues for the military fund were being discovered that suited anybody, but absolutely everybody was vexed because such an attempt was even being made, Augustus in the name of himself and of Tiberius placed money in the treasury which he called the Military Treasury, and commanded that three of the ex-praetors, to be chosen by lot, should administer it for three years, employing two lictors apiece and such further assistance as was fitting. This method was followed with the successive incumbents of the office for many years; but at present they are chosen by the emperor and they go about without lictors. Now Augustus made contribution himself toward the fund and promised to do so annually, and he also accepted voluntary contributions from kings and certain communities; but he took nothing from private citizens, although a considerable number made offers of their own free will, as they at least alleged. But as all this proved very slight in comparison with the amount being spent and there was need of some permanent supply, he ordered each one of the senators to seek out sources of revenue, each independently of the others, to write them in books, and give them to him to consider. This was not because he had no plan of his own, but as the most certain means of persuading them to choose the plan he preferred.

At all events, when different men had proposed different schemes, he approved none of them, but established the tax of five per cent on the inheritances and bequests which should be left by people at their death to any except very near relatives or very poor persons, representing that he had found this tax set down in Caesar's memoranda. It was, in fact, a method which had been introduced once before, but had been abolished later, and was now revived. In this way, then, he increased the revenues; as for the expenditures, he employed three ex-consuls, chosen by lot, by whose help he reduced some of them and altogether abolished others.

FROM VEGETIUS'S *ON MILITARY MATTERS*

ow the Roman army became the ancient world's most formidable fighting force was the subject of a treatise by

Vegetius (Publius – or Flavius – Renatus Vegetius). Living in the late fourth century CE, when Rome's fortunes were very different, Vegetius studied earlier historical accounts for answers. He found them in the writings of Cato the Elder, Cornelius Celsus, Terruntenus Paternus, and Julius Frontinus, and the ordinances and regulations of emperors Augustus, Trajan, and Hadrian. The treatise was addressed to Emperor Valentinian II (r. 375–392 CE).

Book I, Preface
Looking to the Past

My design in this treatise is to exhibit in some order the peculiar customs and usages of the ancients in the choice and discipline of their new levies.

Book I, Chapter 1
Practice and Discipline, The Sources of Roman Military Greatness

Victory in war does not depend entirely upon numbers or mere courage; only skill and discipline will insure it. We find that the Romans owed the conquest of the world to no other cause than continual military training, exact observance of discipline in their camps, and unwearied cultivation of the other arts of war. Without these, what chance would the inconsiderable numbers of the Roman armies have had against the multitudes of the Gauls? Or with what success would their small size have been opposed to the prodigious stature of the Germans? The Iberians surpassed us not only in numbers, but in physical strength. We were always inferior to the Africans in wealth and unequal to them in deception and stratagem. And the Greeks, indisputably, were far superior to us in skill in arts and all kinds of knowledge.

But to all these advantages the Romans opposed unusual care in the choice of their levies and in their military training. They thoroughly understood the importance of hardening them by continual practice, and of training them to every maneuver that might happen in the line and in action. Nor were they less strict in punishing idleness and sloth. The courage of a soldier is heightened by his knowledge of his profession, and he only wants an opportunity to execute what he is convinced he has been perfectly taught. A handful of men, inured to war, proceed to certain victory, while on the contrary numerous armies of raw and undisciplined troops are but multitudes of men dragged to slaughter.

Book I, Chapter 3
The Selection of Recruits

We shall next examine whether the city or the country produces the best and most capable soldiers. No one, I imagine, can doubt that the peasants are the most fit to carry arms for they from their infancy have been exposed to all kinds of weather and have been brought up to the hardest labour. They are able to endure the greatest heat of the sun, are unacquainted with the use of baths, and are strangers to the other luxuries of life. They are simple, content with little, inured to all kinds of fatigue, and prepared in some measure for a military life by their continual employment in their country-work, in handling the spade, digging trenches and carrying burdens. In cases of necessity, however, they are sometimes obliged to make levies in the cities. And these men, as soon as enlisted, should be taught to work on entrenchments, to march in ranks, to carry heavy burdens, and to bear the sun and dust. Their meals should be coarse and moderate; they should be accustomed to lie sometimes in the open air and sometimes in tents. After this, they should be instructed in the use of their arms. And if any long expedition is planned, they should be encamped as far as possible from the temptations of the city. By these precautions their minds, as well as their bodies, will properly be prepared for the service.

Book I, Chapter 9
Initial Training of Recruits

The first thing the soldiers are to be taught is the military step, which can only be acquired by constant practice of marching quick and together. Nor is anything of more consequence either on the march or in the line than that they should keep their ranks with the greatest exactness. For troops who march in an irregular and disorderly manner are always in great danger of being defeated. They should march with the common military step 20 miles in five summer-hours, and with the full step, which is quicker, 24 miles in the same number of hours. If they exceed this pace, they no longer march but run, and no certain rate can be assigned.

But the young recruits, in particular, must be exercised in running, in order to charge the enemy with great vigour; occupy, on occasion, an advantageous post with greater expedition, and prevent the enemy in their designs upon the same; that they may, when sent to reconnoiter, advance with speed, return with greater celerity and more easily come up with the enemy in a pursuit.

Leaping is another very necessary exercise, to enable them to pass ditches or embarrassing eminences of any kind without trouble or difficulty. There is also another very material advantage to be derived from these exercises in time of action; for a soldier who advances with his javelin, running and leaping, dazzles the eyes of his adversary, strikes him with terror, and gives him the fatal stroke before he has time to put himself on his defence. Sallust, speaking of the excellence of Cnaeus Pompeius Magnus in these particulars, tells us that he disputed the superiority in leaping with the most active, in running with the most swift, and in exercises of strength with the most robust. Nor would he ever have been able to have opposed Sertorius with success, if he had not prepared both himself and his soldiers for action by continual exercises of this sort.

Book I, Chapter 11
Training Recruits with Wicker Shields and Posts

We are informed by the writings of the ancients that, among their other exercises, they had that of the post. They gave their recruits round bucklers woven with willows, twice as heavy as those used on real service, and wooden swords double the weight of the common ones. They exercised them with these at the post both morning and afternoon.

This is an invention of the greatest use, not only to soldiers, but also to gladiators. No man of either profession ever distinguished himself in the circus or field of battle, who was not perfect in this kind of exercise. Every soldier, therefore, fixed a post firmly in the ground, about the height of six feet. Against this, as against a real enemy, the recruit was exercised with the above-mentioned arms, as it were with the common shield and sword, sometimes aiming at the head or face, sometimes at the sides, at others endeavouring to strike at the thighs or legs. He was instructed in what manner to advance and retire, and in short how to take every advantage of his adversary; but was thus above all particularly cautioned not to lay himself open to his antagonist while aiming his stroke at him.

Book I, Chapter 12
Training Recruits in the Use of the Sword

They were likewise taught not to cut but to thrust with their swords. For the Romans not only made a jest of those who fought with the edge of that weapon, but always found them an easy conquest. A stroke with the edges, though made with ever so much force, seldom kills, as the vital parts of the body are defended both by the bones and armour. On the contrary, a stab, though it penetrates but two inches, is generally fatal. Besides in the attitude of striking, it is impossible to avoid exposing the right arm and side; but on the other hand, the body is covered while a thrust is given, and the adversary receives the point before he sees the sword. This was the method of fighting principally used by the Romans, and their reason for exercising recruits with arms of such a weight at first was, that when they came to carry the common ones so much lighter, the greater difference might enable them to act with greater security and alacrity in time of action.

FROM EMPEROR AUGUSTUS'S *DEEDS DONE*

Before he died on 19th August 14 CE, Emperor Caesar Augustus wrote the *Res Gestae* or 'Deeds Done', an account of his military and political achievements. He lived 75 years and had led the Roman People for 44 of them, transforming how the *Res Rublica* was ruled ever after.

Part I, Chapters 1–4

The acts of the Deified Augustus by which he placed the whole world under the sovereignty of the Roman People, and of the amounts which he expended upon the state and the Roman people, as engraved upon two bronze columns which have been set up in Rome.

At the age of 19 [44 BCE], on my own initiative and at my own expense, I raised an army by means of which I restored liberty to the *Res Publica*, which had been oppressed by the tyranny of a faction. For which service the senate, with complimentary resolutions, enrolled me in its order, in the consulship of Caius Pansa and Aulus Hirtius [43 BCE], giving me at the same time consular precedence in voting; it also gave me the *imperium*. As propraetor it ordered me, along with the consuls, 'to see that the republic suffered no harm'. In the same year, moreover, as both consuls had fallen in war, the people elected me consul and a triumvir [member of a Commission of three] for settling the constitution.

Those who slew my father I drove into exile, punishing their deed by due process of law, and afterwards when they waged war upon the *Res Publica* I twice defeated them in battle [at Philippi in 42 BCE].

Wars, both civil and foreign, I undertook throughout the world, on sea and land, and when victorious I spared all citizens who sued for pardon. The foreign nations which could with safety be pardoned I preferred to save rather than to destroy. The number of Roman citizens who bound themselves to me by military oath was about 500,000. Of these I settled in colonies or sent back into their own towns, after their term of service, something more than 300,000, and to all I assigned lands, or gave money as a reward for military service. I captured 600 ships, over and above those which were smaller than triremes.

Twice I triumphed with an ovation [40 and 36 BCE], three times I celebrated curule triumphs [29 BCE] and was saluted as *imperator* ['commander'] 21 times. Although the Senate decreed me additional triumphs, I set them aside. When I had performed the vows, which I had undertaken in each war, I deposited upon the Capitol the laurels which adorned my *fasces*. For successful operations on land and sea, conducted either by myself or by my deputies under my auspices, the Senate on 55 occasions decreed that thanks should be rendered to the immortal gods. The days on which such thanks were rendered by Decree of the Senate numbered 890. In my triumphs there were led before my chariot nine kings or children of kings. At the time of writing these words I had been 13 times consul [2 BCE] and was in the thirty-seventh year of my tribunician power [14 CE].

FROM TACITUS'S *ANNALS*

The *Annals of Tacitus* (Publius Cornelius Tacitus, *c.* 56–*c.* 120 CE) is a history of the Roman Empire from the death of Augustus (14 CE) to the end of the reign of Nero (68 CE). His focus was the changing balance of power between the Senate and the emperors, and how the governing classes were corrupted as they adapted to the growing wealth and power of their empire.

Book I, Chapters 1–3
Rome before Augustus. His Attempts at
Securing Power

Rome at the beginning was ruled by kings [753–509 BCE]. Freedom and the consulship were established by Lucius Brutus. Dictatorships were held for a temporary crisis. The power of the decemvirs did not last beyond two years, nor was the consular jurisdiction of the military tribunes of long duration. The despotisms of Cinna [87–82 BCE] and Sulla [82/81–80 BCE] were brief; the rule of Pompeius and of Crassus [60/59–53/52 BCE] soon yielded before Caesar; the arms of Lepidus and Antonius [43–32 BCE] before Augustus; who, when the world was wearied by civil strife, subjected it to empire under the title of *Princeps* ['First Man']. But the successes and reverses of the old Roman People have been recorded by famous historians; and fine intellects were not wanting to describe the times of Augustus, till growing sycophancy scared them away. The histories of Tiberius, Caius [Caligula], Claudius, and Nero, while they were in power [14–68 CE], were falsified through terror, and after their death were written under the irritation of a recent hatred. Hence my purpose is to relate a few facts about Augustus – more particularly his last acts, then the reign of Tiberius [14–37 CE], and all which follows, without either bitterness or partiality, from any motives to which I am far removed.

When after the destruction of Brutus and Cassius [42 BCE] there was no longer any army of the Commonwealth, when [Sextus] Pompeius was crushed in Sicily [36 BCE], and when, with Lepidus pushed aside [36 BCE] and Antonius slain [30 BCE], even the Julian faction had only Caesar left to lead it, then, dropping the title of triumvir, and giving out that he was a Consul, and was satisfied with a tribune's authority for the protection of the people, Augustus won over the soldiers with gifts, the populace with cheap corn, and all men with the sweets of repose, and so grew greater by degrees, while he concentrated in himself the functions of the Senate, the magistrates, and the laws. He was wholly unopposed, for the boldest spirits had fallen in battle, or in the proscription, while the remaining nobles, the readier they were to be slaves, were raised the higher by wealth and promotion, so that, aggrandized by revolution, they preferred the safety of the present to the dangerous past. Nor did the provinces dislike that condition of affairs, for they distrusted the government of the Senate and the people, because of the rivalries between the leading men and the rapacity of the officials, while the protection of the laws was unavailing, as they were continually deranged by violence, intrigue, and finally by corruption.

Augustus, meanwhile, as supports to his despotism, raised to the pontificate and curule aedileship Claudius Marcellus

[23 BCE], his sister's son, while a mere stripling, and Marcus Agrippa, of humble birth, a good soldier, and one who had shared his victory, to two consecutive consulships [28 and 27 BCE], and as Marcellus soon afterwards died [23 BCE], he also accepted him as his son-in-law. Tiberius [Claudius] Nero and [Nero] Claudius Drusus, his stepsons, he honoured with imperial titles, although his own family was as yet undiminished. For he had admitted the children of Agrippa, Caius and Lucius, into the House of the Caesars [17 BCE]; and before they had yet laid aside the dress of boyhood, he had most fervently desired, with an outward show of reluctance, that they should be entitled *Principes Iuventutis* ['Leaders of the Youth'] and be consuls-elect. When Agrippa died [12 BCE], and Lucius Caesar as he was on his way to our armies in Hispania [2 CE], and Caius while returning from Armenia [4 CE], still suffering from a wound, were prematurely cut off by destiny, or by their stepmother Livia's treachery, Drusus too having long been dead [9 BE], [Tiberius Claudius] Nero remained alone of the stepsons, and in him everything tended to centre. He was adopted as a son [4 CE], as a colleague in empire and a partner in the tribunitian power, and paraded through all the armies, no longer through his mother's secret intrigues, but at her open suggestion. For she had gained such a hold on the aged Augustus that he drove out as an exile into the Island of Planasia, his only grandson, Agrippa Postumus [9 CE], who, though devoid of worthy qualities, and having only the brute courage of physical strength, had not been convicted of any gross offence. And yet Augustus had appointed Germanicus, [Nero Claudius] Drusus's offspring, to the command of eight legions on the Rhine [13 CE] and required Tiberius to adopt him [4 CE], although Tiberius had a son [Drusus Julius Caesar], now a young man, in his house; but he did it that he might have several safeguards to rest on. He had no war at the time on his hands except against the Germans, which was rather to wipe out the disgrace of the loss of Quintilius Varus and his army [9 CE] than out of an ambition to extend the empire, or for any adequate recompense. At home all was tranquil, and there were magistrates with the same titles; there was a younger generation, sprung up since the victory of Actium [2 September 31 BCE], and even many of the older men had been born during the civil wars. How few were left who had seen the Republic!

Book IV, Chapter 5
Disposition of the Roman Army Under Tiberius Caesar (24 CE)

Italy on both seas was guarded by fleets, at Misenum and at Ravenna, and the contiguous coast of Gaul by ships of war captured in the victory of Actium and sent by Augustus powerfully manned to the town of Forojulium. But our chief strength was on the Rhine, as a defence alike against Germans and Gauls, and numbered eight legions. Hispania, lately subjugated, was held by three. Mauretania was King Juba's, who had received it as a gift from the Roman people. The rest of Africa was garrisoned by two legions, and Egypt by the same number. Next, beginning with Syria, all within the entire tract of country stretching as far as the Euphrates, was kept in restraint by four legions, and on the frontier were Iberian, Albanian, and other kings, to whom our greatness was a protection against any foreign power. Thrace was held by Rhoemetalces and the children of Cotys; the bank of the Danube by two legions in Pannonia, two in Moesia, and two also were stationed in Dalmatia, which, from the situation of the country, were in the rear of the other four and, should Italy suddenly require aid, not too distant to be summoned.

But the capital was garrisoned by its own special soldiery – three Urban, nine Praetorian Cohorts – levied for the most part in Etruria and Umbria, or ancient Latium and the old Roman colonies. There were besides, in commanding positions in the provinces, allied fleets, cavalry and light infantry, of but little inferior strength; but any detailed account of them would be misleading, since they moved from place to place as circumstances required, and had their numbers increased and sometimes diminished.

Book IV, Chapter 6
Administration of the Empire Under Tiberius Caesar (14–37 CE)

It is, however, I think, a convenient opportunity for me to review the hitherto prevailing methods of administration in the other departments of the State, inasmuch as that year brought with it the beginning of a change for the worse in Tiberius's policy. In the first place, public business and the most important private matters were managed by the Senate: the leading men were allowed freedom of discussion, and when they stooped to flattery, the emperor himself checked them. He bestowed honours with regard to noble ancestry, military renown, or brilliant accomplishments as a civilian, letting it be clearly seen that there were no better men to choose. The consul and the praetor retained their prestige; inferior magistrates exercised their authority; the laws too, with the single exception of cases of treason, were properly enforced.

As to the duties on corn, the indirect taxes and other branches of the public revenue, they were in the hands of companies of Roman knights. The emperor entrusted his own property to men of the most tried integrity or to persons known only by their general reputation, and once appointed they were retained without any limitation, so that most of them grew old in the same employments. The city populace indeed suffered much from high prices, but this was no fault of the emperor, who actually endeavoured to counteract barren soils and stormy seas with every resource of wealth and foresight. And he was also careful not to distress the provinces by new burdens, and to see that in bearing the old they were safe from any rapacity or oppression on the part of governors. Corporal punishments and confiscations of property were unknown.

Book XV, Chapter 38
Fire Breaks Out in Rome Under Nero
(19th–28th July 64 CE)

A disaster followed, whether accidental or treacherously contrived by the emperor, is uncertain, as authors have given both accounts, worse, however, and more dreadful than any which have ever happened to this city by the violence of fire. It had its beginning in that part of the circus which adjoins the Palatine and Caelian Hills, where, amid the shops containing inflammable wares, the conflagration both broke out and instantly became so fierce and so rapid from the wind that it seized in its grasp the entire length of the circus. For here there were no houses fenced in by solid masonry, or temples surrounded by walls, or any other obstacle to interpose delay.

The blaze in its fury ran first through the level portions of the city, then rising to the hills, while it again devastated every place below them, it outstripped all preventive measures; so rapid was the mischief and so completely at its mercy the city, with those narrow winding passages and irregular streets, which characterized old Rome. Added to this were the wailings of terror-stricken women, the feebleness of age, the helpless inexperience of childhood, the crowds who sought to save themselves or others, dragging out the infirm or waiting for them, and by their hurry in the one case, by their delay in the other, aggravating the confusion.

Often, while they looked behind them, they were intercepted by flames on their side or in their face. Or if they reached a refuge close at hand, when this too was seized by the fire, they found that, even places, which they had imagined to be remote, were involved in the same calamity. At last, doubting what they should avoid or whither betake themselves, they crowded the streets or flung themselves down in the fields, while some who had lost their all, even their very daily bread, and others out of love for their kinsfolk, whom they had been unable to rescue, perished, though escape was open to them. And no one dared to stop the mischief, because of incessant menaces from a number of persons who forbade the extinguishing of the flames, because again others openly hurled brands, and kept shouting that there was one who gave them authority, either seeking to plunder more freely, or obeying orders.

Book XV, Chapter 39
Nero Assists in Rescue Efforts

Nero at this time was at Antium and did not return to Rome until the fire approached his house, which he had built to connect the palace with the Gardens of Maecenas. It could not, however, be stopped from devouring the palace, the house, and everything around it. However, to relieve the people, driven out homeless as they were, he threw open to them the *Campus Martius* and the public buildings of [Marcus] Agrippa, and even his own gardens, and raised temporary structures to receive the destitute multitude. Supplies of food were brought up from Ostia and the neighbouring towns, and the price of corn was reduced to three sesterces a peck. These acts, though popular, produced no effect, since a rumour had gone forth everywhere that, at the very time when the city was in flames, the emperor appeared on a private stage and sang of the destruction of Troy, comparing present misfortunes with the calamities of antiquity.

Book XV, Chapter 40
Nero Plans to Build a New Rome Out of the Ashes of the Old

At last, after five days, an end was put to the conflagration at the foot of the Esquiline Hill, by the destruction of all buildings on a vast space, so that the violence of the fire was met by clear ground and an open sky. But before people had laid aside their fears, the flames returned, with no less fury this second time, and especially in the spacious districts of the city.

Consequently, though there was less loss of life, the temples of the gods, and the porticoes which were devoted to enjoyment, fell in a yet more widespread ruin. And to this conflagration there attached the greater infamy because it broke out on the Aemilian property of Tigellinus, and it seemed that Nero was aiming at the glory of founding a new city and calling it by his name. Rome, indeed, is divided into 14 districts, four of which remained uninjured, three were levelled to the ground, while in the other seven were left only a few shattered, half-burnt relics of houses.

Book XV, Chapter 41
Destruction of Historic Artefacts by the Great Fire

It would not be easy to enter into a computation of the private mansions, the blocks of tenements, and of the temples, which were lost. Those with the oldest ceremonial, as that dedicated by Servius Tullius to Luna, the great altar and shrine raised by the Arcadian Evander to the visibly appearing Hercules, the temple of Jupiter the Stayer, which was vowed by Romulus, Numa's royal palace, and the sanctuary of Vesta, with the tutelary deities of the Roman people, were burnt. So too were the riches acquired by our many victories, various beauties of Greek art, then again, the ancient and genuine historical monuments of men of genius, and, notwithstanding the striking splendour of the restored city, old men will remember many things which could not be replaced. Some persons observed that the beginning of this conflagration was on the 19th July, the day on which the Senones captured and fired Rome [c. 387 BCE]. Others have pushed a curious inquiry so far as to reduce the interval between these two conflagrations into equal numbers of years, months and days.

FROM PLINY THE ELDER'S *NATURAL HISTORY*

In the *Natural History*, Pliny the Elder (Caius Plinius Secundus, 23–79 CE) set out to describe anything that could be found in the world, including living things, geology, astronomy, geography, art, and humanity itself.

Book III, Chapter 9
The First Region of Italy: The Tiber River and Rome

The Tiber or Tiberis, formerly called Thybris, and previously Albula, flows down from nearly the central part of the chain of the Apennines, in the territory of the Arretini. It is at first small, and only navigable by means of sluices, in which the water is dammed up and then discharged, in the same manner as the Timia and the Glanis, which flow into it; for which purpose it is found necessary to collect the water for nine days, unless there should happen to be a fall of rain. And even then, the Tiber, by reason of its rugged and uneven channel, is really more suitable for navigation by rafts than by vessels, for any great distance. It winds along for a course of 150 miles, passing not far from Tifernum, Perusia, and Ocriculum, and dividing Etruria from the Umbri and the Sabini, and then, at a distance of less than 16 miles from the city, separating the territory of Veii from that of Crustuminum, and afterwards that of the Fidenates and of Latium from Vaticanum.

Below its union with the Glanis from Arretinum the Tiber is swollen by two and forty streams, particularly the Nar and the Anio, which last is also navigable and shuts in Latium at the back; it is also increased by the numerous aqueducts and springs which are conveyed to the City. Here it becomes navigable by vessels of any burden which may come up from the Italian sea; a most tranquil dispenser of the produce of all parts of the earth and peopled and embellished along its banks with more villas than nearly all the other rivers of the world taken together. And yet there is no river more circumscribed than it, so close are its banks shut in on either side; but still, no resistance does it offer, although its waters frequently rise with great suddenness, and no part is more liable to be swollen than that which runs through the City itself. In such case, however, the Tiber is rather to be looked upon as pregnant with prophetic warnings to us, and in its increase to be considered more as a promoter of religion than a source of devastation.

Latium has preserved its original limits, from the Tiber to Circeii, a distance of 50 miles: so slender at the beginning were the roots from which this our Empire sprang. Its inhabitants have been often changed, and different nations have peopled it at different times, the Aborigines, the Pelasgi, the Arcades, the Seculi, the Aurunci, the Rutuli and, beyond Circeii, the Volsci, the Osci, and the Ausones whence the name of Latium came to be extended as far as the river Liris.

Romulus left the city of Rome, if we are to believe those who state the very greatest number, having three gates and no more. When the Vespasians [father Vespasian and son Titus] were emperors and censors, in the Year 826 From the Founding of the City, the circumference of the walls which surrounded it was 13 miles and two-fifths. Surrounding as it does the Seven Hills, the city is divided into 14 districts, with 265 crossroads under the guardianship of the Lares. If a straight line is drawn from the mile-column placed at the entrance of the Forum, to each of the gates, which are at present 37 in number (taking care to count only once the 12 double gates, and to omit the seven old ones, which no longer exist), the result will be [taking them altogether], a straight line of 20 miles and 765 paces. But if we draw a straight line from the same mile-column to the very last of the houses, including therein the Praetorian Camp, and follow throughout the line of all the streets, the result will then be something more than 70 miles. Add to these calculations the height of the houses, and then a person may form a fair idea of this city and will certainly be obliged to admit that there is not a place throughout the whole world that for size can be compared to it. On the eastern side it is bounded by the *agger* [mound] of Tarquinius Superbus, a work of surpassing grandeur; for he raised it so high as to be on a level with the walls on the side on which the city lay most exposed to attack from the neighbouring plains. On all the other sides it has been fortified either with lofty walls or steep and precipitous hills, but so it is, that its buildings, increasing and extending beyond all bounds, have now united many other cities to it.

Book XXXV, Chapter 9
At What Period Painting Was First Held in High Esteem at Rome, and from What Causes

But it was the Dictator Caesar that first brought the public exhibition of pictures into such high estimation, by consecrating an Ajax and a Medea before the Temple of Venus Genetrix. After him there was M. Agrippa, a man who was naturally more attached to rustic simplicity than to refinement. Still, however, we have a magnificent oration of his, and one well worthy of the greatest of our citizens, on the advantage of exhibiting in public all pictures and statues; a practice which would have been far preferable to sending them into banishment at our country-houses. Severe as he was in his tastes, he paid the people of Cyzicus 1,200,000 sesterces for two paintings, an Ajax and a Venus. He also ordered small paintings to be set in marble in the very hottest part of his Warm Baths; where they remained until they were removed a short time since, when the building was repaired.

Book XXXV, Chapter 10
What Pictures the Emperors Have Exhibited in Public

The late Emperor Augustus did more than all the others; for he placed in the most conspicuous part of his Forum, two pictures, representing War and Triumph. He also placed in the Temple of his father, Caesar, a picture of the Castors, and one of Victory, in addition to those which we shall mention in our account of the works of the different artists. He also inserted two pictures in the wall of the *Curia* which he consecrated in the *Comitium*; one of which was a Nemea seated upon a lion, and bearing a palm in her hand. Close to her is an Old Man, standing with a staff, and above his head hangs the picture of a chariot with two horses. Nicias has written upon this picture that he "inburned" it, such being the word he has employed.

In the second picture the thing to be chiefly admired, is the resemblance that the youth bears to the old man his father, allowing, of course, for the difference in age; above them soars an eagle, which grasps a dragon in its talons. Philochares attests that he is the author of this work, an instance, if we only consider it, of the mighty power wielded by the pictorial art; for here, thanks to Philochares, the senate of the Roman people, age after age, has before its eyes Glaucion and his son Aristippus, persons who would otherwise have been altogether unknown. The Emperor Tiberius, too, a *princeps* who was by no means very gracious, has exhibited in the temple dedicated by him, in his turn, to Augustus, several pictures which we shall describe hereafter.

Book XXXV, Chapter 33
At What Time Combats of Gladiators Were First Painted and Publicly Exhibited

One folly, too, of this age of ours, in reference to painting, I must not omit. The Emperor Nero ordered a painting of himself to be executed upon canvas, of colossal proportions, 120 feet in height; a thing till then unknown. This picture was just completed when it was burnt by lightning, with the greater part of the gardens of Maius, in which it was exhibited.

A freedman of the same prince, on the occasion of his exhibiting a show of gladiators at Antium, had the public porticos hung, as everybody knows, with paintings, in which were represented genuine portraits of the gladiators and all the other assistants. Indeed, at this place, there has been a very prevailing taste for paintings for many ages past. C. Terentius Lucanus was the first who had combats of gladiators painted for public exhibition: in honour of his grandfather, who had adopted him, he provided 30 pairs of gladiators in the Forum, for three consecutive days, and exhibited a painting of their combats in the Grove of Diana.

From the construction of the passage, it is difficult to say whether he means to say that such colossal figures were till then unknown in painting, or whether that the use of canvas in painting was till then unknown. If the latter is the meaning, it is not exactly correct, though it is probable that the introduction of canvas for this purpose was comparatively late; there being no mention of its being employed by the Greek painters of the best periods.

Book XXXVI, Chapter 9
The Method of Cutting Marble into Slabs; the Sand Used in Cutting Marble

But whoever it was that first invented the art of thus cutting marble, and so multiplying the appliances of luxury, he displayed considerable ingenuity, though to little purpose. This division, though apparently effected by the aid of iron is, in reality, effected by sand; the saw acting only by pressing upon the sand within a very fine cleft in the stone, as it is moved to and fro.

The sand of Aethiopia is the most highly esteemed for this purpose; for, to add to the trouble that is entailed, we have to send to Aethiopia for the purpose of preparing our marble – aye, and as far as India even; whereas in former times, the severity of the Roman manners thought it beneath them to repair thither in search of such costly things even as pearls! This Indian sand is held in the next highest degree of estimation, the Aethiopian being of a softer nature, and better adapted for dividing the stone without leaving any roughness on the surface; whereas the sand from India does not leave so smooth a face upon it. Still, however, for polishing marble, we find it recommended to rub it with Indian sand calcined. The sand of Naxos has the same defect; as also that from Coptos, generally known as 'Egyptian' sand.

The above were the several varieties of sand used by the ancients in dividing marble. More recently, a sand has been discovered that is equally approved of for this purpose; in a certain creek of the Adriatic Sea, which is left dry at low water only; a thing that renders it not very easy to be found. At the present day, however, the fraudulent tendencies of our workers in marble have emboldened them to use any kind of river-sand for the purpose; a mischief which very few employers rightly appreciate. For, the coarser the sand, the wider is the division made in the stone, the greater the quantity of material consumed, and the more extensive the labour required for polishing the rough surface that is left; a result of which is that the slabs lose so much more in thickness. For giving the last polish to marble, Thebaic stone is considered well adapted, as also porous stone, or pumice, powdered fine.

Book XXXVI, Chapter 8
At What Period the Various Kinds of Marble Came into Use at Rome

Marcus Lepidus, who was consul with Quintus Catulus, was the first to have the lintels of his house made of Numidian marble, a thing for which he was greatly censured: he was consul in the Year 676 From the Founding of the City [78 BCE]. This is the earliest instance that I can find of the introduction of Numidian marble; not in the form of pillars, however, or of slabs, as was the case with the marble of Carystus, above-mentioned, but in blocks, and that too, for the comparatively ignoble purpose of making the thresholds of doors. Four years after this Lepidus, Lucius Lucullus was consul; the same person who gave its name, it is very evident, to the Lucullan marble; for, taking a great fancy to it, he introduced it at Rome. While other kinds of marble are valued for their spots or their colours, this marble is entirely black. It is found in the island of Melos and is pretty nearly the only marble that has taken its name from the person who first introduced it. Among these personages, Scaurus, in my opinion, was the first to build a theatre with walls of marble: but whether they were only coated with slabs of marble or were made of solid blocks highly polished, such as we now see in the Temple of Jupiter Tonans, in the Capitol, I cannot exactly say: for, up to this period, I cannot find any vestiges of the use of marble slabs in Italy.

Book XXXVI, Chapter 24
Eighteen Marvellous Buildings at Rome

But it is now time to pass on to the marvels in building displayed by our own City, and to make some inquiry into the resources and experience that we have gained in the lapse of 800 years; and so prove that here, as well, the rest of the world has been outdone by us: a thing which will appear, in fact, to have occurred almost as many times as the marvels are in number which I shall have to enumerate. If, indeed, all the buildings of our City are considered in the aggregate, and supposing them, so to say, all thrown together in one vast mass, the united grandeur of them would lead one to suppose that we were describing another world, accumulated in a single spot.

Not to mention among our great works, the *Circus Maximus* [chariot race track] that was constructed by the Dictator [Julius] Caesar, one *stadium* in width and three in length, and occupying, with the adjacent buildings, no less than four *jugera* [measure of area], with room for 260,000 spectators seated; am I not to include in the number of our magnificent constructions, the Basilica of Paulus, with its admirable Phrygian columns; the Forum of the late Emperor Augustus; the Temple of Peace, erected by the Emperor Vespasianus Augustus [r. 69–79 CE] – some of the finest works that the world has ever beheld – the roofing, too, of the *Diribitorium* ['Public Voting Hall'], that was built by [Marcus] Agrippa? Not to forget that, before his time, Valerius of Ostia, the architect, had covered in a theatre at Rome, at the time of the public Games celebrated by Libo?

We behold with admiration pyramids that were built by kings, when the very ground alone, that was purchased by the Dictator Caesar, for the construction of his Forum, cost 100,000,000 sesterces! If, too, an enormous expenditure has its attractions for any one whose mind is influenced by monetary considerations, be it known to him that the house in which Clodius [Pulcher] dwelt, who was slain by Milo, was purchased by him at the price of 14,800,000 sesterces! a thing that, for my part, I look upon as no less astounding than the monstrous follies that have been displayed by kings. And then, as to Milo himself, the sums in which he was indebted, amounted to no less than 70,000,000 sesterces; a state of things, to be considered, in my opinion, as one of the most portentous phenomena in the history of the human mind. But it was in those days, too, that old men still spoke in admiration of the vast proportions of the *agger*, and of the enormous foundations of the Capitol; of the public sewers, too, a work more stupendous than any; as mountains had to be pierced for their construction, and, like the hanging city which we recently mentioned, navigation had to be carried on beneath Rome; an event which happened in the aedileship of Marcus Agrippa, after he had filled the office of consul.

For this purpose, there are seven rivers, made, by artificial channels, to flow beneath the city. Rushing onward, like so many impetuous torrents, they are compelled to carry off and sweep away all the sewage; and swollen as they are by the vast accession of the pluvial waters, they reverberate against the sides and bottom of their channels. Occasionally, too, the Tiber, overflowing, is thrown backward in its course, and discharges itself by these outlets: obstinate is the contest that ensues within between the meeting tides, but so firm and solid is the masonry, that it is enabled to offer an effectual resistance. Enormous as are the accumulations that are carried along above, the work of the channels never gives way. Houses falling spontaneously to ruins, or levelled with the ground by conflagrations, are continually battering against them; the ground, too, is shaken by earthquakes every now and then; and yet, built as they were in the days of Tarquinius Priscus, 700 years ago, these constructions have survived, all but unharmed. We must not omit, too, to mention one remarkable circumstance, and all the more remarkable from the fact, that the most celebrated historians have omitted to mention it. Tarquinius Priscus having commenced the sewers, and set the lower classes to work upon them, the laboriousness and prolonged duration of the employment became equally an object of dread to them; and the consequence was, that suicide was a thing of common occurrence, the citizens adopting this method of escaping their troubles. For this evil, however, the king devised a singular remedy, and one that has never been resorted to either before that time or since: for he ordered the bodies of all who had been thus guilty of self-destruction, to be fastened to a cross, and left there as a spectacle to their fellow – citizens and a prey to birds and wild beasts. The result was, that that sense of propriety which so peculiarly attaches itself to the Roman name, and which more than once has gained a victory when the battle was all but lost, came to the rescue on this occasion as well; though for this once, the Romans were in reality its dupes, as they forgot that, though they felt shocked at the thoughts of such ignominy while alive, they would be quite insensible to any such disgrace when dead. It is said that Tarquinius made these sewers of dimensions sufficiently large to admit of a wagon laden with hay passing along them.

All that we have just described, however, is but trifling when placed in comparison with one marvellous fact, which I must not omit to mention before I pass on to other subjects. In the consulship of Marcus [Aemilius] Lepidus and Quintus [Lutatius] Catulus [78 BCE], there was not at Rome, as we learn from the most trustworthy authors, a finer house than the one which belonged to Lepidus himself: and yet – by Hercules! – within five-and-thirty years from that period, the very same house did not hold the hundredth rank even in the City! Let a person, if he will, in taking this fact into consideration, only calculate the vast masses of marble, the productions of painters, the regal treasures that must have been expended, in bringing these 100 mansions to vie with one that had been in its day the most sumptuous and the most celebrated in all the City; and then let him reflect how that, since that period, and down to the present time, these houses have all of them been surpassed by others without number. There can be no doubt that conflagrations are a punishment inflicted upon us for our luxury; but such are our habits, that despite such warnings as these, we cannot be made to understand that there are things in existence more perishable even than man himself.

But there are still two other mansions by which all these edifices have been eclipsed. Twice have we seen the whole City environed by the palaces of the Emperors Caius [Caligula, r. 37–41 CE] and Nero [r. 54–68 CE]; that of the last, that nothing might be wanting to its magnificence, being coated with gold [*Domus Aurea*, 'The Golden House']. Surely such palaces, as these must have been intended for the abode of those who created this mighty empire, and who left the plough or their native hearth to go forth to conquer nations, and to return laden with triumphs – men, in fact, whose very fields even occupied less space than the audience-chambers of these palaces!

Indeed, one cannot but help reflecting how trifling a portion of these palaces was equal to the sites which the republic granted to its invincible generals, for the erection of their dwellings. The supreme honour, too, attendant upon these grants – as in the case of Publius Valerius Publicola, the first consul with Lucius Brutus [509 BCE], for his many meritorious services; and of his brother, who twice in one consulship defeated the Sabines – was the permission granted, by the terms of the decree, to have the doors of their houses opening from without, and the gates thrown back upon the public street. Such was the most distinguished privilege accorded in those days to triumphal mansions even!

I will not permit, however, these two Caiuses, or two Neros, to enjoy this glory even, such as it is; for I will prove that these extravagant follies of theirs have been surpassed, in the use that was made of his wealth by Marcus [Aemilius] Scaurus [c. 92–52 BCE], a private citizen. Indeed, I am by no means certain that it was not the aedileship of this personage that inflicted the first great blow upon the public manners, and that Sulla was not guilty of a greater crime in giving such unlimited power to his stepson, than in the proscription of so many thousands. During his aedileship, and only for the temporary purposes of a few days, Scaurus executed the greatest work that has ever been made by the hands of man, even when intended to be of everlasting duration; his theatre, I mean. This building consisted of three storeys, supported upon 360 columns; and this, too, in a city which had not allowed without some censure one of its greatest citizens to erect six pillars of Hymettian marble. The ground storey was of marble, the second of glass, a species of luxury which ever since that time has been quite unheard of, and the highest of gilded wood. The lowermost columns, as previously stated, were eight-and-thirty feet in height; and, placed between these columns, as already mentioned, were brazen statues, 3,000 in number. The area of this theatre afforded accommodation for

80,000 spectators; and yet the Theatre of Pompeius, after the City had so greatly increased, and the inhabitants had become so vastly more numerous, was considered abundantly large, with its seating for 40,000 only. The rest of the fittings of it, what with Attalic vestments, pictures, and the other stage-properties, were of such enormous value that, after Scaurus had had conveyed to his Tusculan villa such parts thereof as were not required for the enjoyment of his daily luxuries, the loss was no less than 300,000,000 sesterces, when the villa was burnt by his servants in a spirit of revenge.

The consideration of such prodigality as this quite distracts my attention, and compels me to digress from my original purpose, in order to mention a still greater instance of extravagance, in reference to wood. Caius [Scribonius] Curio [c. 124–53 BCE], who died during the civil wars, fighting on the side of Caesar, found, to his dismay, that he could not, when celebrating the funeral games in honour of his father, surpass the riches and magnificence of Scaurus – for where, in fact, was to be found such a step sire as Sulla, and such a mother as Metella, that bidder at all auctions for the property of the proscribed? Where, too, was he to find for his father, Marcus [Aemilius] Scaurus [c. 159–c. 89 BCE], so long the principal man in the city, and one who had acted, in his alliance with Marius, as a receptacle for the plunder of whole provinces? Indeed, Scaurus himself was now no longer able to rival himself; and it was at least one advantage which he derived from this destruction by fire of so many objects brought from all parts of the earth, that no one could ever after be his equal in this species of folly. Curio, consequently, found himself compelled to fall back upon his own resources, and to think of some new device of his own.

It is really worth our while to know what this device was, if only to congratulate ourselves upon the manners of the present day, and to reverse the ordinary mode of expression, and term ourselves the men of the olden time.

He caused to be erected, close together, two theatres of very large dimensions, and built of wood, each of them nicely poised, and turning on a pivot. Before midday, a spectacle of games was exhibited in each; the theatres being turned back-to-back, in order that the noise of neither of them might interfere with what was going on in the other. Then, in the latter part of the day, all on a sudden, the two theatres were swung round, and, the corners uniting, brought face to face; the outer frames, too, were removed and, thus, an amphitheatre was formed, in which combats of gladiators were presented to the view; men whose safety was almost less compromised than was that of the Roman people, in allowing itself to be thus whirled round from side to side. Now, in this case, which have we most reason to admire, the inventor or the invention? the artist, or the author of the project? him who first dared to think of such an enterprise, or him who ventured to undertake it? him who obeyed the order, or him who gave it? But the thing that surpasses all is, the frenzy that must have possessed the public, to take their seats in a place which must, of necessity, have been so unsubstantial and so insecure. Lo and behold! Here is a people that has conquered the whole earth, that has subdued the universe, that divides the spoils of kingdoms and of nations, that sends its laws to foreign lands, that shares in some degree the attributes of the immortal gods in common with mankind, suspended aloft in a machine, and showering plaudits even upon its own peril!

This is, indeed, holding life cheap; and can we, after this, complain of our disasters at Cannae [216 BCE]? How vast the catastrophe that might have ensued! When cities are swallowed up by an earthquake, it is looked upon by mankind as a general calamity; and yet, here have we the whole Roman people, embarked, so to say, in two ships, and sitting suspended on a couple of pivots; the grand spectacle being its own struggle with danger, and its liability to perish at any moment that the overstrained machinery may give way! And then the object, too, of all this – that public favour may be conciliated for the tribune's harangues at a future day, and that, at the Rostra, he may still have the power of shaking the tribes, nicely balanced as they are! And really, what may he not dare with those who, at his persuasion, have braved such perils as these? Indeed, to confess the truth, at the funeral games celebrated at the tomb of his father, it was no less than the whole Roman people that shared the dangers of the gladiatorial combats. When the pivots had now been sufficiently worked and wearied, he gave another turn to his magnificent displays. For, upon the last day, still preserving the form of the amphitheatre, he cut the stage in two through the middle, and exhibited a spectacle of athletes; after which, the stage being suddenly withdrawn on either side, he exhibited a combat, upon the same day, between such of the gladiators as had previously proved victorious. And yet, with all this, Curio was no king, no ruler of the destinies of a nation, nor yet a person remarkable for his opulence even; seeing that he possessed no resources of his own, beyond what he could realize from the discord between the leading men.

But let us now turn our attention to some marvels which, justly appreciated, may be truthfully pronounced to remain unsurpassed. Quintus Marcius Rex, upon being commanded by the senate to repair the Appian Aqueduct, and those of the Anio and Tepula, constructed during his praetorship a new aqueduct, which bore his name, and was brought hither by a channel pierced through the sides of mountains. Agrippa, in his aedileship, united the Marcia with the Virgo Aqueduct, and repaired and strengthened the channels of the others. He also formed 700 wells, in addition to 500 fountains, and 130 reservoirs, many of them magnificently adorned. Upon these works, too, he erected 300 statues of marble or bronze, and 400 marble columns; and all this in the space of a single year! In the work which he has written in commemoration of his aedileship, he also informs us that public games were celebrated for the space of 59 days, and that 170 gratuitous baths were opened. The number of these last at Rome, has increased to an infinite extent since his time.

The preceding aqueducts, however, have all been surpassed by the costly work which was more recently commenced by the Emperor Caius [Caligula], and completed by Claudius [r. 41–54 CE]. Under these princes, the Curtian and Caerulean Waters, with the New Anio, were brought from a distance of 40 miles, and at so high a level that all the hills were supplied with water, on which the City is built. The sum expended on these works was 350,000,000 sesterces. If we only take into consideration the abundant supply of water to the public, for baths, ponds, canals, household purposes, gardens, places in the suburbs, and country-houses; and then reflect upon the distances that are traversed, the arches that have been constructed, the mountains that have been pierced, the valleys that have been levelled, we must of necessity admit that there is nothing to be found more worthy of our admiration throughout the whole universe.

Among the most memorable works, too, I, for my own part, should include another undertaking of the Emperor Claudius, although it was afterwards abandoned in consequence of the hatred borne him by his successor; I mean the channel that was cut through a mountain as an emissary for Lake Fucinus; a work which cost a sum beyond all calculation, and employed a countless multitude of workmen for many years. In those parts where the soil was found to be terreous, it was necessary to pump up the water by the aid of machinery; in other parts, again, the solid rock had to be hewn through. All this, too, had to be done in the midst of darkness within; a series of operations which can only be adequately conceived by those who were witnesses of them, and which no human language can possibly describe.

I pass in silence the harbour that has been formed at Ostia; the various roads, too, that have been cut across mountains; the Tyrrhenian Sea separated by an embankment from Lake Lucrinus; and vast numbers of bridges constructed at an enormous expense. Among the many other marvels, too, of Italy, we are informed by Papirius Fabianus [first century CE], a most diligent enquirer into the operations of Nature, that the marble there grows in the quarries; and those who work in the quarries assure us that the wounds thus inflicted upon the mountains fill up spontaneously. If such is the fact, luxury has good grounds for hoping that it will never be at a loss for a supply of materials for its gratification.

FROM JULIUS FRONTINUS'S
AQUEDUCTS OF THE CITY OF ROME

In 97 CE, Julius Frontinus (Sextus Julius Frontinus, *c.* 40–103 CE) was appointed by Emperor Nerva (r. 96–98 CE) to supervise management of Rome's public water system. Based on his experience in that role, he wrote a book to explain how the distribution network operated.

Book I, Chapters 4–16
Sources and Distribution of Water in Rome

For 441 years from the Foundation of the City, the Romans were satisfied with the use of such waters as they drew from the Tiber, from wells, or from springs. Esteem for springs still continues and is observed with veneration. They are believed to bring healing to the sick, as, for example, the springs of the Camenae, of Apollo, and of Juturna. But there now run into the City: the *Aqua Appia* ['Appian Aqueduct'], *Anio Vetus* ['Old Anio'], *Marcia* ['Marcian'], *Tepula* ['Tepulan'], *Julia* ['Julian'], *Virgo* ['Virgin'], *Alsietina*, which is also called *Augusta* ['Augustan'], *Claudia* ['Claudian'], *Anio Novus* ['New Anio'].

In the consulship of Marcus Valerius Maximus and Publius Decius Mus [312 BCE], in the thirtieth year after the beginning of the Samnite War, the Appian Aqueduct was brought into the City by Appius Claudius Crassus the Censor, who afterwards received the surname of *Caecus* ['the Blind'], the same man who had charge of constructing the *Via Appia* ['Appian Way'] from the Porta Capena as far as the City of Capua. As colleague in the censorship Appius had Caius

Plautius, to whom was given the name of *Venox* ('the Hunter') for having discovered the springs of this water; but since Plautius resigned the censorship within a year and six months, under the mistaken impression that his colleague would do the same, the honour of giving his name to the aqueduct fell to Appius alone, who, by various subterfuges, is reported to have extended the term of his censorship, until he should complete both the Way and this aqueduct. The intake of the *Appia* is on the Lucullan estate, between the 7th and 8th milestones, on the Praenestine Way, on a crossroad, 780 paces to the left. From its intake to the Salinae at the *Porta Trigemina* ['Trigeminan Gate'], its channel has a length of 11,190 paces, of which 11,130 paces run underground, while above ground 60 paces are carried on substructures and, near the *Porta Capena*, on arches. Near *Spes Vetus* [an ancient shrine on the Esquiline Hill], on the edge of the Torquatian and Epaphroditian Gardens, there joins it a branch of *Augusta*, added by Augustus as a supplementary supply [...]. This branch has its intake at the 6th milestone, on the Praenestine Way, on a crossroad, 980 paces to the left, near the Collatian Way. Its course, by underground channel, extends to 6,380 paces before reaching The Twins. The distribution of *Appia* begins at the foot of the Publician Ascent, near the *Porta Trigemina*, at the place designated as the Salinae.

Forty years after *Appia* was brought in, in the Year 481 from the Founding of the City [273 BCE], Manius Curius Dentatus, who held the censorship with Lucius Papirius Cursor, contracted to have the waters of what is now called *Anio Vetus* brought into the City, with the proceeds of the booty captured from Pyrrhus. This was in the second consulship of

Spurius Carvilius and Lucius Papirius. Then two years later the question of completing the aqueduct was discussed in the Senate on the motion of the praetor [...]. At the close of the discussion, Curius, who had let the original contract, and Fulvius Flaccus were appointed by Decree of the Senate as Duumvirs ['Members of a Commission of Two'] to bring in the water. Within five days of the time he had been appointed, one of the two commissioners, Curius, died; thus the credit of achieving the work rested with Flaccus. The intake of *Anio Vetus* is above Tibur at the 20th milestone outside the [...] Gate, where it gives a part of its water to supply the Tiburtines. Owing to the exigence of elevation, its conduit has a length of 43,000 paces. Of this, the channel runs underground for 42,779 paces, while there are above ground substructures for 221 paces.

One hundred and twenty-seven years later, that is in the Year 608 From the Founding of the City [actually 146 BCE], in the consulship of Servius Sulpicius Galba and Lucius Aurelius Cotta, when the conduits of *Appia* and *Anio Vetus* had become leaky by reason of age, and water was also being diverted from them unlawfully by individuals, the Senate commissioned Marcius, who at that time administered the law as praetor between citizens, to reclaim and repair these conduits; and since the growth of the City was seen to demand a more bountiful supply of water, the same man was charged by the Senate to bring into the City other waters so far as he could. [...] He restored the old channels and brought in a third supply, more wholesome than these, [...] which is called *Marcia* after the man who introduced it. We read in Fenestella [a Roman historian], that 180,000,000 sesterces were granted to

Marcius for these works, and since the term of his praetorship was not sufficient for the completion of the enterprise, it was extended for a second year. At that time, the Decemvirs ['Commission of Ten'], on consulting the Sibylline Books for another purpose, are said to have discovered that it was not right for the Marcian water, or rather the *Anio* (for tradition more regularly mentions this) to be brought to the Capitol. The matter is said to have been debated in the Senate in the consulship of Appius Claudius and Quintus Caecilius [143 BCE], Marcus Lepidus acting as spokesman for the Commission of Decemvirs; and three years later the matter is said to have been brought up again by Lucius Lentulus, in the consulship of Caius Laelius and Quintus Servilius [140 BCE]; but on both occasions the influence of Marcius Rex carried the day, and thus the water was brought to the Capitol. The intake of *Marcia* is at the 36th milestone on the Valerian Way, on a crossroad, three miles to the right as you come from Rome. But on the Sublacensian Way, which was first paved under the Emperor Nero, at the 38th milestone, within 200 paces to the left [a view of its source may be seen]. Its waters stand like a tranquil pool, of deep green hue. Its conduit has a length, from the intake to the City, of 61,710½ paces; 54,247½ paces of underground conduit; 7,463 paces on structures above ground, of which, at some distance from the City, in several places where it crosses valleys, there are 463 paces on arches; nearer the City, beginning at the 7th milestone, 528 paces on substructures, and the remaining 6,472 paces on arches.

The Censors, Cnaeus Servilius Caepio and Lucius Cassius Longinus (called Ravilla), in the year 627 From the Founding of the City [127 BCE], in the consulate of Marcus Plautus

Hypsaeus and Marcus Fulvius Flaccus, had the water called *Tepula* brought to Rome and to the Capitol, from the estate of Lucullus, which some persons hold to belong to Tusculan territory. The intake of *Tepula* is at the 10th milestone on the Latin Way, near a crossroad, two miles to the right as you proceed from Rome […] From that point it was conducted in its own channel to the City.

Later […] in the second consulate of the Emperor Caesar Augustus, when Lucius Volcatius was his colleague, in the year 719 From the Founding of the City [33 BCE], [Marcus] Agrippa, when aedile, after his first consulship, took another independent source of supply, at the 12th milestone from the City on the Latin Way, on a crossroad two miles to the right as you proceed from Rome, and also tapped *Tepula*. The name *Julia* was given to the new aqueduct by its builder, but since the waters were again divided for distribution, the name *Tepula* remained. The conduit of *Julia* has a length of 15,426½ paces; 7,000 paces on masonry above ground, of which 528 paces next the City, beginning at the 7th milestone, are on substructures, the other 6,472 paces being on arches. Past the intake of *Julia* flows a brook, which is called Crabra. Agrippa refrained from taking in this brook either because he had condemned it, or because he thought it ought to be left to the proprietors at Tusculum, for this is the water which all the estates of that district receive in turn, dealt out to them on regular days and in regular quantities. But our watermen, failing to practise the same restraint, have always claimed a part of it to supplement *Julia*, not, however, thus increasing the actual flow of *Julia*, since they habitually exhausted it by diverting its waters for their own profit. I therefore shut off the Crabra brook and, at the Emperor's command, restored it entirely to the Tusculan proprietors, who now, possibly not without surprise, take its waters, without knowing to what cause to ascribe the unusual abundance. The *Aqua Julia*, on the other hand, by reason of the destruction of the branch pipes through which it was secretly plundered, has maintained its normal quantity even in times of most extraordinary drought. In the same year, Agrippa repaired the conduits of *Appia*, *Anio Vetus*, and *Marcia*, which had almost worn out, and with unique forethought provided the City with a large number of fountains.

The same man, after his own third consulship, in the consulship of Caius Sentius and Quintus Lucretius [19 BCE], 12 years after he had constructed the Julian aqueduct, also brought Virgo to Rome, taking it from the estate of Lucullus. We learn that 9th June was the day that it first began to flow in the City. It was called *Virgo*, because a young girl pointed out certain springs to some soldiers hunting for water, and when they followed these up and dug, they found a copious supply. A small temple, situated near the spring, contains a painting which illustrates this origin of the aqueduct. The intake of *Virgo* is on the Collatian Way at the 8th milestone, in a marshy spot, surrounded by a concrete enclosure for the purpose of confining the gushing waters. Its volume is augmented by several tributaries. Its length is 14,105 paces. For 12,865 paces of this distance it is carried in an underground channel, for 1,240 paces above ground. Of these 1,240 paces, it is carried for 540 paces on substructures at various points, and for 700 paces on arches. The underground conduits of the tributaries measure 1,405 paces.

I fail to see what motive induced Augustus, a most sagacious sovereign, to bring in the Alsietinian water, also called *Augusta*. For this has nothing to commend it – is in fact positively unwholesome, and for that reason is nowhere delivered for consumption by the people. It may have been that when Augustus began the construction of his *Naumachia* [an artificial lake used for mock sea battles, constructed before 2 BCE], he brought this water in a special conduit, in order not to encroach on the existing supply of wholesome water, and then granted the surplus of the *Naumachia* to the adjacent gardens and to private users for irrigation. It is customary, however, in the district across the Tiber, in an emergency, whenever the bridges are undergoing repairs and the water supply is cut off from this side of the river, to draw from *Alsietina* to maintain the flow of the public fountains. Its source is the Alsietinian Lake, at the 14th milestone, on the Claudian Way, on a crossroad, six miles and a half to the right. Its conduit has a length of 22,172 paces, with 358 paces on arches.

To supplement *Marcia*, whenever dry seasons required an additional supply, Augustus also, by an underground channel, brought to the conduit of *Marcia* another water of the same excellent quality, called Augusta from the name of its donor. Its source is beyond the Springs of Marcia; its conduit, up to its junction with *Marcia*, measures 800 paces.

After these aqueducts, Caius Caesar [Caligula], the successor of Tiberius, in the second year of his reign, in the consulate of Marcus Aquila Julianus and Publius Nonius Asprenas, in the Year 791 From the Founding of the City [38 CE], began two others, inasmuch as the seven then existing seemed insufficient to meet both the public needs and the luxurious private demands of the day. These works Claudius completed on the most magnificent scale, and dedicated in the consulship of Sulla and Titianus, on the 1st of August in the Year 803 From the Founding of the City [50 CE]. To the one water, which had its sources in the Caerulean and Curtian Springs, was given the name *Claudia*. This is next to *Marcia* in excellence. The second began to be designated as *Anio Novus*, in order the more readily to distinguish by title the two *Anios* that had now begun to flow to the City. To the former *Anio* the name of *Vetus* ['Old'] was added.

The intake of *Claudia* is at the 38th milestone on the Sublacensian Way, on a crossroad, less than 300 paces to the left. The water comes from two very large and beautiful springs, the Caerulean, so designated from its appearance, and the Curtian. *Claudia* also receives the spring which is called Albudinus, which is of such excellence that, when *Marcia*, too, needs supplementing, this water answers the purpose so admirably that by its addition there is no change in *Marcia's* quality. The spring of *Augusta* was turned into *Claudia*, because it was plainly evident that Marcia was of sufficient volume by itself. But *Augusta* remained, nevertheless, a reserve supply to *Marcia*, the understanding being that *Augusta* should run into *Claudia* only when the conduit of *Marcia* would not carry it. *Claudia's* conduit has a length of 46,606 paces, of which 36,230 are in a subterranean channel, 10,176 on structures above ground; of these last there are at various points in the upper reaches 3,076 paces on arches; and near the City, beginning at the 7th milestone, 609 paces on substructures and 6,491 on arches.

The intake of *Anio Novus* is at the 42nd milestone on the Sublacensian Way, in the district of Simbruvium. The water is taken from the river, which, even without the effect of rainstorms, is muddy and discoloured, because it has rich and cultivated fields adjoining it, and in consequence loose banks. For this reason, a settling reservoir was put in beyond the inlet of the aqueduct, in order that the water might settle there and clarify itself, between the river and the conduit. But even despite this precaution, the water reaches the City in a discoloured condition whenever there are rains. It is joined by the Herculanean brook, which has its source on the same Way, at the 38th milestone, opposite the springs of *Claudia*, beyond the river and the highway. This is naturally very clear but loses the charm of its purity by admixture with *Anio Novus*. The conduit of *Anio Novus* measures 58,700 paces, of which 49,300 are in an underground channel, 9,400 paces above ground on masonry; of these, at various points in the upper reaches are 2,300 paces on substructures or arches; while nearer the City, beginning at the 7th milestone, are 609 paces on substructures, 6,491 paces on arches. These are the highest arches, rising at certain points to 109 feet.

With such an array of indispensable structures carrying so many waters, compare, if you will, the idle Pyramids or the useless, though famous, works of the Greeks!

Book II, Chapters 105
Rules for Provision of Water for Private Consumption from Public Aqueducts

Whoever wishes to draw water for private use must seek for a grant and bring to the Commissioner a writing from the sovereign; the Commissioner must then immediately expedite the grant of Caesar, and appoint one of Caesar's freedmen as his deputy for this service. [Emperor] Tiberius Claudius appears to have been the first man to appoint such a deputy after he introduced *Claudia* and *Anio Novus*. The overseers must also be made acquainted with the contents of the writing, that they may not excuse their negligence or fraud on the plea of ignorance. The deputy must call in the levellers and provide that the *calix* [a bronze nozzle which regulated the supply to a private consumer] is stamped as conforming to the deeded quantity, and must study the size of the ajutages we have enumerated above, as well as have knowledge of their location, lest it rest with the caprice of the levellers to approve a *calix* of sometimes greater, or sometimes smaller, interior area, according as they interest themselves in the parties. Neither must the deputy permit the free option of connecting directly to the ajutages any sort of lead pipe, but there must rather be attached for a length of 50 feet one of the same interior area as that which the ajutage has been certified to have, as has been ordained by a vote of the Senate.

FROM PLINY THE YOUNGER'S *LETTERS*

Pliny the Younger (Caius Plinius Caecilius Secundus, 61/62– c. 113 CE) was a lawyer who served as praetor (93 CE), consul (100 CE), prefect of the Military Treasury (104 CE), curator of the Tiber's beds and banks and Rome's sewer system (104–106 CE), and as propraetorian governor of Bithynia-Pontus (c. 110 CE). Many of his letters survive, including the one describing the death of his uncle during the eruption of Vesuvius, and the exchange with Emperor Trajan (r. 98–117 CE) about the Christians.

Book I, Letter 1
Pliny To Septicius

You have constantly urged me to collect and publish the more highly finished of the letters that I may have written. I have made such a collection, but without preserving the order in which they were composed, as I was not writing a historical narrative. So I have taken them as they happened to come to hand. I can only hope that you will not have cause to regret the advice you gave, and that I shall not repent having followed it; for I shall set to work to recover such letters as have up to now been tossed on one side, and I shall not keep back any that I may write in the future.

Farewell.

Book III, Letter 14
Pliny to Acilius

A shocking affair, worthy of more publicity than a letter can bestow, has befallen Largius Macedo, a man of praetorian rank, at the hands of his own slaves. He was known to be an overbearing and cruel master, and one who forgot – or rather remembered too keenly – that his own father had been a slave.

He was bathing at his villa near Fromiae, when he was suddenly surrounded by his slaves. One seized him by the throat, another struck him on the forehead, and others smote him in the chest, belly, and even – I am shocked to say – in the private parts. When they thought the breath had left his body they flung him on to the hot tiled floor to see if he was still alive. Whether he was insensible, or merely pretended to be so, he certainly did not move, and lying there at full length, he made them think that he was actually dead. At length they carried him out as though he had been overcome by the heat and handed him over to his more trusty servants, while his mistresses ran shrieking and wailing to his side.

Aroused by their cries and restored by the coolness of the room where he lay, he opened his eyes and moved his limbs, betraying thereby that he was still alive, as it was then safe to do so. His slaves took to flight; most of them have been captured, but some are still being hunted for. Thanks to the attentions he received, Macedo was kept alive for a few days and had the satisfaction of full vengeance before he died, for he exacted the same punishment while he still lived as is usually taken when the victim of a murder dies. You see the dangers, the affronts and insults we are exposed to, and no one can feel at all secure because he is an easy and mild-tempered master, for villainy not deliberation murders masters.

But enough of that subject! Have I any other news to tell you? Let me see! No, there is nothing. If there were, I would tell you, for I have room enough on this sheet, and, as today is a holiday, I should have plenty of time to write more. But I will just add an incident which I chance to recall that happened to the same Macedo. When he was in one of the public baths in Rome, a curious and – the event has shown – an ominous accident happened to him. Macedo's servant lightly tapped a Roman knight with his hand to induce him to make room for them to pass, and the knight turned round and struck, not the slave who had touched him but Macedo himself, such a heavy blow with his fist that he almost felled him. So one may say that the bath has been by certain stages the scene first of humiliation to him and then of death.

Farewell.

Book IV, Letter 2
Pliny to Attius Clemens

Regulus has lost his son – the only misfortune he did not deserve, because I doubt whether he considers it as such. He was a sharp-witted youth, whatever use he might have made of his talents, though he might have followed honourable courses if he did not take after his father. Regulus freed him from his parental control in order that he might succeed to his mother's property, but after freeing him – and those who knew the character of the man spoke of it as a release from slavery – he endeavoured to win his affections by treating him with a pretended indulgence which was as disgraceful as it was unusual in a father. It seems incredible, but remember that it was Regulus. Yet now that his son is dead, he is mad with grief at his loss.

The boy had a number of ponies, some in harness and others not broken in, dogs both great and small, nightingales, parrots and blackbirds – all these Regulus slaughtered at his pyre. Yet an act like that was no token of grief; it was but a mere parade of it. It is strange how people are flocking to call upon him. Everyone detests and hates him, yet they run to visit him in shoals as though they both admired and loved him.

To put in a nutshell what I mean, people in paying court to Regulus are copying the example he set. He does not move from his gardens across the Tiber, where he has covered an immense quantity of ground with colossal porticos and littered the riverbank with his statues, for, though he is the meanest of misers, he flings his money broadcast, and though his name is a byword, he is forever vaunting his glories. Consequently, in this the most sickly season of the year, he is upsetting everyone's arrangements and thinks it soothes his grief to inconvenience everybody. He says he is desirous of taking a wife, and here again, as in other matters, he shows the perversity of his nature. You will hear soon that the mourner is married, that the old man has taken a wife, displaying unseemly haste as the former and undue delay as the latter. If you ask what makes me think he will take this step, I reply that it is not because he says he will – for there is no greater liar than he – but because it is quite certain that Regulus will do what he ought not to do.

Farewell.

Book IV, Letter 7
Pliny to Catius Lepidus

I am constantly writing to tell you what energy Regulus possesses. It is wonderful the way he carries through anything which he has set his mind upon. It pleased him to mourn for his son – and never man mourned like him; it pleased him to erect a number of statues and busts to his memory, and the result is that he is keeping all the workshops busy; he is having his boy represented in colours, in wax, in bronze, in silver, in gold, ivory, and marble – always his boy. He himself just lately got together a large audience and read a memoir of his life – of the boy's life; he read it aloud, and yet had 1,000 copies written out which he has scattered broadcast over Italy and the provinces.

He wrote at large to the decurions and asked them to choose one of their number with the best voice to read the memoir to the people, and it was done. What good he might have effected with this energy of his – or whatever name we should give to such dauntless determination on his part to get his own way – if he had only turned it into a better channel! But then, as you know, good men rarely have this faculty so well developed as bad men; the Greeks say, "Ignorance makes a man bold; calculation gives him pause," and just in the same way modesty cripples the force of an upright mind, while unblushing confidence is a source of strength to a man without conscience.

Regulus is a case in point. He has weak lungs, he never looks you straight in the face, he stammers, he has no imaginative power, absolutely no memory, no quality at all, in short, except a wild, frantic genius, and yet, thanks to his effrontery, and even just to this frenzy of his, he has got people to regard him as an orator. Herennius Senecio very neatly turned against him Cato's well-known definition of an orator by saying, "An orator is a bad man who knows nothing of the art of speaking," and I really think that he thereby gave a better definition of Regulus than Cato did of the really true orator.

Have you any equivalent to send me for a letter like this? Yes, indeed, you have, if you will write and say whether any one of my friends in your township, or whether you yourself have read this pitiful production of Regulus in the forum, like a Cheap Jack, pitching your voice high, as Demosthenes says, shouting with delight, and straining every muscle in your throat. For it is so absurd that it will make you laugh rather than sigh, and you would think it was written not about a boy but by a boy.

Farewell.

Book VI, Letter 16
Pliny to Tacitus

You ask me to send you an account of my uncle's death, so that you may be able to give posterity an accurate description of it. I am much obliged to you, for I can see that the immortality of his fame is well assured, if you take in hand to write of it. For although he perished in a disaster which devastated some of the fairest regions of the land, and though he is sure of eternal remembrance like the peoples and cities that fell with him in that memorable calamity, though too he had written a large number of works of lasting value, yet the undying fame of which your writings are assured will secure for his a still further lease of life. For my own part, I think that those people are highly favoured by Providence who are capable either of performing deeds worthy of the historian's pen or of writing histories worthy of being read, but that they are peculiarly favoured who can do both. Among the latter I may class my uncle, thanks to his own writings and to yours. So, I am all the more ready to fulfil your injunctions – nay, I am even prepared to beg to be allowed to undertake them!

My uncle was stationed at Misemum, where he was in active command of the fleet, with full powers. On 24th August, about the seventh hour, my mother drew his attention to the fact that a cloud of unusual size and shape had made its appearance. He had been out in the sun, followed by a cold bath, and after a light meal he was lying down and reading. Yet he called for his sandals, and climbed up to a spot from which he could command a good view of the curious phenomenon. Those who were looking at the cloud from some distance could not make out from which mountain it was rising – it was afterwards discovered to have been Mount Vesuvius – but in likeness and form it more closely resembled a pine tree than anything else, for what corresponded to the trunk was of great length and height, and then spread out into a number of branches, the reason being, I imagine, that while the vapour was fresh, the cloud was borne upwards, but when the vapour became wasted, it lost its motion, or even became dissipated by its own weight, and spread out laterally. At times it looked white, and at other times dirty and spotted, according to the quantity of earth and cinders that were shot up.

To a man of my uncle's learning, the phenomenon appeared one of great importance, which deserved a closer study. He ordered a Liburnian galley to be got ready, and offered to take me with him, if I desired to accompany him, but I replied that I preferred to go on with my studies, and it so happened that he had assigned me some writing to do. He was just leaving the house when he received a written message from Rectina, the wife of Tascus, who was terrified at the peril threatening her – for her villa lay just beneath the mountain, and there were no means of escape save by shipboard – begging him to save her from her perilous position. So he changed his plans, and carried out with the greatest fortitude the task, which he had started as a scholarly inquiry.

He had the galleys launched and went on board himself, in the hope of succouring, not only Rectina, but many others, for there were a number of people living along the shore owing to its delightful situation. He hastened, therefore, towards the place whence others were fleeing, and steering a direct course, kept the helm straight for the point of danger, so utterly devoid of fear that every movement of the looming portent and every change in its appearance he described and had noted down by his secretary, as soon as his eyes detected it. Already ashes were beginning to fall upon the ships, hotter and in thicker showers as they approached more nearly, with pumice-stones and black flints, charred and cracked by the heat of the flames, while their way was barred by the sudden shoaling of the sea bottom and the litter of the mountain on the shore. He hesitated for a moment whether to turn back, and then, when the helmsman warned him to do so, he exclaimed, 'Fortune favours the bold; try to reach Pomponianus.' The latter was at Stabiae, separated by the whole width of the bay, for the sea there pours in upon a gently rounded and curving shore. Although the danger was not yet close upon him, it was nonetheless clearly seen, and it travelled quickly as it came nearer, so Pomponianus had got his baggage together on shipboard, and had determined upon flight, and was waiting for the wind which was blowing on shore to fall. My uncle sailed in with the wind fair behind him, and embraced Pomponianus, who was in a state of fright, comforting and cheering him at the same time. Then in order to calm his friend's fears by showing how composed he was himself, he ordered the servants to carry him to the bath, and, after his ablutions, he sat down and had dinner in the best of spirits, or with that assumption of good spirits which is quite as remarkable as the reality.

In the meantime, broad sheets of flame, which rose high in the air, were breaking out in a number of places on Mount Vesuvius and lighting up the sky, and the glare and brightness seemed all the more striking owing to the darkness of the night. My uncle, in order to allay the fear of his companions, kept declaring that the country people in their terror had left their fires burning, and that the conflagration they saw arose from the blazing and empty villas. Then he betook himself to rest and enjoyed a very deep sleep, for his breathing, which, owing to his bulk, was rather heavy and loud, was heard by those who were waiting at the door of his chamber. But by this time the courtyard leading to the room he occupied was so full of ashes and pumice-stones mingled together, and covered to such a depth, that if he had delayed any longer in the bedchamber there would have been no means of escape. So my uncle was aroused, and came out and joined Pomponianus and the rest who had been keeping watch. They held a consultation whether they should remain indoors or wander forth in the open; for the buildings were beginning to shake with the repeated and intensely severe shocks of earthquake and seemed to be rocking to and fro as though they had been torn from their foundations. Outside again there was danger to be apprehended from the pumice-stones, though these were light and nearly burnt through, and thus, after weighing the two perils, the latter course was determined upon. With my uncle it was a choice of reasons which prevailed, with the rest a choice of fears.

They placed pillows on their heads and secured them with cloths, as a precaution against the falling bodies. Elsewhere the day had dawned by this time, but there it was still night, and the darkness was blacker and thicker than any ordinary night. This, however, they relieved as best they could by a number of torches and other kinds of lights. They decided to make their way to the shore, and to see from the nearest point whether the sea would enable them to put out, but it was still running high and contrary. A sheet was spread on the ground, and on this my uncle lay, and twice he called for a draught of cold water, which he drank. Then the flames, and the smell of sulphur which gave warning of them, scattered the others in flight and roused him. Leaning on two slaves, he rose to his feet and immediately fell down again, owing, as I think, to his breathing being obstructed by the thickness of the fumes and congestion of the stomach, that organ being naturally weak and narrow, and subject to inflammation. When daylight returned – two days after the last day he had seen – his body was found untouched, uninjured, and covered, dressed just as he had been in life. The corpse suggested a person asleep rather than a dead man.

Meanwhile my mother and I were at Misenum. But that is of no consequence for the purposes of history, nor indeed did you express a wish to be told of anything except of my uncle's death. So, I will say no more, except to add that I have given you a full account both of the incidents, which I myself witnessed, and of those narrated to me immediately afterwards, when, as a rule, one gets the truest account of what has happened. You will pick out what you think will answer your purpose best, for to write a letter is a different thing from writing a history, and to write to a friend is not like writing to all and sundry.

Farewell.

Book X, Letter 96
Pliny to Emperor Trajan

It is my custom, Sir, to refer to you in all cases where I do not feel sure, for who can better direct my doubts or inform my ignorance? I have never been present at any legal examination of the Christians, and I do not know, therefore, what are the usual penalties passed upon them, or the limits of those penalties, or how searching an inquiry should be made. I have hesitated a great deal in considering whether any distinctions should be drawn according to the ages of the accused; whether the weak should be punished as severely as the more robust; whether if they renounce their faith they should be pardoned, or whether the man who has once been a Christian should gain nothing by recanting; whether the name itself, even though otherwise innocent of crime, should be punished, or only the crimes that gather round it.

In the meantime, this is the plan which I have adopted in the case of those Christians who have been brought before me. I ask them whether they are Christians; if they say yes, then I repeat the question a second and a third time, warning them of the penalties it entails, and if they still persist, I order them to be taken away to prison. For I do not doubt that, whatever the character of the crime may be which they confess, their pertinacity and inflexible obstinacy certainly ought to be punished. There were others who showed similar mad folly whom I reserved to be sent to Rome, as they were Roman citizens. Subsequently, as is usually the way, the very fact of my taking up this question led to a great increase of accusations, and a variety of cases were brought before me.

A pamphlet was issued anonymously, containing the names of a number of people. Those who denied that they were or had been Christians and called upon the gods in the usual formula, reciting the words after me, those who offered incense and wine before your image, which I had given orders to be brought forward for this purpose, together with the statues of the deities – all such I considered should be discharged, especially as they cursed the name of Christ, which, it is said, those who are really Christians cannot be induced to do. Others, whose names were given me by an informer, first said that they were Christians and afterwards denied it, declaring that they had been but were so no longer, some of them having recanted many years before, and more than one so long as 20 years back. They all worshipped your image and the statues of the deities and cursed the name of Christ. But they declared that the sum of their guilt or their error only amounted to this, that on a stated day they had been accustomed to meet before daybreak and to recite a hymn among themselves to Christ, as though he were a god, and that so far from binding themselves by oath to commit any crime, their oath was to abstain from theft, robbery, adultery, and from breach of faith, and not to deny trust money placed in their keeping when called upon to deliver it. When this ceremony was concluded, it had been their custom to depart and meet again to take food, but it was of no special character and quite harmless, and they had ceased this practice after the edict in which, in accordance with your orders, I had forbidden all secret societies. I thought it the more necessary, therefore, to find out what truth there was in these statements by submitting two women, who were called deaconesses, to the torture, however, I found nothing, but a debased superstition carried to great lengths.

So, I postponed my examination, and immediately consulted you. The matter seems to me worthy of your consideration, especially as there are so many people involved in the danger. Many persons of all ages, and of both sexes alike, are being brought into peril of their lives by their accusers, and the process will go on. For the contagion of this superstition has spread not only through the free cities, but into the villages and the rural districts, and yet it seems to me that it can be checked and set right. It is beyond doubt that the temples, which have been almost deserted, are beginning again to be thronged with worshippers, that the sacred rites which have for a long time been allowed to lapse are now being renewed, and that the food for the sacrificial victims is once more finding a sale, whereas, up to recently, a buyer was hardly to be found. From this it is easy to infer what vast numbers of people might be reclaimed, if only they were given an opportunity of repentance.

Book X, Letter 97
Emperor Trajan to Pliny

You have adopted the proper course, my dear Pliny, in examining into the cases of those who have been denounced to you as Christians, for no hard and fast rule can be laid down to meet a question of such wide extent. The Christians are not to be hunted out; if they are brought before you and the offence is proved, they are to be punished, but with this reservation – that if anyone denies that he is a Christian and makes it clear that he is not, by offering prayers to our deities, then he is to be pardoned because of his recantation, however suspicious his past conduct may have been. But pamphlets published anonymously must not carry any weight whatsoever, no matter what the charge may be, for they are not only a precedent of the very worst type, but they are not in consonance with the spirit of our age.

FROM THE *HISTORIA AUGUSTA*

The *Historia Augusta* is a collection of biographies of 30 Roman emperors reigning during the years 117 to 284 CE in the style of Suetonius's *Twelve Caesars* but written by up to six different authors in the fourth century CE. Modern scholars argue over the authorship and accuracy of the accounts, some believing the profiles – or at least some of them – to be satirical.

Life of Hadrian
(Attributed to Aelius Spartianus)

Chapter 5
Hadrian Assumes Power, Makes Domestic and Foreign Policy Changes

On taking possession of the imperial power [11th August 117 CE], Hadrian at once resumed the policy of the early emperors and devoted his attention to maintaining peace throughout the world. For the nations which Trajan had conquered began to revolt; the Moors, moreover, began to make attacks, and the Sarmatians to wage war, the Britons could not be kept under Roman sway, Egypt was thrown into disorder by riots, and finally Libya and Judaea showed the spirit of rebellion. Whereupon he relinquished all the conquests east of the Euphrates and the Tigris, following, as he used to say, the example of Cato, who urged that the Macedonians, because they could not be held as subjects, should be declared free and independent. And Parthamasiris, appointed king of the

Parthians by Trajan, he assigned as ruler to the neighbouring tribes, because he saw that the man was held in little esteem by the Parthians.

Chapter 10
Hadrian Tours the Roman Provinces, Reviews the Army

After this he travelled to the provinces of Gaul [122 CE], and came to the relief of all the communities with various acts of generosity; and from there he went over into Germania [121–122 CE]. Though more desirous of peace than of war, he kept the soldiers in training just as if war were imminent, inspired them by proofs of his own powers of endurance, actually led a soldier's life among the maniples, and, after the example of Scipio Aemilianus, Metellus, and his own adoptive father Trajan, cheerfully ate out of doors such camp-fare as bacon, cheese and vinegar. And that the troops might submit more willingly to the increased harshness of his orders, he bestowed gifts on many and honours on a few. For he re-established the discipline of the camp, which since the time of Octavian [Augustus] had been growing slack through the laxity of his predecessors. He regulated, too, both the duties and the expenses of the soldiers, and now no one could get a leave of absence from camp by unfair means, for it was not popularity with the troops but just deserts that recommended a man for appointment as tribune. He incited others by the example of his own soldierly spirit; he would walk as much as 20 miles fully armed; he cleared the camp of banqueting-rooms, porticoes, grottos, and bowers, generally wore the commonest clothing, would have no gold ornaments on his sword-belt or jewels on the clasp, would scarcely consent to have his sword furnished with an ivory hilt, visited the sick soldiers in their quarters, selected the sites for camps, conferred the centurion's wand on those only who were hardy and of good repute, appointed as tribunes only men with full beards or of an age to give to the authority of the tribuneship the full measure of prudence and maturity, permitted no tribune to accept a present from a soldier, banished luxuries on every hand, and, lastly, improved the soldiers' arms and equipment. Furthermore, with regard to length of military service he issued an order that no one should violate ancient usage by being in the service at an earlier age than his strength warranted, or at a more advanced one than common humanity permitted. He made it a point to be acquainted with the soldiers and to know their numbers.

Chapter 10
Hadrian Builds at Wall in Britannia

Besides this, he strove to have an accurate knowledge of the military stores, and the receipts from the provinces he examined with care in order to make good any deficit that might occur in any particular instance. But more than any other emperor he made it a point not to purchase or maintain anything that was not serviceable. And so, having reformed the army quite in the manner of a monarch, he set out for Britannia [122 CE], and there he corrected many abuses and was the first to construct a wall [119/122–c. 130 CE], 80 miles [73 modern miles] in length, which was to separate the barbarians from the Romans.

Life of Antoninus Pius
(Attributed to Julius Capitolinus)

Chapter 5
Antoninus Pius Assumes Power, Makes Domestic
Policy Changes, and Builds a Wall in Britannia

His father, as long as he lived, he obeyed most scrupulously and, when Hadrian passed away at Baiae [10th July 138 CE], he bore his remains to Rome with all piety and reverence, and buried him in the Gardens of Domitia; moreover, though all opposed the measure, he had him placed among the deified. On his wife Faustina he permitted the Senate to bestow the name of *Augusta*, and for himself accepted the surname *Pius* [139 CE]. The statues decreed for his father, mother, grandparents and brothers, then dead, he accepted readily; nor did he refuse the circus-games ordered for his birthday, though he did refuse other honours. In honour of Hadrian, he set up a superb shield and established a college of priests.

After his accession to the throne [138 CE] he removed none of the men whom Hadrian had appointed to office, and, indeed, was so steadfast and loyal that he retained good men in the government of provinces for terms of seven and even nine years. He waged a number of wars, but all of them through his legates. For Lollius Urbicus, his legate, overcame the Britons and built a second wall [142 CE], one of turf, after driving back the barbarians. Through other legates or governors, he forced the Moors to sue for peace [145/150 CE], and crushed the Germans [140 CE] and the Dacians [around 157 CE] and many other tribes, and also the Jews, who were in revolt. In

Achaea also and in Egypt he put down rebellions and many a time sharply checked the Alani in their raiding.

Chapter 6
Antoninus Pius Runs a Light-touch, No-frills Administration

His procurators were ordered to levy only a reasonable tribute, and those who exceeded a proper limit were commanded to render an account of their acts, nor was he ever pleased with any revenues that were onerous to the provinces. Moreover, he was always willing to hear complaints against his procurators. He besought the Senate to pardon those men whom Hadrian had condemned, saying that Hadrian himself had been about to do so. The imperial pomp he reduced to the utmost simplicity and thereby gained the greater esteem, though the palace-attendants opposed this course, for they found that since he made no use of go-betweens, they could in no wise terrorize men or take money for decisions about which there was no concealment.

In his dealings with the Senate, he rendered it, as emperor, the same respect that he had wished another emperor to render him when he was a private man. When the Senate offered him the title of *Pater Patriae* ['Father of his Country'], he at first refused it, but later accepted it [139 CE] with an elaborate expression of thanks. On the death of his wife Faustina, in the third year of his reign [141 CE], the senate deified her, and voted her games and a temple and priestesses and statues of silver and of gold. These the Emperor accepted, and furthermore granted permission that her statue be erected in all the circuses; and when the Senate voted her a golden statue, he undertook to erect it himself. At the instance of the Senate, Marcus Antoninus, now quaestor, was made consul; also Annius Verus [Lucius Verus], he who was afterwards entitled Antoninus, was appointed quaestor before the legal age. Never did he resolve on measures about the provinces or render a decision on any question without previously consulting his friends, and in accordance with their opinions he drew up his final statement. And, indeed, he often received his friends without the robes of state and even in the performance of domestic duties.

Life of Marcus Aurelius the Philosopher
(Attributed to Julius Capitolinus)

Chapter 12
Early Life of Marcus Aurelius

Toward the people he [Marcus Antonius] acted just as one acts in a free state. He was at all times exceedingly reasonable both in restraining men from evil and in urging them to good, generous in rewarding and quick to forgive, thus making bad men good, and good men very good, and he even bore with unruffled temper the insolence of not a few. For example, when he advised a man of abominable reputation, who was running for office, a certain Vetrasinus, to stop the town-talk about himself, and Vetrasinus replied that many who had fought with him in the arena were now praetors, the Emperor took it with good grace. Again, in order to avoid taking an easy revenge on anyone, instead of ordering a praetor who had acted very badly in certain matters to resign his office, he merely entrusted the administration of the law to the man's colleague. The privy-purse never influenced his judgment in lawsuits involving money. Finally, if he was firm, he was also reasonable. After his brother had returned victorious from Syria, the title *Pater Patriae* was decreed to both, inasmuch as Marcus in the absence of [his colleague Lucius] Verus had conducted himself with great consideration toward both senators and commons. Furthermore, the *corona civica* ['civic crown' made of oak leaves, presented to a man who had saved the life of a fellow citizen in battle] was offered to both; and Lucius demanded that Marcus triumph with him, and demanded also that the name Caesar should be given to Marcus's sons [12 October 166 CE]. But Marcus was so free from love of display that though he triumphed with Lucius, nevertheless after Lucius's death he called himself only *Germanicus* [from 172 CE], the title he had won in his own war. In the triumphal procession, moreover, they carried with them Marcus's children of both sexes, even his unmarried daughters; and they viewed the games held in honour of the triumph clad in the triumphal robe. Among other illustrations of his unfailing consideration towards others this act of kindness is to be told: After one lad, a ropedancer, had fallen, he ordered mattresses spread under all ropedancers. This is the reason why a net is stretched them today. While the Parthian War [161–166 CE] was still in progress, the Marcomannic War [166–180 CE] broke out, after having been postponed for a long time by the diplomacy of the men who were in charge there, in order that the Marcomannic War might not be waged until Rome was done with the war in the East. Even at the time of the famine the Emperor had hinted at this war to the people, and when his brother returned after five years' service, he brought the matter up in the Senate, saying that both emperors were needed for the German War.

Chapter 13
War and Pestilence

So great was the dread of this Marcomannic War, that Antoninus summoned priests from all sides, performed foreign religious ceremonies, and purified the city in every way, and he was delayed thereby from setting out to the seat of war. The Roman ceremony of the Feast of the Gods was celebrated for seven days. And there was such a pestilence [180 CE], besides, that the dead were removed in carts and wagons. About this time, also, the two emperors ratified certain very stringent laws on burial and tombs, in which they even forbade any one to build a tomb at his country-place, a law still in force. Thousands were carried off by the pestilence, including many nobles, for the most prominent of whom Antoninus erected statues. Such, too, was his kindliness of heart that he had funeral ceremonies performed for the lower classes even at the public expense; and in the case of one foolish fellow, who, in a search with divers confederates for an opportunity to plunder the city, continually made speeches from the wild fig tree on the *Campus Martius*, to the effect that fire would fall down from heaven and the end of the world would come should he fall from the tree and be turned into a stork, and finally at the appointed time did fall down and free a stork from his robe, the Emperor, when the wretch was hailed before him and confessed all, pardoned him.

Chapter 14
Marcus Aurelius at War

Clad in the military cloak the two emperors finally set forth, for now not only were the Victuali and Marcomanni throwing everything into confusion, but other tribes, who had been driven on by the more distant barbarians and had retreated before them, were ready to attack Italy if not peaceably received. And not a little good resulted from that expedition, even by the time they had advanced as far as Aquileia, for several kings retreated, together with their peoples, and put to death the authors of the trouble. And the Quadi, after they had lost their king, said that they would not confirm the successor who had been elected until such a course was approved by our emperors. Nevertheless, Lucius went on, though reluctantly, after a number of peoples had sent ambassadors to the legates of the emperors asking pardon for the rebellion. Lucius, it is true, thought they should return, because Furius Victorinus, the Prefect of the Praetorian Cohorts, had been lost, and part of his army had perished; Marcus, however, held that they should press on, thinking that the barbarians, in order that they might not be crushed by the size of so great a force, were feigning a retreat and using other ruses which afford safety in war, held that they should persist in order that they might not be overwhelmed by the mere burden of their vast preparations. Finally, they crossed the Alps, and pressing further on, completed all measures necessary for the defence of Italy and Illyricum. They then decided, at Lucius's insistence, that letters should first be sent ahead to the Senate and that Lucius should then return to Rome. But on the way, after they had set out upon their journey, Lucius died from a stroke of apoplexy [169 CE] while riding in the carriage with his brother.

Chapter 16
Marcus Aurelius, Family Man and Stoic

Such was Marcus's kindness toward his own family that he bestowed the insignia of every office on all his kin, while on his son [Commodus], and an accursed and foul one he was, he hastened to bestow the name of Caesar, then afterward the priesthood [175 CE], and, a little later, the title of *imperator* and a share in a triumph [27th November 176 CE] and the consulship. It was at this time that Marcus, though acclaimed *imperator*, ran on foot in the Circus by the side of the triumphal car in which his son was seated.

After the death of Verus, Marcus Antoninus held the empire alone, a nobler man by far and more abounding in virtues, especially as he was no longer hampered by Verus's faults, neither by those of excessive candour and hot-headed plain speaking, from which Verus suffered through natural folly, nor by those others which had particularly irked Marcus Antoninus even from his earliest years, the principles and habits of a depraved mind. Such was Marcus's own repose of spirit that neither in grief nor in joy did he ever change countenance, being wholly given over to the Stoic philosophy, which he had not only learned from all the best masters, but also acquired for himself from every source. For this reason, Hadrian would have taken him for his own successor to the throne had not his youth prevented. This intention, indeed, seems obvious from the fact that he chose Marcus to be the son-inlaw of Pius, in order that the direction of the Roman state might some time at least come into his hands, as to those of one well worthy.

Chapter 28
The Death of Marcus Aurelius

He died in the following manner: When he began to grow ill, he summoned his son and besought him first of all not to think lightly of what remained of the war, lest he seem a traitor to the state. And when his son replied that his first desire was good health, he allowed him to do as he wished, only asking him to wait a few days and not leave at once. Then, being eager to die, he refrained from eating or drinking, and so aggravated the disease. On the sixth day he summoned his friends, and with derision for all human affairs and scorn for death, said to them, 'Why do you weep for me, instead of thinking about the pestilence and about death which is the common lot of us all?' And when they were about to retire he groaned and said: 'If you now grant me leave to go, I bid you farewell and pass on before.' And when he was asked to whom he commended his son he replied: 'To you, if he prove worthy, and to the immortal gods.'

The army, when they learned of his sickness, lamented loudly, for they loved him singularly. On the seventh day he was weary and admitted only his son, and even him he at once sent away in fear that he would catch the disease. And when his son had gone, he covered his head as though he wished to sleep and during the night he breathed his last [17th March 180 CE]. It is said that he foresaw that after his death

Commodus would turn out as he actually did, and expressed the wish that his son might die, lest, as he himself said, he should become another Nero, Caligula, or Domitian.

FROM AMMIANUS MARCELLINUS'S *ROMAN HISTORY*

A soldier by profession, Ammianus Marcellinus (*c.* 330–*c.* 391/400 CE) wrote a history of Rome from the accession of Nerva (96 CE) to the death of Valens at the Battle of Adrianople (378 CE), thereby continuing the work of Tacitus. Only the books covering the years 353–378 CE survive.

Book XXXV, Chapter 4
Julian, the Soldier Emperor Who Restored Rome to the Old Gods

He [Julian, r. 361–363 CE] was thoroughly skilled in the arts of war and peace, greatly inclined to courtesy, and claiming for himself only so much deference as he thought preserved him from contempt and insolence. He was older in virtue than in years. He gave great attention to the administration of justice, and was sometimes an unbending judge; also a very strict censor in regulating conduct, with a calm contempt for riches, scorning everything mortal; in short, he often used to declare that it was shameful for a wise man, since he possessed a soul, to seek honour from bodily gifts.

By what high qualities he was distinguished in his administration of justice is clear from many indications. Firstly, because taking into account circumstances and persons, he was awe-inspiring but free from cruelty. Secondly, because he checked vice by making examples of a few, and also because he more frequently threatened men with the sword than actually used it. Finally, to be brief, it is well known that he was so merciful towards some open enemies who plotted against him, that he corrected the severity of their punishment by his inborn mildness.

His fortitude is shown by the great number of his battles and by his conduct of wars, as well as by his endurance of excessive cold and heat. And although bodily duty is demanded from a soldier, but mental duty from a general, yet he once boldly met a savage enemy in battle and struck him down, and when our men gave ground, he several times alone checked their flight by opposing his breast to them. When destroying the kingdoms of the raging Germans and on the burning sands of Persia he added to the confidence of his soldiers by fighting among the foremost. There are many notable evidences of his knowledge of military affairs: the sieges of cities and fortresses, undertaken amid the extremest dangers, the varied forms in which he arranged the lines of battle, the choice of safe and healthful places for camps, the wisely planned posting of frontier guards and field pickets. His authority was so well established that, being feared as well as deeply loved as one who shared in the dangers and hardships of his men, he both in the heat of fierce battles condemned cowards to punishment, and, while he was still only a Caesar, he controlled his men even without pay, when they were fighting with savage tribes, as I have long ago said. And when they were armed and mutinous, he did not fear to address them and threaten to return to private life, if they continued to be insubordinate. Finally, one thing it will be enough to know in token of many, namely, that merely by a speech he induced his Gallic troops, accustomed to snow and to the Rhine, to traverse long stretches of country and follow him through torrid Assyria to the very frontiers of the Medes.

His success was so conspicuous that for a long time he seemed to ride on the shoulders of Fortune herself, his faithful guide as he in victorious career surmounted enormous difficulties. And after he left the western region, so long as he was on earth all nations preserved perfect quiet, as if a kind of earthly wand of Mercury were pacifying them.

There are many undoubted tokens of his generosity. Among these are his very light imposition of tribute, his remission of the *coronarium* ['crown-money' presented to the emperor personally by the provinces on his ascension], the cancellation of many debts made great by long standing, the impartial treatment of disputes between the privy purse and private persons, the restoration of the revenues from taxes to various states along with their lands, except such as previous high officials [praetorian prefects] had alienated by a kind of legal sale; furthermore, that he was never eager to increase his wealth, which he thought was better secured in the hands of its possessors; and he often remarked that Alexander the Great, when asked where his treasures were, gave the kindly answer, 'In the hands of my friends.'

Having set down his good qualities, so many as I could know, let me now come to an account of his faults, although they can be summed up briefly. In disposition he was somewhat inconsistent, but he controlled this by the excellent habit of submitting, when he went wrong, to correction. He was somewhat talkative, and very seldom silent; also too much given to the consideration of omens and portents, so that in this respect he seemed to equal the Emperor Hadrian. Superstitious rather than truly religious, he sacrificed innumerable victims without regard to cost, so that one might believe that if he had returned from the Parthians, there would soon have been a scarcity of cattle; like the Caesar Marcus [Aurelius], of whom (as we learn) the following Greek couplet was written:

> *We the white steers do Marcus Caesar greet.*
> *Win once again, and death we all must meet.*

FROM OROSIUS'S *HISTORIES AGAINST THE PAGANS*

The *History Against the Pagans* by Paulus Orosius (c. 375/385–c. 420 CE) tells Roman history from an entirely Christian viewpoint. He rewrote the story to diminish the achievements of Pagan Romans and to celebrate the attainments of the Followers of Jesus Christ.

Book VII, Chapter 25
The Division of the Roman Empire into West and East

In the Year 1041 [284 CE], Diocletian was chosen by the army as the thirty-third emperor. He reigned for 20 years. Upon assuming full command, he at once killed with his own hand Aper, the murderer of Numerianus. He next defeated Carinus in a stubbornly contested battle. This man had been leading a dissolute life in Dalmatia, where Carus had left him as Caesar.

Later Amandus and Aelianus in Gaul gathered together a band of farmers, who were called Bacaudae, and stirred up destructive insurrections. Diocletian appointed Maximianus, surnamed Herculius, Caesar and sent him into the Gallic provinces. Here, by his military prowess, he easily put down the inexperienced and disorderly company of peasants.

At this time a certain Carausius, a man of lowly birth to be sure, but quick in thought and action, was in charge of the defence of the coasts of the ocean, which were infested by the Franks and Saxons. He did more to injure than to help the government, for he did not restore to its true owners any of the booty recovered from the pirates but claimed it for himself alone. In this way he aroused the suspicion that it was his deliberate neglect that had allowed the enemy to make raids. For this reason, Maximianus ordered his execution. Carausius at once assumed the purple and seized control of the British provinces [286 CE].

Thus, the thunders of strife suddenly reverberated throughout the territories of the Roman Empire. Carausius was leading a rebellion in Britannia, and Achilleus one in Egypt; the Quinquegentiani were attacking Africa, and Narseus [Narseh, r. 293–303 CE], king of the Persians, was waging destructive wars in the East. In view of this dangerous situation, Diocletian advanced Maximianus Herculius from the rank of Caesar to that of Augustus and appointed Constantius [Chlorus] and Galerius Maximianus Caesars. Constantius now married Theodora, the stepdaughter of Herculius Maximianus, and by her had six sons, the brothers of Constantine. Carausius, after laying claim to Britannia, held it firmly in his grasp for seven years [to 293 CE]. Finally, however, he was treacherously killed by his comrade Allectus. The latter held for three years the island that he had taken away from his friend. The praetorian prefect Asclepiodotus then overthrew him and regained Britannia [296 CE], 10 years after it had been lost.

In Gaul, in the first encounter, the Alemanni routed Constantius Caesar's army. He himself barely managed to escape. In the second battle [288 CE], however, he won a complete victory. It is said that 60,000 of the Alemanni were slain in the course of a few hours. Maximianus Augustus subdued the Quinquegentiani in Africa. Then Diocletian besieged Achilleus at Alexandria for eight months. He finally captured and killed him [297 CE]; but, far from showing moderation in his victory, he gave Alexandria over to pillage, and made life in all Egypt hideous with proscriptions and massacres.

Galerius Maximianus fought two battles against Narseus. In a third engagement, which took place somewhere between the cities of Callinicus and Carrhae, Narseus defeated him [297 CE]. After losing his troops, Galerius took refuge with Diocletian, who received him with extreme arrogance. The story goes that though clad in scarlet robes he was forced to run before the Emperor's carriage for several miles. Nevertheless, Galerius made this insult serve as a whetstone to his valour. Spurred on by this treatment, when the rust of kingly pride was rubbed off, he was able to sharpen his mind to a keen edge. He at once made a general levy of troops throughout Illyricum and Moesia, and hurriedly returning to meet the enemy, he overwhelmed Narseus by skilful strategy and superior forces. After annihilating the Persian army and putting Narseus himself to flight, he seized the latter's camp, made prisoners of his wives, sisters, and children, appropriated an immense amount of Persian treasure, and led away many of the Persian nobles into captivity. On his return to Mesopotamia, he was welcomed by Diocletian and given the highest honours. Later these same generals fought vigorously against the Carpi and the Basternae. They then conquered the Sarmatians and distributed a great number of captives from this people among the garrisons of the Roman frontiers.

In the meantime, Diocletian in the East and Maximianus Herculius in the West ordered the churches to be destroyed and the Christians persecuted and put to death [303 CE]. This persecution, the tenth in succession from Nero's, was longer and more cruel than any other that had preceded it. For 10 years it was carried on without interruption; churches were burned, the innocent were proscribed, and martyrs were slaughtered. Then followed an earthquake in Syria. Thousands of people throughout Tyre and Sidon were crushed by falling buildings. In the second year of the persecution [304 CE], Diocletian suggested to the unwilling Maximianus that both of them should at the same time lay aside the purple and the imperial power and, after substituting younger men for themselves in the government, pass their declining years in the leisure of private life. Accordingly, on the day agreed they laid aside the power and trappings of empire – Diocletian at Nicomedia, and Maximianus at Mediolanum.

The *Augusti*, Galerius and Constantius, were the first to divide the Roman Empire in two [286 CE]: the former took Illyricum, Asia, and the East; the latter took Italy, Africa, and the Gallic provinces. Constantius, however, who was of an extremely mild disposition, was satisfied with Gaul and Spain alone and permitted Galerius to take the other districts. Galerius chose two *Caesares*: Maximinus, whom he stationed in the East, and Severus, to whom he entrusted Italy. He himself established his government in Illyricum. Constantius Augustus, a mild-tempered man and one skilled in the conduct of government, died in Britannia [306 CE], leaving Constantine, a son by his concubine Helena, as *imperator* of the Gallic provinces.

Book VII, Chapter 28
Constantine the Great, Rome's First
Christian Emperor

Now, as I have said, after the death of Constantius in Britannia, Constantine was proclaimed emperor [25th July 306 CE]. He was the first Christian emperor – with the exception of Philip [the Arab], whose Christian reign of a very few years [r. 244–249 CE] was, in my opinion, established only to the end that the 1,000th anniversary of Rome should be dedicated to Christ rather than to idols. From the time of Constantine, however, all the emperors have been Christians up to the present day [420 CE] – with the exception of Julian, whose pernicious life, it is said, was cut off while he was plotting shameful deeds. This is the slow but inevitable punishment of pagans. This is why they rave, though in their right mind. This is why they are goaded by the stings of conscience, though they have not been hurt. This is why they groan, though they laugh. This is why they begin to fail, though they are still in sound health. This is why they are tortured in secret, though no one persecutes them. Finally, this is why there are now but few left, though they have never been punished by any persecutor.

ANCIENT
KINGS & LEADERS

Ancient cultures often traded with and influenced
each other, while others grew independently.
This section provides the key leaders from a
number of regions, to offer comparative insights
into developments across the ancient world.

SUMERIAN KING LIST

This list is based on the *Sumerian King List* or *Chronicle of the One Monarchy*. The lists were often originally carved into clay tablets and several versions have been found, mainly in southern Mesopotamia. Some of these are incomplete and others contradict one another. Dates are based on archaeological evidence as far as possible but are thus approximate. There may also be differences in name spellings between different sources. Nevertheless, the lists remain an invaluable source of information.

As with many civilizations, lists of leaders often begin with mythological and legendary figures before they merge into the more solidly historical, hence why you will see some reigns of seemingly impossible length.

After the kingship descended from heaven, the kingship was in Eridug.

Alulim	28,800 years (8 *sars**)
Alalngar	36,000 years (10 *sars*)

Then Eridug fell and the kingship was taken to Bad-tibira.

En-men-lu-ana	43,200 years (12 *sars*)
En-mel-gal-ana	28,800 years (8 *sars*)
Dumuzid the Shepherd (or Tammuz)	36,000 years (10 *sars*)

Then Bad-tibira fell and the kingship was taken to Larag.

En-sipad-zid-ana   28,800 years (8 *sars*)

Then Larag fell and the kingship was taken to Zimbir.

En-men-dur-ana   21,000 years (5 *sars* and 5 *ners*)

Then Zimbir fell and the kingship was taken to Shuruppag.

Ubara-Tutu   18,600 years (5 *sars* and 1 *ner**)

Then the flood swept over.

*A *sar* is a numerical unit of 3,600; a *ner* is a numerical unit of 600.

FIRST DYNASTY OF KISH

After the flood had swept over, and the kingship had descended from heaven, the kingship was in Kish.

Jushur	1,200 years	Zuqaqip	900 years
Kullassina-bel	960 years	Atab (or A-ba)	600 years
Nangishlisma	1,200 years	Mashda (son of	
En-tarah-ana	420 years	Atab)	840 years
Babum	300 years	Arwium (son of	
Puannum	840 years	Mashda)	720 years
Kalibum	960 years	Etana the Shepherd	1,500 years
Kalumum	840 years	Balih (son of Etana)	400 years

En-me-nuna	660 years	Iltasadum	1,200 years
Melem-Kish (son of Enme-nuna)	900 years	Enmebaragesi (earliest proven ruler based on archaeological sources; Early Dynastic Period, 2900–2350 BCE)	900 years
Barsal-nuna (son of Enme-nuna)	1,200 years		
Zamug (son of Barsal-nuna)	140 years		
Tizqar (son of Zamug)	305 years	Aga of Kish (son of Enmebaragesi) (Early Dynastic Period, 2900–2350 BCE)	625 years
Ilku	900 years		

Then Kish was defeated and the kingship was taken to E-anna.

FIRST RULERS OF URUK

Mesh-ki-ang-gasher (son of Utu)	324 years (Late Uruk Period, 4000–3100 BCE)
Enmerkar (son of Mesh-ki-ang-gasher)	420 years (Late Uruk Period, 4000–3100 BCE)
Lugal-banda the shepherd	1200 years (Late Uruk Period, 4000–3100 BCE)
Dumuzid the fisherman	100 years (Jemdet Nasr Period, 3100–2900 BCE)
Gilgamesh	126 years (Early Dynastic Period, 2900–2350 BCE)
Ur-Nungal (son of Gilgamesh)	30 years
Udul-kalama (son of Ur-Nungal)	15 years
La-ba'shum	9 years
En-nun-tarah-ana	8 years

Mesh-he	36 years
Melem-ana	6 years
Lugal-kitun	36 years

Then Unug was defeated and the kingship was taken to Urim (Ur).

FIRST DYNASTY OF UR

Mesh-Ane-pada	80 years
Mesh-ki-ang-Nuna (son of Mesh-Ane-pada)	36 years
Elulu	25 years
Balulu	36 years

Then Urim was defeated and the kingship was taken to Awan.

DYNASTY OF AWAN

Three kings of Awan	356 years

Then Awan was defeated and the kingship was taken to Kish.

SECOND DYNASTY OF KISH

Susuda the fuller	201 years
Dadasig	81 years
Mamagal the boatman	360 years
Kalbum (son of Mamagal)	195 years

Tuge	360 years
Men-nuna (son of Tuge)	180 years
Enbi-Ishtar	290 years
Lugalngu	360 years

Then Kish was defeated and the kingship was taken to Hamazi.

DYNASTY OF HAMAZI

Hadanish	360 years

Then Hamazi was defeated and the kingship was taken to Unug (Uruk).

SECOND DYNASTY OF URUK

En-shag-kush-ana	60 years (*c.* 25th century BCE)
Lugal-kinishe-dudu	120 years
Argandea	7 years

Then Unug was defeated and the kingship was taken to Urim (Ur).

SECOND DYNASTY OF UR

Nanni	120 years
Mesh-ki-ang-Nanna II (son of Nanni)	48 years

Then Urim was defeated and the kingship was taken to Adab.

DYNASTY OF ADAB

Lugal-Ane-mundu   90 years (*c.* 25th century BCE)

Then Adab was defeated and the kingship was taken to Mari.

DYNASTY OF MARI

Anbu	30 years	Zizi of Mari, the fuller	20 years
Anba (son of Anbu)	17 years	Limer the 'gudug'	
Bazi the		priest	30 years
leatherworker	30 years	Sharrum-iter	9 years

Then Mari was defeated and the kingship was taken to Kish.

THIRD DYNASTY OF KISH

Kug-Bau (Kubaba)   100 years (*c.* 25th century BCE)

Then Kish was defeated and the kingship was taken to Akshak.

DYNASTY OF AKSHAK

Unzi	30 years	Ishu-Il	24 years
Undalulu	6 years	Shu-Suen (son of	
Urur	6 years	Ishu-Il)	7 years
Puzur-Nirah	20 years		

Then Akshak was defeated and the kingship was taken to Kish.

FOURTH DYNASTY OF KISH

Puzur-Suen (son of Kug-bau)	25 years (*c.* 2350 BCE)
Ur-Zababa (son of Puzur-Suen)	400 years (*c.* 2300 BCE)
Zimudar	30 years
Usi-watar (son of Zimudar)	7 years
Eshtar-muti	11 years
Ishme-Shamash	11 years
Shu-ilishu	15 years
Nanniya the jeweller	7 years

Then Kish was defeated and the kingship was taken to Unug (Uruk).

THIRD DYNASTY OF URUK

Lugal-zage-si	25 years (*c.* 2296–2271 BCE)

Then Unug was defeated and the kingship was taken to Agade (Akkad).

DYNASTY OF AKKAD

Sargon of Akkad	56 years (*c.* 2270–2215 BCE)
Rimush of Akkad (son of Sargon)	9 years (*c.* 2214–2206 BCE)
Manishtushu (son of Sargon)	15 years (*c.* 2205–2191 BCE)

Naram-Sin of Akkad (son of
Manishtushu)   56 years (c. 2190–2154 BCE)
Shar-kali-sharri (son of Naram-Sin) 24 years (c. 2153–2129 BCE)

Then who was king? Who was not the king?

Irgigi, Nanum, Imi and Ilulu   3 years (four rivals who fought
                                  to be king during a three-year
                                  period; c. 2128–2125 BCE)
Dudu of Akkad   21 years (c. 2125–2104 BCE)
Shu-Durul (son of Duu)   15 years (c. 2104–2083 BCE)

Then Agade was defeated and the kingship was taken to Unug (Uruk).

FOURTH DYNASTY OF URUK

Ur-ningin   7 years (c. 2091?–2061? BCE)
Ur-gigir (son of Ur-ningin)   6 years
Kuda   6 years
Puzur-ili   5 years
Ur-Utu (or Lugal-melem; son of Ur-gigir) 6 years

Unug was defeated and the kingship was taken to the army of Gutium.

GUTIAN RULE

Inkišuš   6 years (c. 2147–2050 BCE)
Sarlagab (or Zarlagab)   6 years

Shulme (or Yarlagash)	6 years
Elulmeš (or Silulumeš or Silulu)	6 years
Inimabakeš (or Duga)	5 years
Igešauš (or Ilu-An)	6 years
Yarlagab	3 years
Ibate of Gutium	3 years
Yarla (or Yarlangab)	3 years
Kurum	1 year
Apilkin	3 years
La-erabum	2 years
Irarum	2 years
Ibranum	1 year
Hablum	2 years
Puzur-Suen (son of Hablum)	7 years
Yarlaganda	7 years
Si'um (or Si-u)	7 years
Tirigan	40 days

Then the army of Gutium was defeated and the kingship taken to Unug (Uruk).

FIFTH DYNASTY OF URUK

Utu-hengal	427 years / 26 years / 7 years
	(conflicting dates; c. 2055–2048 BCE)

THIRD DYNASTY OF UR

Ur-Namma (or Ur-Nammu)	18 years (c. 2047–2030 BCE)
Shulgi (son of Ur-Namma)	48 years (c. 2029–1982 BCE)
Amar-Suena (son of Shulgi)	9 years (c. 1981–1973 BCE)
Shu-Suen (son of Amar-Suena)	9 years (c. 1972–1964 BCE)
Ibbi-Suen (son of Shu-Suen)	24 years (c. 1963–1940 BCE)

Then Urim was defeated. The very foundation of Sumer was torn out. The kingship was taken to Isin.

DYNASTY OF ISIN

Ishbi-Erra	33 years (c. 1953–1920 BCE)
Shu-Ilishu (son of Ishbi-Erra)	20 years
Iddin-Dagan (son of Shu-Ilishu)	20 years
Ishme-Dagan (son of Iddin-Dagan)	20 years
Lipit-Eshtar (son of Ishme-Dagan or Iddin Dagan)	11 years
Ur-Ninurta (son of Ishkur)	28 years
Bur-Suen (son of Ur-Ninurta)	21 years
Lipit-Enlil (son of Bur-Suen)	5 years
Erra-imitti	8 years
Enlil-bani	24 years
Zambiya	3 years
Iter-pisha	4 years
Ur-du-kuga	4 years
Suen-magir	11 years
Damiq-ilishu (son of Suen-magir)	23 years

ANCIENT EGYPTIAN PHARAOHS

There is dispute about the dates and position of pharaohs within dynasties due to several historical sources being incomplete or inconsistent. This list aims to provide an overview of the ancient Egyptian dynasties, but is not exhaustive and dates are approximate. There may also be differences in name spellings between different sources. Also please note that the throne name is given first, followed by the personal name – more commonly they are known by the latter.

ANCIENT EGYPTIAN DEITIES

Ancient Egyptian gods and goddesses were worshipped as deities. They were responsible for maat (divine order or stability), and different deities represented different natural forces, such as Ra the Sun God. After the Egyptian state was first founded in around 3100 BCE, pharaohs claimed to be divine representatives of these gods and were thought to be successors of the gods.

While there are many conflicting Egyptian myths, some of the significant gods and goddesses and their significant responsibilities are listed here.

Amun/Amen/Amen-Ra	Creation
Atem/Tem	Creation, the sun

Ra	The sun
Isis	The afterlife, fertility, magic
Osiris	Death and resurrection, agriculture
Hathor	The sky, the sun, motherhood
Horus	Kingship, the sky
Set	Storms, violence, deserts
Maat	Truth and justice, she personifies *maat*
Anubis	The dead, the underworld

PREDYNASTIC AND EARLY DYNASTIC PERIODS
(*c.* 3000–2686 BCE)

First Dynasty (*c.* 3150–2890 BCE)
The first dynasty begins at the unification of Upper and Lower Egypt.

Narmer (Menes/M'na?)	c. 3150 BCE
Aha (Teti)	c. 3125 BCE
Djer (Itej)	54 years
Djet (Ita)	10 years
Merneith (possibly the first female Egyptian pharaoh)	c. 2950 BCE
Khasti (Den)	42 years
Merybiap (Adjib)	10 years
Semerkhet (Iry)	8.5 years
Qa'a (Qebeh)	34 years
Sneferka	c. 2900 BCE
Horus-Ba (Horus Bird)	c. 2900 BCE

Second Dynasty (*c.* 2890–2686 BCE)
Little is known about the second dynasty of Egypt.

Hetepsekhemwy (Nebtyhotep)	15 years
Nebra	14 years
Nynetjer (Banetjer)	43–45 years
Ba	unknown
Weneg-Nebty	c. 2740 BCE
Wadjenes (Wadj-sen)	c. 2740 BCE
Nubnefer	unknown
Senedj	c. 47 years
Peribsen (Seth-Peribsen)	unknown
Sekhemib (Sekhemib-Perenmaat)	c. 2720 BCE
Neferkara I	25 years
Neferkasokkar	8 years
Horus Sa	unknown
Hudejefa (real name missing)	11 years
Khasekhemwy (Bebty)	18 years

OLD KINGDOM (c. 2686–2181 BCE)

Third Dynasty (c. 2686–2613 BCE)

The third dynasty was the first dynasty of the Old Kingdom. Its capital was at Memphis.

Djoser (Netjerikhet)	c. 2650 BCE
Sekhemkhet (Djoser-Teti)	2649–2643 BCE
Nebka? (Sanakht)	c. 2650 BCE
Qahedjet (Huni?)	unknown
Khaba (Huni?)	2643–2637 BCE
Huni	2637–2613 BCE

Fourth Dynasty (*c.* 2613–2498 BCE)

The fourth dynasty is sometimes known as the 'golden age' of Egypt's Old Kingdom.

Snefru (Nebmaat)	2613–2589 BCE
Khufu, or Cheops (Medjedu)	2589–2566 BCE
Djedefre (Kheper)	2566–2558 BCE
Khafre (Userib)	2558–2532 BCE
Menkaure (Kakhet)	2532–2503 BCE
Shepseskaf (Shepeskhet)	2503–2498 BCE

Fifth Dynasty (*c.* 2498–2345 BCE)

There is some doubt over the succession of pharaohs in the fifth dynasty, especially Shepseskare.

Userkaf	2496/8–2491 BCE
Sahure	2490–2477 BCE
Neferirkare-Kakai	2477–2467 BCE
Neferefre (Izi)	2460–2458 BCE
Shepseskare (Netjeruser)	few months between 2458 and 2445 BCE
Niuserre (Ini)	2445–2422 BCE
Menkauhor (Kaiu)	2422–2414 BCE
Djedkare (Isesi)	2414–2375 BCE
Unis (Wenis)	2375–2345 BCE

Sixth Dynasty (*c.* 2345–2181 BCE)

Teti	2345–2333 BCE
Userkare	2333–2332 BCE
Meryre (Pepi I)	2332–2283 BCE

Merenre I (Nemtyemsaf I)	2283–2278 BCE
Neferkare (Pepi II)	2278–2183 BCE
Merenre II (Nemtyemsaf II)	2183 or 2184 BCE
Netjerkare (Siptah I) or Nitocris	2182–2179 BCE

FIRST INTERMEDIATE PERIOD (c. 2181–2040 BCE)

Seventh and Eighth Dynasties (c. 2181–2160 BCE)

There is little evidence on this period in ancient Egyptian history, which is why many of the periods of rule are unknown.

Menkare	c. 2181 BCE
Neferkare II	unknown
Neferkare III (Neby)	unknown
Djedkare (Shemai)	unknown
Neferkare IV (Khendu)	unknown
Merenhor	unknown
Sneferka (Neferkamin I)	unknown
Nikare	unknown
Neferkare V (Tereru)	unknown
Neferkahor	unknown
Neferkare VI (Peiseneb)	unknown to 2171 BCE
Neferkamin (Anu)	c. 2170 BCE
Qakare (Ibi)	2175–2171 BCE
Neferkaure	2167–2163 BCE
Neferkauhor (Khuwihapi)	2163–2161 BCE
Neferiirkkare (Pepi)	2161–2160 BCE

Ninth Dynasty (*c.* 2160–2130 BCE)

There is little evidence on this period in ancient Egyptian history which is why many of the periods of rule are unknown.

Maryibre (Khety I)	2160 BCE to unknown
Name unknown	unknown
Naferkare VII	unknown
Seneh (Setut)	unknown

The following pharaohs and their dates of rule are unknown or widely unconfirmed.

Tenth Dynasty (*c.* 2130–2040 BCE)

Rulers in the Tenth dynasty were based in Lower Egypt.

Meryhathor	2130 BCE to unknown
Neferkare VIII	2130–2040 BCE
Wahkare (Khety III)	unknown
Merykare	unknown to 2040 BCE
Name unknown	unknown

Eleventh Dynasty (*c.* 2134–1991 BCE)

Rulers in the eleventh dynasty were based in Upper Egypt.

Intef the Elder	unknown
Tepia (Mentuhotep I)	unknown to 2133 BCE
Sehertawy (Intef I)	2133–2117 BCE
Wahankh (Intef II)	2117–2068 BCE
Nakhtnebtepefer (Intef III)	2068–2060/40 BCE

MIDDLE KINGDOM (c. 2040-1802 BCE)

Eleventh Dynasty Continued (c. 2134-1991 BCE)

This period is usually known as the beginning of the Middle Kingdom.

Nebhepetre (Mentuhotep II)   2060–2040 BCE as king of Upper
    Egypt, 2040–2009 BCE as King of Upper and Lower Egypt
Sankhkare (Mentuhotep III)   2009–1997 BCE
Nebtawyre (Mentuhotep IV)   1997–1991 BCE

Twelfth Dynasty (c. 1991-1802 BCE)

The twelfth dynasty was one of the most stable prior to the New Kingdom, and is often thought to be the peak of the Middle Kingdom.

Sehetepibre (Amenemhat I)	1991–1962 BCE
Kheperkare (Senusret I / Sesostris I)	1971–1926 BCE
Nubkaure (Amenemhat II)	1929–1895 BCE
Khakheperre (Senusret II / Sesostris II)	1898–1878 BCE
Khakaure (Senusret III / Sesostris III)	1878–1839 BCE
Nimaatre (Amenemhat III)	1860–1815 BCE
Maakherure (Amenemhat IV)	1815–1807 BCE
Sobekkare (Sobekneferu/Nefrusobek)	1807–1802 BCE

SECOND INTERMEDIATE PERIOD (c. 1802-1550 BCE)

Thirteenth Dynasty (c. 1802-c. 1649 BCE)

There is some ambiguity on the periods of rule of the thirteenth dynasty, but it is marked by a period of several short rules. This dynasty is often combined with the eleventh, twelfth and fourteenth dynasties under the Middle Kingdom.

Sekhemre Khutawy (Sobekhotep I)	1802–1800 BCE
Mehibtawy Sekhemkare (Amenemhat Sonbef)	1800–1796 BCE
Nerikare (Sobek)	1796 BCE
Sekhemkare (Amenemhat V)	1796–1793 BCE
Ameny Qemau	1795–1792 BCE
Hotepibre (Qemau Siharnedjheritef)	1792–1790 BCE
Lufni	1790–1788 BCE
Seankhibre (Amenemhat VI)	1788–1785 BCE
Semenkare (Nebnuni)	1785–1783 BCE
Sehetepibre (Sewesekhtawy)	1783–1781 BCE
Sewadjkare I	1781 BCE
Nedjemibre (Amenemhat V)	1780 BCE
Khaankhre (Sobekhotep)	1780–1777 BCE
Renseneb	1777 BCE
Awybre (Hor)	1777–1775 BCE
Sekhemrekhutawy Khabaw	1775–1772 BCE
Djedkheperew	1772–1770 BCE
Sebkay	unknown
Sedjefakare (Kay Amenemhat)	1769–1766 BCE
Khutawyre (Wegaf)	c. 1767 BCE
Userkare (Khendjer)	c. 1765 BCE
Smenkhkare (Imyremeshaw)	started in 1759 BCE
Sehetepkare (Intef IV)	c. 10 years
Meribre (Seth)	ended in 1749 BCE
Sekhemresewadjtawy (Sobekhotep III)	1755–1751 BCE
Khasekhemre (Neferhotep I)	1751–1740 BCE

Menwadjre (Sihathor)	1739 BCE
Khaneferre (Sobekhotep IV)	1740–1730 BCE
Merhotepre (Sobekhotep V)	1730 BCE
Knahotepre (Sobekhotep VI)	c. 1725 BCE
Wahibre (Ibiau)	1725–1714 BCE
Merneferre (Ay I)	1714–1691 BCE
Merhotepre (Ini)	1691–1689 BCE
Sankhenre (Sewadjtu)	1675–1672 BCE
Mersekhemre (Ined)	1672–1669 BCE
Sewadjkare II (Hori)	c. 5 years
Merkawre (Sobekhotep VII)	1664–1663 BCE
Seven kings (names unknown)	1663–? BCE

Note: the remaining pharaohs of the thirteenth dynasty are not listed here as they are either unknown or there is a lot of ambiguity about when they ruled.

Fourteenth Dynasty (*c.* 1805/1710–1650 BCE)

Rulers in the fourteenth dynasty were based at Avaris, the capital of this dynasty.

Sekhaenre (Yakbim)	1805–1780 BCE
Nubwoserre (Ya'ammu)	1780–1770 BCE
Khawoserre (Qareh)	1770–1745 BCE
Aahotepre ('Ammu)	1760–1745 BCE
Maaibre (Sheshi)	1745–1705 BCE
Aasehre (Nehesy)	c. 1705 BCE
Khakherewre	unknown
Nebefawre	c. 1704 BCE
Sehebre	1704–1699 BCE

Merdjefare   *c.* 1699 BCE

Note: the remaining pharaohs of the fourteenth dynasty are not listed here as they are either unknown or there is a lot of ambiguity about when they ruled.

Fifteenth Dynasty (*c.* 1650–1544 BCE)

The fifteenth dynasty was founded by Salitas and covered a large part of the Nile region.

Salitas	*c.* 1650 BCE
Semqen	1649 BCE to unknown
'Aper-'Anat	unknown
Sakir-Har	unknown
Seuserenre (Khyan)	*c.* 30 to 35 years
Nebkhepeshre (Apepi)	1590 BCE?
Nakhtyre (Khamudi)	1555–1544 BCE

Sixteenth Dynasty (*c.* 1650–1580 BCE)

Rulers in the sixteenth dynasty were based at Thebes, the capital of this dynasty. The name and date of rule of the first pharaoh is unknown.

Sekhemresementawy (Djehuti)	3 years
Sekhemresemeusertawy (Sobekhotep VIII)	16 years
Sekhemresankhtawy (Neferhotep III)	1 year
Seankhenre (Mentuhotepi)	less than a year
Sewadjenre (Nebiryraw)	26 years
Neferkare (?) (Nebiryraw II)	*c.* 1600 BCE
Semenre	*c.* 1600 BCE

Seuserenre (Bebiankh)	12 years
Djedhotepre (Dedumose I)	c. 1588–1582 BCE
Djedneferre (Dedumose II)	c. 1588–1582 BCE
Djedankhre (Montensaf)	c. 1590 BCE
Merankhre (Mentuhotep VI)	c. 1585 BCE
Seneferibre (Senusret IV)	unknown
Sekhemre (Shedwast)	unknown

Seventeenth Dynasty (c. 1650–1550 BCE)
Rulers in the seventeenth dynasty ruled Upper Egypt.

Sekhemrewahkhaw (Rahotep)	c. 1620 BCE
Sekhemre Wadjkhaw (Sobekemsaf I)	c. 7 years
Sekhemre Shedtawy (Sobekemsaf II)	unknown to c. 1573 BCE
Sekhemre-Wepmaat (Intef V)	c. 1573–1571 BCE
Nubkheperre (Intef VI)	c. 1571–1565 BCE
Sekhemre-Heruhirmaat (Intef VII)	late 1560s BCE
Senakhtenre (Ahmose)	c. 1558 BCE
Seqenenre (Tao I)	1558–1554 BCE
Wadkheperre (Kamose)	1554–1549 BCE

NEW KINGDOM (c. 1550–1077 BCE)

Eighteenth Dynasty (c. 1550–1292 BCE)
The first dynasty of Egypt's New Kingdom marked the beginning of ancient Egypt's highest power and expansion.

Nebpehtire (Ahmose I)	c. 1550–1525 BCE
Djeserkare (Amenhotep I)	1541–1520 BCE

Aakheperkare (Thutmose I)	1520–1492 BCE
Aakheperenre (Thutmose II)	1492–1479 BCE
Maatkare (Hatshepsut)	1479–1458 BCE
Menkheperre (Thutmose III)	1458–1425 BCE
Aakheperrure (Amenhotep II)	1425–1400 BCE
Menkheperure (Thutmose IV)	1400–1390 BCE
Nebmaatre 'the Magnificent'	
(Amehotep III)	1390–1352 BCE
Neferkheperure Waenre (Amenhotep IV)	1352–1336 BCE
Ankhkheperure (Smenkhkare)	1335–1334 BCE
Ankhkheperure mery Neferkheperure	
(Neferneferuaten III)	1334–1332 BCE
Nebkheperure (Tutankhamun)	1332–1324 BCE
Kheperkheperure (Aya II)	1324–1320 BCE
Djeserkheperure Setpenre (Haremheb)	1320–1292 BCE

Nineteenth Dynasty (c. 1550–1292 BCE)

The nineteenth dynasty is also known as the Ramessid dynasty as it includes Ramesses II, one of the most famous and influential Egyptian pharaohs.

Menpehtire (Ramesses I)	1292–1290 BCE
Menmaatre (Seti I)	1290–1279 BCE
Usermaatre Setpenre 'the Great',	
'Ozymandias' (Ramesses II)	1279–1213 BCE
Banenre (Merneptah)	1213–1203 BCE
Menmire Setpenre (Amenmesse)	1203–1200 BCE
Userkheperure (Seti II)	1203–1197 BCE
Sekhaenre (Merenptah Siptah)	1197–1191 BCE
Satre Merenamun (Tawosret)	1191–1190 BCE

Twentieth Dynasty (c. 1190–1077 BCE)

This, the third dynasty of the New Kingdom, is generally thought to mark the start of the decline of ancient Egypt.

Userkhaure (Setnakht)	1190–1186 BCE
Usermaatre Meryamun (Ramesses III)	1186–1155 BCE
Heqamaatre Setpenamun (Ramesses IV)	1155–1149 BCE
Heqamaatre Setpenamun (Ramesses IV)	1155–1149 BCE
Usermaatre Sekheperenre (Ramesses V)	1149–1145 BCE
Nebmaatre Meryamun (Ramesses VI)	1145–1137 BCE
Usermaatre Setpenre Meryamun (Ramesses VII)	1137–1130 BCE
Usermaatre Akhenamun (Ramesses VIII)	1130–1129 BCE
Neferkare Setpenre (Ramesses IX)	1128–1111 BCE
Khepermaatre Setpenptah (Ramesses X)	1111–1107 BCE
Menmaatre Setpenptah (Ramesses XI)	1107–1077 BCE

Twenty-first Dynasty (c. 1077–943 BCE)

Rulers in the twenty-first dynasty were based at Tanis and mainly governed Lower Egypt.

Hedjkheperre-Setpenre (Nesbanadjed I)	1077–1051 BCE
Neferkare (Amenemnisu)	1051–1047 BCE
Aakkheperre (Pasebakhenniut I)	1047–1001 BCE
Usermaatre (Amenemope)	1001–992 BCE
Aakheperre Setepenre (Osorkon the Elder)	992–986 BCE
Netjerikheperre-Setpenamun (Siamun)	986–967 BCE
Titkheperure (Pasebakhenniut II)	967–943 BCE

Twenty-second Dynasty (c. 943–728 BCE)

Sometimes called the Bubastite dynasty. Its pharaohs came from Libya.

Hedjkheneperre Setpenre (Sheshonq I)	943–922 BCE
Sekhemkheperre Setepenre (Osorkon I)	922–887 BCE
Heqakheperre Setepenre (Sheshonq II)	887–885 BCE
Tutkheperre (Sheshonq Llb)	c. the 880s BCE
Hedjkheperre Setepenre (Takelot I Meriamun)	885–872 BCE
Usermaatre Setpenre (Sheshonq III)	837–798 BCE
Hedjkheperre Setepenre (Sheshonq IV)	798–785 BCE
Usermaatre Setpenre (Pami Meriamun)	785–778 BCE
Aakheperre (Sheshonq V)	778–740 BCE
Usermaatre (Osorkon IV)	740–720 BCE

Twenty-third and Twenty-fourth Dynasties (c. 837–720 BCE)

These dynasties were led mainly by Libyans and mainly ruled Upper Egypt.

Hedjkheperre Setpenre (Takelot II)	837–813 BCE
Usermaatre Setpenamun (Meriamun Pedubaste I)	826–801 BCE
Usermaatre Meryamun (Sheshonq VI)	801–795 BCE
Usermaatre Setpenamun (Osorkon III)	795–767 BCE
Usermaatre-Setpenamun (Takelot III)	773–765 BCE
Usermaatre-Setpenamun (Meriamun Rudamun)	765–762 BCE
Shepsesre (Tefnakhte)	732–725 BCE
Wahkare (Bakenrenef)	725–720 BCE

Twenty-fifth Dynasty (c. 744–656 BCE)

Also known as the Kushite period, the twenty-fifth dynasty follows the Nubian invasions.

Piankhy (Piye)	744–714 BCE
Djedkaure (Shebitkku)	714–705 BCE
Neferkare (Shabaka)	705–690 BCE
Khuinefertemre (Taharqa)	690–664 BCE

LATE PERIOD (c. 664–332 BCE)

Twenty-sixth Dynasty (c. 664 – 525 BCE)

Also known as the Saite period, the twenty-sixth dynasty was the last native period before the Persian invasion in 525 BCE.

Wahibre (Psamtik I)	664–610 BCE
Wehemibre (Necho II)	610–595 BCE
Neferibre (Psamtik II)	595–589 BCE
Haaibre (Apreis)	589–570 BCE
Khemibre (Amasis II)	570–526 BCE
Ankhkaenre (Psamtik III)	526–525 BCE

Twenty-seventh Dynasty (c. 525–404 BCE)

The twenty-seventh dynasty is also known as the First Egyptian Satrapy and was ruled by the Persian Achaemenids.

Mesutre (Cambyses II)	525–1 July 522 BCE
Seteture (Darius I)	522–November 486 BCE
Kheshayarusha (Xerxes I)	November 486–December 465 BCE
Artabanus of Persia	465–464 BCE
Arutakhshashas (Artaxerxes I)	464–424 BCE
Ochus (Darius II)	July 423–March 404 BCE

Twenty-eighth Dynasty (*c.* 404–398 BCE)

The twenty-eighth dynasty consisted of a single pharaoh.

Amunirdisu (Amyrtaeus)   404–398 BCE

Twenty-ninth Dynasty (*c.* 398–380 BCE)

The twenty-ninth dynasty was founded following the overthrow of Amyrtaeus.

Baenre Merynatjeru (Nepherites I)   398–393 BCE
Khnemmaatre Setepenkhnemu (Hakor)   *c.* 392–391 BCE
Userre Setepenptah (Psammuthis)   *c.* 391 BCE
Khnemmaatre Setepenkhnemu (Hakor)   *c.* 390–379 BCE
Nepherites II   *c.* 379 BCE

Thirtieth Dynasty (*c.*379–340 BCE)

The thirtieth dynasty is thought to be the final native dynasty of ancient Egypt.

Kheperkare (Nectanebo I)   *c.* 379–361 BCE
Irimaatenre (Teos)   *c.* 361–359 BCE
Snedjemibre Setepenanhur (Nectanebo II)   *c.* 359–340 BCE

Thirty-first Dynasty (*c.* 340–332 BCE)

The thirty-first dynasty is also known as the Second Egyptian Satrapy and was ruled by the Persian Achaemenids.

Ochus (Artaxerxes III)   *c.* 340–338 BCE
Arses (Artaxerxes IV)   338–336 BCE
Darius III   336–332 BCE

MACEDONIAN/ARGEAD DYNASTY (*c.* 332–309 BCE)

Alexander the Great conquered Persia and Egypt in 332 BCE.

Setpenre Meryamun (Alexander III of Macedon 'the Great')	332–323 BCE
Setpenre Meryamun (Philip Arrhidaeus)	323–317 BCE
Khaibre Setepenamun (Alexander IV)	317–309 BCE

PTOLEMAIC DYNASTY (*c.* 305–30 BCE)

The Ptolemaic dynasty in Egypt was the last dynasty of ancient Egypt before it became a province of Rome.

Ptolemy I Soter	305–282 BCE
Ptolemy II Philadelphos	284–246 BCE
Arsinoe II	*c.* 277–270 BCE
Ptolemy III Euergetes	246–222 BCE
Berenice II	244/243–222 BCE
Ptolemy IV Philopater	222–204 BCE
Arsinoe III	220–204 BCE
Ptolemy V Epiphanes	204–180 BCE
Cleopatra I	193–176 BCE
Ptolemy VI Philometor	180–164, 163–145 BCE
Cleopatra II	175–164 BCE, 163–127 BCE and 124–116 BCE
Ptolemy VIII Physcon	171–163 BCE, 144–131 BCE and 127–116 BCE
Ptolemy VII Neos Philopator	145–144 BCE

Cleopatra III	142–131 BCE, 127–107 BCE
Ptolemy Memphites	113 BCE
Ptolemy IX Soter	116–110 BCE
Cleopatra IV	116–115 BCE
Ptolemy X Alexander	110–109 BCE
Berenice III	81–80 BCE
Ptolemy XI Alexander	80 BCE
Ptolemy XII Auletes	80–58 BCE, 55–51 BCE
Cleopatra V Tryphaena	79–68 BCE
Cleopatra VI	58–57 BCE
Berenice IV	58–55 BCE
Cleopatra VII	52–30 BCE
Ptolemy XIII Theos Philopator	51–47 BCE
Arsinoe IV	48–47 BCE
Ptolemy XIV Philopator	47–44 BCE
Ptolemy XV Caesar	44–30 BCE

In 30 BCE, Egypt became a province of the Roman Empire.

ANCIENT GREEK MONARCHS

This list is not exhaustive and dates are approximate. Where dates of rule overlap, emperors either ruled jointly or ruled in opposition to one another. There may also be differences in name spellings between different sources.

Because of the fragmented nature of Greece prior to its unification by Philip II of Macedon, this list includes mythological and existing rulers of Thebes, Athens and Sparta as some of the leading ancient Greek city-states. These different city-states had some common belief in the mythological gods and goddesses of ancient Greece, although their accounts may differ.

KINGS OF THEBES (c. 753-509 BCE)

These rulers are mythological. There is much diversity over who the kings actually were, and the dates they ruled.

Calydnus (son of Uranus)
Ogyges (son of Poseidon, thought to be king of Boeotia or Attica)
Cadmus (Greek mythological hero known as the founder of Thebes, known as Cadmeia until the reign of Amphion and Zethus)
Pentheus (son of Echion, one of the mythological Spartoi, and Agave, daughter of Cadmus)

Polydorus (son of Cadmus and Harmonia, goddess of harmony)

Nycteus (like his brother Lycus, thought to be the son of a Spartoi and a nymph, or a son of Poseidon)

Lycus (brother of Nyceteus)

Labdacus (grandson of Cadmus)

Lycus (second reign as regent for Laius)

Amphion and Zethus (joint rulers and twin sons of Zeus, constructed the city walls of Thebes)

Laius (son of Labdacus, married to Jocasta)

Oedipus (son of Laius, killed his father and married his mother, Jocasta)

Creon (regent after the death of Laius)

Eteocles and Polynices (brothers/sons of Oedipus; killed each other in battle)

Creon (regent for Laodamas)

Laodamas (son of Eteocles)

Thersander (son of Polynices)

Peneleos (regent for Tisamenus)

Tisamenus (son of Thersander)

Autesion (son of Tisamenes)

Damasichthon (son of Peneleos)

Ptolemy (son of Damasichton, 12 century BCE)

Xanthos (son of Ptolemy)

KINGS OF ATHENS

Early legendary kings who ruled before the mythological flood caused by Zeus, which only Deucalion (son of Prometheus) and a few others survived (date unknown).

Periphas (king of Attica, turned into an eagle by Zeus)

Ogyges (son of Poseidon, thought to be king of either Boeotia or Attica)

Actaeus (king of Attica, father-in-law to Cecrops I)

Erechtheid Dynasty (1556–1127 BCE)

Cecrops I (founder and first king of Athens; half-man, half-serpent who married Actaeus' daughter) 1556–1506 BCE

Cranaus   1506–1497 BCE

Amphictyon (son of Deucalion)   1497–1487 BCE

Erichthonius (adopted by Athena)   1487–1437 BCE

Pandion I (son of Erichthonius)   1437–1397 BCE

Erechtheus (son of Pandion I)   1397–1347 BCE

Cecrops II (son of Erechtheus)   1347–1307 BCE

Pandion II (son of Cecrops II)   1307–1282 BCE

Aegeus (adopted by Pandion II, gave his name to the Aegean Sea)   1282–1234 BCE

Theseus (son of Aegeus, killed the minotaur)   1234–1205 BCE

Menestheus (made king by Castor and Pollux when Theseus was in the underworld)   1205–1183 BCE

Demophon (son of Theseus)   1183–1150 BCE

Oxyntes (son of Demophon)   1150–1136 BCE

Apheidas (son of Oxyntes)   1136–1135 BCE

Thymoetes (son of Oxyntes)   1135–1127 BCE

Melanthid Dynasty (1126–1068 BCE)

Melanthus (king of Messenia, fled to Athens when expelled)   1126–1089 BCE

Codrus (last of the semi-mythological Athenian kings)   1089–1068 BCE

LIFE ARCHONS OF ATHENS (1068–753 BCE)

These rulers held public office up until their deaths.

Medon	1068–1048 BCE	Pherecles	864–845 BCE
Acastus	1048–1012 BCE	Ariphon	845–825 BCE
Archippus	1012–993 BCE	Thespieus	824–797 BCE
Thersippus	993–952 BCE	Agamestor	796–778 BCE
Phorbas	952–922 BCE	Aeschylus	778–755 BCE
Megacles	922–892 BCE	Alcmaeon	755–753 BCE
Diognetus	892–864 BCE		

From this point, archons led for a period of 10 years up to 683 BCE, then a period of one year up to 485 CE. Selected important leaders – including archons and tyrants – in this later period are as follows:

SELECTED LATER LEADERS OF ATHENS

Peisistratos 'the Tyrant of Athens'	561, 559–556, 546–527 BCE
Cleisthenes (archon)	525–524 BCE
Themistocles (archon)	493–492 BCE
Pericles	c. 461–429 BCE

KINGS OF SPARTA

These rulers are mythological and are thought to be descendants of the ancient tribe of Leleges. There is much diversity over who the kings actually were, and the dates they ruled.

Lelex (son of Poseidon or Helios, ruled Laconia) c. 1600 BCE
Myles (son of Lelex, ruled Laconia) c. 1575 BCE
Eurotas (son of Myles, father of Sparta) c. 1550 BCE

From the Lelegids, rule passed to the Lacedaemonids when Lacedaemon married Sparta.
Lacedaemon (son of Zeus, husband of Sparta)
Amyklas (son of Lacedaemon)
Argalus (son of Amyklas)
Kynortas (son of Amyklas)
Perieres (son of Kynortas)
Oibalos (son of Kynortas)
Tyndareos (first reign; son of Oibalos, father of Helen of Troy)
Hippocoon (son of Oibalos)
Tyndareos (second reign; son of Oibaos, father of Helen of Troy)

From the Lacedaemons, rule passed to the Atreids when Menelaus married Helen of Troy.

Menelaus (son of Atreus, king of Mycenae,
    and husband of Helen) c. 1250 BCE
Orestes (son of Agamemnon, Menelaus' brother) c. 1150 BCE
Tisamenos (son of Orestes)
Dion c. 1100 BCE

From the Atreids, rule passed to the Heraclids following war.

Aristodemos (son of Aristomachus, great-great-grandson of Heracles)

Theras (served as regent for Aristodemes' sons, Eurysthenes and Procles)

Eurysthenes   *c.* 930 BCE

From the Heraclids, rule passed to the Agiads, founded by Agis I. Only major kings during this period are listed here.

Agis I (conceivably the first historical Spartan king)	*c.* 930–900 BCE
Alcamenes	*c.* 740–700 BCE, during First Messenian War
Cleomenes I (important leader in the Greek resistance against the Persians)	524 – 490 BCE
Leonidas I (died while leading the Greeks – the 300 Spartans – against the Persians in the Battle of Thermopylae, 480 BCE)	490–480 BCE
Cleomenes III (exiled following the Battle of Sellasia)	*c.* 235–222 BCE

KINGS OF MACEDON

Argead Dynasty (808–309 BCE)

Karanos	*c.* 808–778 BCE	Alcetas I	*c.* 576–547 BCE
Koinos	*c.* 778–750 BCE	Amyntas I	*c.* 547–498 BCE
Tyrimmas	*c.* 750–700 BCE	Alexander I	*c.* 498–454 BCE
Perdiccas I	*c.* 700–678 BCE	Alcetas II	*c.* 454–448 BCE
Argaeus I	*c.* 678–640 BCE	Perdiccas II	*c.* 448–413 BCE
Philip I	*c.* 640–602 BCE	Archelaus I	*c.* 413–339 BCE
Aeropus I	*c.* 602–576 BCE	Craterus	*c.* 399 BCE

Orestes	c. 399–396 BCE	Perdiccas III	c. 368–359 BCE
Aeropus II	c. 399–394/93 BCE	Amyntas IV	c. 359 BCE
Archelaus II	c. 394–393 BCE	Philip II	c. 359–336 BCE
Amyntas II	c. 393 BCE	Alexander III 'the Great'	
Pausanias	c. 393 BCE	(also King of Persia and	
Amyntas III	c. 393 BCE; first reign	Pharaoh of Egypt by end of reign)	c. 336–323 BCE
Argeus II	c. 393–392 BCE	Philip III	c. 323–317 BCE
Amyntas III	c. 392–370 BCE	Alexander IV	c. 323/
Alexander II	c. 370–368 BCE		317–309 BCE

Note: the Corinthian League or Hellenic League was created by Philip II and was the first time that the divided Greek city-states were unified under a single government.

Post-Argead Dynasty (309–168 BCE, 149–148 BCE)

Cassander	c. 305–297 BCE
Philip IV	c. 297 BCE
Antipater II	c. 297–294 BCE
Alexpander V	c. 297–294 BCE

Antigonid, Alkimachid and Aeacid Dynasties (294–281 BCE)

Demetrius	c. 294–288 BCE
Lysimachus	c. 288–281 BCE
Pyrrhus	c. 288–285 BCE; first reign

Ptolemaic Dynasty (281–279 BCE)

Ptolemy Ceraunus (son of Ptolemy I of Egypt)	c. 281–279 BCE
Meleager	279 BCE

Antipatrid, Antigonid, Aeacid Dynasties, Restored
(279–167 BCE)

Antipater	c. 279 BCE
Sosthenes	c. 279–277 BCE
Antigonus II	c. 277–274 BCE; first reign
Pyrrhus	c. 274–272 BCE; second reign
Antigonus II	c. 272–239 BCE; second reign
Demetrius II	c. 239–229 BCE
Antigonus III	c. 229–221 BCE
Philip V	c. 221–179 BCE
Perseus (deposed by Romans)	c. 179–168 BCE
Revolt by Philip VI (Andriskos)	c. 149–148 BCE

SELEUCID DYNASTY (c. 320 BCE–63 CE)

Seleucus I Nicator	c. 320–315, 312–305, 305–281 BCE
Antiochus I Soter	c. 291, 281–261 BCE
Antiochus II Theos	c. 261–246 BCE
Seleucus II Callinicus	c. 246–225 BCE
Seleucus III Ceraunus	c. 225–223 BCE
Antiochus III 'the Great'	c. 223–187 BCE
Seleucus IV Philopator	c. 187–175 BCE
Antiochus (son of Seleucus IV)	c. 175–170 BCE
Antiochus IV Epiphanes	c. 175–163 BCE
Antiochus V Eupater	c. 163–161 BCE
Demetrius I Soter	c. 161–150 BCE
Alexander I Balas	c. 150–145 BCE
Demetrius II Nicator	c. 145–138 BCE; first reign
Antiochus VI Dionysus	c. 145–140 BCE

Diodotus Tryphon	c. 140–138 BCE
Antiochus VII Sidetes	c. 138–129 BCE
Demetrius II Nicator	c. 129–126 BCE; second reign
Alexander II Zabinas	c. 129–123 BCE
Cleopatra Thea	c. 126–121 BCE
Seleucus V Philometor	c. 126/125 BCE
Antiochus VIII Grypus	c. 125–96 BCE
Antiochus IX Cyzicenus	c. 114–96 BCE
Seleucus VI Epiphanes	c. 96–95 BCE
Antiochus X Eusebes	c. 95–92/83 BCE
Demetrius III Eucaerus	c. 95–87 BCE
Antiochus XI Epiphanes	c. 95–92 BCE
Philip I Philadelphus	c. 95–84/83 BCE
Antiochus XII Dionysus	c. 87–84 BCE
Seleucus VII	c. 83–69 BCE
Antiochus XIII Asiaticus	c. 69–64 BCE
Philip II Philoromaeus	c. 65–63 BCE

Ptolemaic Dynasty (305–30 BCE)

The Ptolemaic dynasty in Greece was the last dynasty of ancient Egypt before it became a province of Rome.

Ptolemy I Soter	305–282 BCE
Ptolemy II Philadelphos	284–246 BCE
Arsinoe II	c. 277–270 BCE
Ptolemy III Euergetes	246–222 BCE
Berenice II	244/243–222 BCE
Ptolemy IV Philopater	222–204 BCE
Arsinoe III	220–204 BCE
Ptolemy V Epiphanes	204–180 BCE

Cleopatra I   193–176 BCE
Ptolemy VI Philometor   180–164, 163–145 BCE
Cleopatra II   175–164 BCE, 163–127 BCE and 124–116 BCE
Ptolemy VIII Physcon   171–163 BCE, 144–131 BCE and 127–116 BCE
Ptolemy VII Neos Philopator   145–144 BCE
Cleopatra III   142–131 BCE, 127–107 BCE
Ptolemy Memphites   113 BCE
Ptolemy IX Soter   116–110 BCE
Cleopatra IV   116–115 BCE
Ptolemy X Alexander   110–109 BCE
Berenice III   81–80 BCE
Ptolemy XI Alexander   80 BCE
Ptolemy XII Auletes   80–58 BCE, 55–51 BCE
Cleopatra V Tryphaena   79–68 BCE
Cleopatra VI   58–57 BCE
Berenice IV   58–55 BCE

In 27 BCE, Caesar Augustus annexed Greece and it became integrated into the Roman Empire.

ANCIENT ROMAN LEADERS

This list is not exhaustive and some dates are approximate. The legitimacy of some rulers is also open to interpretation. Where dates of rule overlap, emperors either ruled jointly or ruled in opposition to one another. There may also be differences in name spellings between different sources.

KINGS OF ROME (753–509 BCE)

Romulus (mythological founder and first ruler of Rome)	753–716 BCE
Numa Pompilius (mythological)	715–672 BCE
Tullus Hostilius (mythological)	672–640 BCE
Ancus Marcius (mythological)	640–616 BCE
Lucius Tarquinius Priscus (mythological)	616–578 BCE
Servius Tullius (mythological)	578–534 BCE
Lucius Tarquinius Superbus (Tarquin the Proud; mythological)	534–509 BCE

ROMAN REPUBLIC (509-27 BCE)

During this period, two consuls were elected to serve a joint one-year term. Therefore, only a selection of significant consuls are included here.

Lucius Junius Brutus (semi-mythological)	509 BCE
Marcus Porcius Cato (Cato the Elder)	195 BCE
Scipio Africanus	194 BCE
Cnaeus Pompeius Magnus (Pompey the Great)	70, 55 and 52 BCE
Marcus Linius Crassus	70 and 55 BCE
Marcus Tullius Cicero	63 BCE
Caius Julius Caesar	59 BCE
Marcus Aemilius Lepidus	46 and 42 BCE
Marcus Antonius (Mark Anthony)	44 and 34 BCE
Marcus Agrippa	37 and 28 BCE

PRINCIPATE (27 BCE-284 CE)

Julio-Claudian Dynasty (27 BCE–68 CE)

Augustus (Caius Octavius Thurinus, Caius Julius Caesar, Imperator Caesar Divi filius)	27 BCE–14 CE
Tiberius (Tiberius Julius Caesar Augustus)	14–37 CE
Caligula (Caius Caesar Augustus Germanicus)	37–41 CE
Claudius (Tiberius Claudius Caesar Augustus Germanicus)	41–54 CE
Nero (Nero Claudius Caesar Augustus Germanicus)	54–68 CE

Year of the Four Emperors (68–69 CE)

Galba (Servius Sulpicius Galba Caesar Augustus)	68–69 CE
Otho (Marcus Salvio Otho Caesar Augustus)	Jan–Apr 69 CE
Vitellius (Aulus Vitellius Germanicus Augustus)	Apr–Dec 69 CE

Note: the fourth emperor, Vespasian, is listed below.

Flavian Dynasty (66–96 CE)

Vespasian (Caesar Vespasianus Augustus)	69–79 CE
Titus (Titus Caesar Vespasianus Augustus)	79–81 CE
Domitian (Caesar Domitianus Augustus)	81–96 CE

Nerva-Antonine Dynasty (69–192 CE)

Nerva (Nerva Caesar Augustus)	96–98 CE
Trajan (Caesar Nerva Traianus Augustus)	98–117 CE
Hadrian (Caesar Traianus Hadrianus Augustus)	138–161 CE
Antonius Pius (Caesar Titus Aelius Hadrianus Antoninus Augustus Pius)	138–161 CE
Marcus Aurelius (Caesar Marcus Aurelius Antoninus Augustus)	161–180 CE
Lucius Verus (Lucius Aurelius Verus Augustus)	161–169 CE
Commodus (Caesar Marcus Aurelius Commodus Antoninus Augustus)	180–192 CE

Year of the Five Emperors (193 CE)

Pertinax (Publius Helvius Pertinax)	Jan–Mar 193 CE
Didius Julianus (Marcus Didius Severus Julianus)	Mar–Jun 193 CE

Note: Pescennius Niger and Clodius Albinus are generally regarded as usurpers, while the fifth, Septimius Severus, is listed below

Severan Dynasty (193–235 CE)

Septimius Severus (Lucius Septimus Severus Pertinax)	193–211 CE
Caracalla (Marcus Aurelius Antonius)	211–217 CE
Geta (Publius Septimius Geta)	Feb–Dec 211 CE
Macrinus (Caesar Marcus Opellius Severus Macrinus Augustus)	217–218 CE
Diadumenian (Marcus Opellius Antonius Diadumenianus)	May–Jun 218 CE
Elagabalus (Caesar Marcus Aurelius Antoninus Augustus)	218–222 CE
Severus Alexander (Marcus Aurelius Severus Alexander)	222–235 CE

Crisis of the Third Century (235–285 CE)

Maximinus 'Thrax' (Caius Julius Verus Maximus)	235–238 CE
Gordian I (Marcus Antonius Gordianus Sempronianus Romanus)	Apr–May 238 CE
Gordian II (Marcus Antonius Gordianus Sempronianus Romanus)	Apr–May 238 CE
Pupienus Maximus (Marcus Clodius Pupienus Maximus)	May–Aug 238 CE
Balbinus (Decimus Caelius Calvinus Balbinus)	May–Aug 238 CE
Gordian III (Marcus Antonius Gordianus)	Aug 238–Feb 244 CE
Philip I 'the Arab' (Marcus Julius Philippus)	244–249 CE
Philip II 'the Younger' (Marcus Julius Severus Philippus)	247–249 CE
Decius (Caius Messius Quintus Traianus Decius)	249–251 CE
Herennius Etruscus (Quintus Herennius Etruscus Messius Decius)	May/Jun 251 CE

Trebonianus Gallus (Caius Vibius Trebonianus Gallus)   251–253 CE
Hostilian (Caius Valens Hostilianus Messius
   Quintus)   Jun–Jul 251 CE
Volusianus (Caius Vibius Afinius Gallus
   Veldumnianus Volusianus)   251–253 CE
Aemilian (Marcus Aemilius Aemilianus)   Jul–Sep 253 CE
Silbannacus (Marcus Silbannacus)   Sep/Oct 253 CE
Valerian (Publius Licinius Valerianus)   253–260 CE
Gallienus (Publius Licinius Egnatius Gallienus)   253–268 CE
Saloninus (Publius Licinius Cornelius
   Saloninus Valerianus)   Autumn 260 CE
Claudius II Gothicus (Marcus Aurelius Claudius)   268–270 CE
Quintilus (Marcus Aurelius Claudias
   Quintillus)   Apr–May/Jun 270 CE
Aurelian (Lucius Domitius Aurelianus)   270–275 CE
Tacitus (Marcus Claudius Tacitus)   275–276 CE
Florianus (Marcus Annius Florianus)   276–282 CE
Probus (Marcus Aurelius Probus Romanus;
   in opposition to Florianus)   276–282 CE
Carus (Marcus Aurelias Carus)   282–283 CE
Carinus (Marcus Aurelius Carinus)   283–285 CE
Numerian (Marcus Aurelius Numerianus)   283–284 CE

DOMINATE (284–610)

Tetrarchy (284–324)

Diocletian 'Iovius' (Caius Aurelius Valerius Diocletianus)   284–305
Maximian 'Herculius' (Marcus Aurelius Valerius
   Maximianus; ruled the western provinces)   286–305/late 306–308

Galerius (Caius Galerius Valerius Maximianus; ruled the eastern provinces)	305–311
Constantius I 'Chlorus' (Marcus Flavius Valerius Constantius; ruled the western provinces)	305–306
Severus II (Flavius Valerius Severus; ruled the western provinces)	306–307
Maxentius (Marcus Aurelius Valerius Maxentius)	306–312
Licinius (Valerius Licinanus Licinius; ruled the western, then the eastern provinces)	308–324
Maximinus II 'Daza' (Aurelius Valerius Valens; ruled the western provinces)	316–317
Martinian (Marcus Martinianus; ruled the western provinces)	Jul–Sep 324

Constantinian Dynasty (306–363)

Constantine I 'the Great' (Flavius Valerius Constantinus; ruled the western provinces then whole)	306–337
Constantine II (Flavius Claudius Constantinus)	337–340
Constans I (Flavius Julius Constans)	337–350
Constantius II (Flavius Julius Constantius)	337–361
Magnentius (Magnus Magnentius)	360–353
Nepotianus (Julius Nepotianus)	Jun 350
Vetranio	Mar–Dec 350
Julian 'the Apostate' (Flavius Claudius Julianus)	361–363
Jovian (Jovianus)	363–364

Valentinianic Dynasty (364–392)

Valentinian I 'the Great' (Valentinianus)	364–375
Valens (ruled the eastern provinces)	364–378

Procopius (revolted against Valens)	365–366
Gratian (Flavius Gratianus Augustus; ruled the western provinces then whole)	375–383
Magnus Maximus	383–388
Valentinian II (Flavius Valentinianus)	388–392
Eugenius	392–394

Theodosian Dynasty (379–457)

Theodosius I 'the Great' (Flavius Theodosius)	Jan 395
Arcadius	383–408
Honorius (Flavius Honorius)	395–432
Constantine III	407–411
Theodosius II	408–450
Priscus Attalus; usurper	409–410
Constantius III	Feb–Sep 421
Johannes	423–425
Valentinian III	425–455
Marcian	450–457

Last Emperors in the West (455–476)

Petronius Maximus	Mar–May 455
Avitus	455–456
Majorian	457–461
Libius Severus (Severus III)	461–465
Anthemius	467–472
Olybrius	Apr–Nov 472
Glycerius	473–474
Julius Nepos	474–475
Romulus Augustulus (Flavius Momyllus Romulus Augustulus)	475–476

Leonid Dynasty (East, 457–518)

Leo I (Leo Thrax Magnus)	457–474
Leo II	Jan–Nov 474
Zeno	474–475
Basiliscus	475–476
Zeno (second reign)	476–491
Anastasius I 'Dicorus'	491–518

Justinian Dynasty (East, 518–602)

Justin I	518–527
Justinian I 'the Great' (Flavius Justinianus, Petrus Sabbatius)	527–565
Justin II	565–578
Tiberius II Constantine	578–582
Maurice (Mauricius Flavius Tiberius)	582–602
Phocas	602–610

LATER EASTERN EMPERORS (610–1059)

Heraclian Dynasty (610–695)

Heraclius	610–641
Heraclius Constantine (Constantine III)	Feb–May 641
Heraclonas	Feb–Nov 641
Constans II Pogonatus ('the Bearded')	641–668
Constantine IV	668–685
Justinian II	685–695

Twenty Years' Anarchy (695–717)

Leontius	695–698
Tiberius III	698–705

Justinian II 'Rhinometus' (second reign)	705–711
Philippicus	711–713
Anastasius II	713–715
Theodosius III	715–717

Isaurian Dynasty (717–803)

Leo III 'the Isaurian'	717–741
Constantine V	741–775
Artabasdos	741/2–743
Leo V 'the Khazar'	775–780
Constantine VI	780–797
Irene	797–802

Nikephorian Dynasty (802–813)

Nikephoros I 'the Logothete'	802–811
Staurakios	July–Oct 811
Michael I Rangabé	813–820

Amorian Dynasty (820–867)

Michael II 'the Amorian'	820–829
Theophilos	829–842
Theodora	842–856
Michael III 'the Drunkard'	842–867

Macedonian Dynasty (867–1056)

Basil I 'the Macedonian'	867–886
Leo VI 'the Wise'	886–912
Alexander	912–913
Constantine VII Porphyrogenitus	913–959
Romanos I Lecapenus	920–944

Romanos II	959–963
Nikephoros II Phocas	963–969
John I Tzimiskes	969–976
Basil II 'the Bulgar-Slayer'	976–1025
Constantine VIII	1025–1028
Romanus III Argyros	1028–1034
Michael IV 'the Paphlagonian'	1034–1041
Michael V Kalaphates	1041–1042
Zoë Porphyrogenita	Apr–Jun 1042
Theodora Porphyrogenita	Apr–Jun 1042
Constantine IX Monomachos	1042–1055
Theodora Porphyrogenita (second reign)	1055–1056
Michael VI Bringas 'Stratioticus'	1056–1057
Isaab I Komnenos	1057–1059

COLLECTOR'S EDITIONS

FLAME TREE

A wide range of new and classic fiction, including short story anthologies, *Collectable Classics*, *Gothic Fantasy* collections and *Epic Tales* of mythology.

•

Available at all good bookstores, and online at *flametreepublishing.com*

FLAME TREE PUBLISHING